GREAT ROMANTIC RUINS
of England and Wales

GREAT ROMANTIC

RUINS *of England and Wales*

Brian Bailey

Photographs by Rita Bailey

Crown Publishers, Inc., New York

FRONT ENDPAPER *An eighteenth-century view of Fountains Abbey, North Yorkshire, across the lake in the gardens at Studley Royal.*

BACK ENDPAPER *Dunstanburgh Castle, Northumberland, by Turner, who drew and painted several views of this dramatic coastal ruin.*

HALF-TITLE *Interlaced wall arcading in the chapter house of Wenlock Priory, Shropshire.*

TITLE PAGE *Late evening light on the ruins of Kenilworth Castle, Warwickshire.*

RIGHT *The red-brick ruins of Bradgate House, built by the Marquess of Dorset at the end of the fifteenth century in one of England's most romantic landscapes.*

Copyright © 1984 by Brian Bailey

Published in the United States by Crown Publishers, Inc., One Park Avenue, New York, New York 10016

Published in Great Britain by George Weidenfeld & Nicolson Ltd.

Printed in Italy

Library of Congress Cataloging in Publication Data

Bailey, Brian J.
    Great romantic ruins of England and Wales.

    1. Historic sites—England—Guide-books.
2. Historic sites—Wales—Guide-books.
3. England—Antiquities—Guide-books. 4. Wales
—Antiquities—Guide-books. 5. England—
Description and travel—1971– —Guide books.
6. Wales—Description and travel—1981– —
Guide-books. I. Title.
DA660.B164 1984   914.2   84–7107

ISBN 0–517–55151–9

10 9 8 7 6 5 4 3 2 1

First American Edition

Author's Note

THE LINES on page 27 are from 'June Thunder' by Louis MacNeice, and are quoted by kind permission of Faber & Faber, publishers of the *Collected Poems of Louis MacNeice*.

The anecdote by Gwyn Thomas on page 143 is from *A Welsh Eye*, and is quoted by kind permission of Mrs Lyn Thomas and Felix de Wolfe.

My wife and I are deeply indebted to Wendy Dallas of Weidenfeld & Nicolson, and to Robin Wright of the National Trust, and my own thanks are due, not for the first time, to Van Phillips, who read the typescript and made many valuable comments and criticisms.

Finally, a word of greeting to my old friend William MacQuitty, whose fine books on the ruins of Abu Simbel and Philae remind me that, according to the ancient Egyptians, 'to speak of the dead is to make them live again'.

Brian Bailey, 1984

Acknowledgments

THE PUBLISHERS would like to thank David Worth of Line and Line for supplying artwork for the maps which appear on pages 12, 44, 126 and 196.

All the photographs in the book were taken by Rita Bailey except for those listed below, for which we would like to thank the photographers and galleries who kindly loaned them for reproduction:

Aerofilms Limited: 19, 132, 155, 158–9, 161
John Bethell: 7 top right, 195
Courtauld Institute: 9, 111, 114
Bob Estall: 2–3
Mansell Collection: 163, 230
Swan Gallery, Sherborne: 90, 190–1, 217, back endpaper
Weidenfeld and Nicolson Archive: front endpaper, 33, 65, 183

Contents

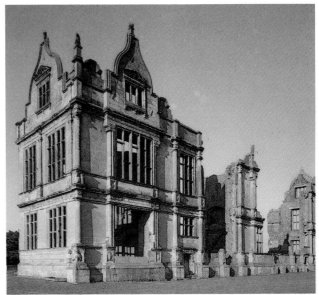

Military Ruins: The Mighty Fallen

Domestic Ruins: Silent Halls

Introduction:

ECHOES OF THE PAST

WHAT IS A RUIN but a useless heap of stones? For centuries it would have been regarded as such by most people. Lords of manors, masons and farmers, among others, saw ruins merely as convenient sources of building material, and they plundered them not with any guilty consciousness of despoliation (for how could you despoil something that was already a wreck?) but with what they regarded as practical common sense. Why pay for quarrying and transportation when tons of stone were lying near at hand, serving no purpose and just waiting to be utilized? There is hardly an ancient ruin in England or Wales whose stones have not made some contribution to local houses, bridges or field walls. But that was before the Romantic Movement invested ruins with a touch of the sublime.

Modern appreciation of ruins is, to a large extent, an English invention. Although painters, poets and philosophers have mused on ruins all through the ages, it was in England in the eighteenth century that the intrinsic beauty of forlorn buildings was given meaning for a wide public. The Romantic Movement began in the second half of the century, using nature to fill a void left by the decline of religion. One of the new movement's prophets was Edmund Burke, who in 1757, at the age of twenty-eight, published *A Philosophical Enquiry into the Origin of our Ideas of the Sublime and the Beautiful*. 'Whatever is fitted in any sort to excite the ideas of pain, and danger,' he wrote, 'that is to say, whatever is in any sort terrible, or is conversant about terrible objects, or operates in a manner analogous to terror, is a source of the *sublime*; that is, it is productive of the strongest emotions which the mind is capable of feeling.'

This concept, not far removed from what in drama is called tragedy, superseded that which identified the sublime with the beauty of classical perfection. It was a psychological rather than an objective approach, emphasizing spiritual values and emotions instead of the universal virtues of flawless form and symmetry which had long been taken almost as absolute truths.

Imagination was henceforth given full rein, and no image in the freshly perceived landscape fed the imagination more than a finely situated ruin. It fitted the new perception of the sublime because, far from being perfect or serene, as the images of the classical world were, it possessed an awful splendour in decay, melancholy but undoubtedly picturesque. The ivy-clad walls of ancient castles and crumbling abbeys were soon prominent features of the newly discovered Romantic imagery, and it was not long before descendants of those who had carelessly dismantled old ruins were engaging expensive architects to design sham ruins in order to improve the views from their drawing room windows.

Oscar Wilde said that 'a really well-made buttonhole is the only link between art and nature', but I venture to suggest that a ruin built of stone and mantled with ivy is another candidate. Not content with enhancing nature with artfully contrived ruins, the eighteenth-century imagination went so far as to perceive nature imitating art. Fanciful visitors to the Lake District, whose scenery Defoe had described not a century before as 'the wildest, most barren and frightful of any that I have passed over in England', were only too eager to follow Sir Walter Scott in seeing a fairly ordinary projecting crag as the 'Castle Rock

The Bard *by John Martin. No painter responded with more gusto to the romantic notion of the sublime than this Northumberland artist, sometimes known as 'Mad Martin'. Here, he planted Harlech Castle in a dramatic imaginary landscape to show the last Welsh bard defying the slaughtering army of Edward I.*

of Triermain', which a local historian described as 'making an awful, rude and Gothic appearance with its lofty turrets and ruined battlements'.

Painters were soon leaping on the bandwagon that poets had set in motion, and the Romantic artists usually exaggerated the dramatic qualities of their subjects. John Martin's *The Bard* is a typical piece of Merlin-like wizardry – spiriting Harlech Castle into a fantastic mountain landscape, inspired by Thomas Gray's poem about Edward I's alleged massacre of the Celtic bards.

I suppose the culmination of this kind of overblown imagination took place before the Second World War, when bizarre discussions took place between the megalomaniac Adolf

Hitler and his architect Albert Speer about how their grandiose building projects would appear when the 'Thousand-Year Reich' had finally passed away. What greater folly could there be than planning buildings which, regardless of their practical purposes, were aimed to rival those of Athens and Rome when they had been brought to ruin?

It is not surprising, then, that Frederick Raphael has described the cult of ruins as 'a suspect passion', and long before him Henry James talked of ruin-seeking as 'a heartless pastime' tinged with perversity. But do we merely enjoy ruins as a spectacle of decay?

Rose Macaulay, in her famous book *Pleasure of Ruins*, sought to penetrate to the essence of the matter. She cited among the pleasures to be derived from ruins a morbid satisfaction in images of decay, as well as the historical and literary associations of the remains, and of course less sophisticated pleasures such as looting fragments and scratching one's initials on the ancient walls. But Dame Rose's sights were set chiefly on the crumbling remnants of lost civilizations, and the 'backward-looking dreams' she wrote of so well, deriving from the 'stunning impact of world history on its amazed heirs', seem to me to be slightly self-indulgent exercises in escapism. My own view coincides with that of a forgotten clergyman in the early years of Romanticism: 'If we look backwards to antiquity, it should be as those that are winning a race.'

If one sees ruins merely as heaps of stone, then all ruins are the same. It is our psychological response which gives them holiness or heroism. But is there a more deeply felt and compelling need for silence at Fountains Abbey than at Corfe Castle only because we know that one was a monastery and the other a fortress, or does the fine tracery of a Gothic window inspire, of its own accord, more reverence than a battlemented wall? Are we victims of self-hypnosis even before we arrive, conditioned by our own expectations? What is certain is that our reaction to ruins is highly complex.

Of course, one must view a ruin entirely

alone in order to feel a sense of communion with the past, and this may indicate that one needs a melancholy temperament to appreciate ruins fully. Nothing dispels the lingering sanctity of an ancient temple or abbey so instantly as a coachload of tourists clicking their cameras and reading the guide-book aloud. Alone among the crumbling stones, one can listen to the whispering walls and share the silence with the ghosts. So serious ruin-seekers should stay at home at weekends and bank holidays. It seems to me a sorry thing that there is no collective name for the connoisseur of ruins. 'Dilettante' will not do, for we are not necessarily connoisseurs of art or architecture – it is the sense of the past that appeals to us, not the pointing of the brickwork. Perhaps 'olethrophile' is the word, from the Greek 'olethros' for ruins or destruction.

There may be nothing in England to match the overwhelming sense of awe felt at the beauty of the Acropolis, the fantastic mountain site of Macchu Picchu, or the jungle-gripped ruins of Angkor Wat. But what there is is closer to the people not only in the obvious physical and cultural senses, but in its ability to evoke responses from the collective unconscious. You can flavour ruins to your own taste, and hopefully gain wisdom from them. Their appeal is by no means an entirely negative one, and in this fact lies the importance of preserving what is left.

If I were asked to say in a word what positive lesson we should learn from looking at these crippled monuments to our violent and stumbling progress towards what we are pleased to call civilization, I would answer, 'Tolerance'. For how absurd in retrospect seem the greed, petty quarrels and ambitions which have caused these fine buildings to topple and crumble into dust. Ruins evoke in us a cosmic philosophy, a paradoxical sense of mortality and eternal values.

They also present a tantalizing glimpse of something we recognize as a source of uplift and enrichment. We are always entranced but never satisfied. A ruin is like an unfinished symphony or novel, or alternatively, something which is frozen in the very process of dissolving. We yearn for whatever else there was, or should have been, but we know that only our imaginations can supply it. A ruin feeds our dreams, and is a challenge to our senses, creating within us a tension between what we see and what we know. And in an age when we are all threatened with a more complete destruction than any of us can truly comprehend, these echoes of the past remind us of the need to learn from what has been and to strive for survival. 'One sees the storm', wrote the German dramatist Gotthold Lessing, 'in the wreckage and corpses it has cast upon the shore.'

Whatever our individual reactions to the ruins we see, whether the overriding emotion is one of anger or sadness, admiration or excitement, we should defy the destructive inclinations of our time and ensure that these treasures are preserved, for they are more than our heritage, they are a link in our lifeline.

A few practical and explanatory words may be necessary before we set out on our explorations. I have chosen one hundred ruins for discussion in this volume. It would have been two hundred if space had allowed – three hundred even – and some readers may be disappointed not to find a particular favourite here. A choice had to be made, and it involved difficult decisions, especially in the case of abbeys and castles, but I have tried to aim at good geographical coverage and variety of size, style and period, so that the book, if far from comprehensive, is at least representative of the ruins to be found in England and Wales.

My wife and I have visited *every* ruin mentioned, and a lot more besides – she to photograph them and I to absorb the particular atmosphere of each place. At the end of each piece, I have given directions and the National Grid reference. Opening times and admission charges are not given as they are subject to change, but the majority of ruins open to the public are open throughout the year except Sunday mornings. It is, however, advisable to check before making a visit.

Prehistoric and Roman Ruins:
WHISPERING WALLS

THE RUINS of prehistory and the Roman occupation are among the most mysterious and occasionally intimidating of our fallen buildings. When Wordsworth came upon the stone circle in Cumbria known as 'Long Meg and Her Daughters', he wrote:

A weight of awe not easy to be borne
Fell suddenly upon my spirit, cast
From the dread bosom of the unknown past
When first I saw that sisterhood forlorn.

And Walter de la Mare was driven from Cornwall by the pagan spirit of the area, with a determination never to stay there again. There are plenty of other testimonies to the effect of ancient remains on those who are sensitive to whatever forces their venerable stones harbour, if indeed they harbour *any*.

My own position is one of disbelief in supernatural forces, whether Christian or pagan. But I have felt the thrill of communication with people of whom we know very little, through the presence of their works, as one might feel, looking at Rembrandt's self-portraits, that one knows the painter. To touch the massive monoliths of Stonehenge is almost like shaking hands with a Neolithic mason, and to stand on Hadrian's Wall looking across to the Cheviot Hills is to share an experience with a Roman soldier.

If only the touch of a Stone Age hand, the resounding echo of a Roman officer's shout, the blood of an executed criminal and the footsteps of a slave-girl had made permanent impressions on the enduring stones, which we could tap as easily as we induce music from the grooves of a gramophone record, I suspect we should not be so apprehensive of prehistory. But imagination has to feed an appetite for knowledge that archaeology cannot fully satisfy, and the remains before us – strange temples, megaliths and burial mounds – were left by a people with whom we cannot identify. Yet if Hamlet's imagination may 'trace the noble dust of Alexander till he find it stopping a bung-hole', why may not our minds make similar leaps of fancy?

A stone quarried by Romans for use in one of their forts, plundered centuries afterwards, may have been incorporated in the walls of a monastery, left there after the Dissolution until taken for another building, and from there found its way into the wall of a modern house. Thus a twentieth-century schoolboy may exercise his penknife on a stone knocked into shape by a Roman soldier who had cheered the Emperor Claudius in Rome, led military elephants across the Thames to subdue the tribes of Britain, and suffered from rheumatism in his old age in this cold, damp corner of the empire. This is not by any means an impossible scenario. I remember being taken as a boy to see a Roman mosaic pavement which formed the cellar floor of a corset shop in Leicester.

Fear of the unknown is what makes prehistoric ruins intimidating, not sinister presences. We look at an alien architecture and signs of alien culture and, by seizing on the differences between 'them' and 'us', conjure up visions of hostile beings – savages even. If we could only seize on the similarities between us instead, discomfiture would give way to the shock of recognition.

Aquae Sulis

Avon

THE ROMAN RUINS at Bath have been called 'the most remarkable remains of this kind north of the Alps', yet as one enters the museum containing the baths, from the modern city street of a Georgian spa, there is little feeling of going back in time to a remote civilization. One pays the admission price and proceeds into dimly-lit exhibition galleries as if one were going to the cinema – to see a re-creation of Roman Britain, not the real thing. The uncomfortable feeling that this is not a genuine ruin, however, evaporates like water from the hot spring after a few minutes. Despite all modern distractions – throngs of

The Great Bath at Aquae Sulis. Restored columns reflected in the steaming water from hot springs which soothed and refreshed citizens of Rome in the greatest days of their empire.

visitors; modern building and reconstruction above and all round the baths; views through glass as if the place were an aquarium – a sense of the Roman Empire in all its splendour gradually seeps into one's consciousness.

It was not until the middle of the eighteenth century, when Bath was already internationally famous as a gracefully built health resort, that demolition and excavation work revealed Saxon remains. And not until more than a century later was proper excavation carried out to uncover the ruins of a Roman spa unmatched in northern Europe, with steaming hot water issuing from the rock, as it has done for millions of years, at the rate of half a million gallons a day and a constant temperature of 120° Fahrenheit.

According to legend, Bath was founded by Bladud (father of King Lear) who was cured of leprosy after fortuitously immersing himself in the water from the hot mineral springs. The Romans dedicated the place to Sulis, the local Celtic goddess of the springs, identified with the Roman Minerva, and called it Aquae Sulis. They built five baths and two swimming pools, with hypocausts, steam rooms, cooling rooms, reservoirs, a temple, ornamental

sculpture and all the other requirements of what the Romans regarded, with some justice, as high civilization. For if there was one thing the Romans were addicted to, it was cleanliness. In Rome alone there were already a hundred and seventy public baths in Julius Caesar's time.

Their engineers channelled the hot water bubbling up from the bowels of the earth into conduits made of lead, which they mined in the Mendip Hills (where the springs themselves originate), and some of their plumbing is still in use after nearly two thousand years. The most imposing part of the complex is the so-called Great Bath, occupying a hall 110 by 68 feet, and now open to the sky, but in the Roman period roofed with a great tunnel-vault supported on massive piers and having open lunettes at each end to let the steam out. The floor of the bath was lined with sheets of lead, and the floor of the hall with tessellated paving. The hall had dressing rooms and seats in recesses round its walls, and stone steps descending into the pale green water.

Other baths are in cavern-like rooms below ground level, in a series of hot baths and cold plunges which were famous abroad even in Roman times. It was not only native aristocrats and imperial patricians who came here to bathe regularly – and who did so as a matter of course after exercise and before the main meal of the day – but also pilgrims from across the Channel, coming to try the effect of the medicinal water on ailments that we should now identify, no doubt, as gout and rheumatism, sciatica, scrofula and the like.

A woman called Rusonia Aventina came to Aquae Sulis from Gaul and died here. Was she, one wonders, faithfully but vainly seeking a cure for some disease from the hot springs, as Christian believers now reverse the traffic in seeking miracles at Lourdes?

Craftsmen also came from abroad to work on what was clearly a place of great importance and prestige in the northern empire. One of them was Priscus, a mason from the Chartres area, who erected a dedication to Sulis Minerva, among other works. There were priests and soothsayers here, and rogues, too, for a Latin graffito was found inscribed on a piece of lead in one of the reservoirs cursing whoever had kidnapped Vilbia, presumably a woman, probably a slave, perhaps a lover.

When the Romans left Britain in the fifth century, the healing properties of the springs lost their significance and were soon forgotten. The Anglo-Saxons took Bath in AD 577 with much death and destruction, and soon the Roman baths were buried under the rubble of the Dark Ages, a Saxon cemetery usurping the ground dedicated to Sulis Minerva, which remained hidden for over a thousand years.

Winding through the rediscovered steamy labyrinth today, among carved stones heaped up from excavations and pools where rich and poor alike immersed their bodies in the soothing waters, a vision of this cosmopolitan spa of classical times comes easily after a few minutes of acclimatization. A lost world of luxury is evoked by the broken stones and columns whose eloquence is beyond words.

Bath is twelve miles south-east of Bristol. The remains of the Roman baths are the property of the town, and are incorporated in the Museum adjoining the Pump Room at the town centre near the abbey. There are several car parks in the vicinity. ST 751647.

Bryn-celli-ddu

Gwynedd

WE TREKKED DUTIFULLY, on a hot day, across the treeless island of Anglesey to this rudimentary pyramid, thinking of cold drinks and shady woods. After all, it was not

Bryn-celli-ddu. An entrance to the excavated chamber where Celtic settlers on Anglesey buried their dead.

Fountains Abbey or a great castle we were heading for – only a prehistoric burial mound. But this small and isolated ruin is a sacred place almost as compelling – to anyone who is not afraid of alien religion – as any altar of Christendom.

Bryn-celli-ddu is the best example in England and Wales of a megalithic passage grave. It qualifies as a ruin because it has been excavated and restored, and is no longer in the state intended by its builders. The round cairn itself it surrounded by a circle of stones and a ditch. At the entrance to one end of the chamber there is a standing stone on which it is still just possible to detect inscriptions in the form of spirals and wavy lines, which doubtless had magical significance for the benefit of the souls interred here. The spirals may symbolize the sun and the wavy lines may represent serpents – both ancient symbols of life. Inside the chamber, built of upright stone slabs infilled with rubble, there is a smoothly dressed monolith which may be a phallic symbol.

The most striking single fact about this monument's builders, who may have been primitive farmers but were certainly not simple, is that they expended a great deal more energy and skill in protecting their departed than in housing the living. Their graves have survived longer than their homes. This argues a powerful cult of the dead, and the fertility symbols they carved on their tombs suggest that the souls of their ancestors were believed to have some influence on the growth of their crops and the fertility of their womenfolk, among other things.

The chamber may well have had the same function as a family vault – a place which could be reopened when necessary to admit the dead members of an upper-class family through succeeding generations, and as a shrine for ancestor-worship.

It is impossible not to feel here an intimation of pagan sanctity. The New Stone Age men who buried their dead here more than three thousand years ago did so with just as much sombre ritual as attends the lowering of Christian corpses into the earth to the incantations of a solemn churchman.

Bryn-celli-ddu is in the protection of the Welsh Office. It stands on farmland one mile east of Llanddaniel Fab, and is reached by a minor road between that village and A4080 west of Menai Bridge. You must park your car on the road at the end of the signposted farm lane and walk the half mile to the monument, which is in a field near the farmhouse. SH 507702.

Chedworth Villa

Gloucestershire

IF WE COULD summon up the ghosts of those who occupied this magnificent villa in the late Roman period, what sort of people would we find before us? Probably a dark-haired Romano-British family, with some Celtic blood in their veins, one of their military ancestors having married a woman of the British Dobunni tribe which ruled these parts before the invasion. They would be of no more than average height by today's standards. We imagine Romans as tall because of what the awe-struck Anglo-Saxons could only regard as the work of giants. This much is speculation. What is certain is that they were wealthy, with some appreciation of the finer things of life, and despite the traditional pagan images in their superb mosaic floors, they may well have been Christians.

The villa's remains were discovered in 1864, by a gamekeeper digging for his ferret, in the area of intense Roman activity surrounding Cirencester. They stood in rural isolation, in a fine situation at the edge of Chedworth Woods, not far from a spot where Bronze Age men had buried an urn of cremated bones beneath a round barrow. The villa site was one of the best preserved in Britain. Some of its walls were still standing a few feet high.

Since their discovery, the ruins have been properly excavated and carefully preserved, and they form one of the most fascinating glimpses into the Britain of the imperial occupation – the comfortable and stylish home of a rich and no doubt powerful local family before the Roman departure left the people to descend into the Dark Ages.

We know very little about rural life in Roman Britain, but it seems a reasonable assumption that the villa was the head-quarters of an agricultural estate engaged chiefly in sheep-farming, and it may be that the family derived its wealth, as so many later Cotswold families were to do, from wool. It was thought at one time that one of the villa's rooms had been a fullery, but subsequent research showed it to have been a bath-house.

The villa was evidently built early in the second century, but considerably enlarged in the third, to form a large house round two courtyards, with corridors and verandas linking reception rooms, dining room and bathroom suites for both Turkish and sauna baths. The two-storey house had underfloor central heating, and was roofed with Cotswold stone tiles.

It is not easy for us, standing among these fragments of a lost civilization, to reconstruct in imagination the sort of life that people led here, but what these walls and floors tell us unmistakably across sixteen centuries is that this was a luxurious mansion, the inside of which was probably never seen by the humble Britons (except for the house servants) who worked for its owner, either in the nearby fields or at his business in the town.

The tessellated floors were made by paviours from Cirencester, whose style was so distinctive that their work has been recognized at several sites throughout the district. One of the favourite themes of their mosaics was Orpheus, charming the birds and beasts with his lute. One floor at Chedworth showed nymphs and satyrs among figures representing the seasons, one of whom was a man in a cloth cap, well wrapped up against the winter cold, carrying a dead hare. (It is a nice irony that the gamekeeper who dug up the remains also unearthed a poacher.) Celtic deities were

also represented. The floors were made mostly with local materials: the Oolitic and Liassic limestone of which modern villages in the Cotswolds are built was used for the paler colours, with baked tiles and red sandstone brought from elsewhere for the reds and purples.

In the fourth century the villa's water supply was reorganized, being channelled from the spring into a stone cistern, or *nymphaeum*. The Chi-Rho symbol on the stones of the tank wall is one of the few pieces of evidence of British Christianity in the Cotswolds, suggesting that the family may have been converts. Perhaps it was Censorinus, a supposed owner of the villa whose

A broken column and stone foundations of the villa at Chedworth where a wealthy Roman family enjoyed life in what today might be called a 'sought-after location'.

name was found engraved on a silver spoon, who embraced the new faith.

Who can tell what became of the family? If we could make these stones give up their secrets, we should not hear the music of Orpheus, but we might detect the homesick sighs of a Roman officer far from his origins in sunny Italy, or perhaps even the voice of the lady of the house telling the removal men where to put the furniture. There would be little sound of conflict in this rural retreat, I dare say, until the Anglo-Saxons came burning and plundering, but by that time the villa's walls may already have been half buried beneath the soil.

Chedworth Villa is in the protection of the National Trust. It lies just north of Chedworth village in woodland also in the Trust's ownership, and is best reached via A429 turning north towards Yanworth at Fossebridge and following the well-signposted route. There is a car park, a National Trust shop and a museum at the site. SP 053135.

Chysauster

Cornwall

IT HAS been said that the British did not know how to build houses until taught by the Romans, but Chysauster refutes that allegation. Celtic settlers lived here a century before Caesar set foot on British soil, in stone-built houses flanking the wide curving street of the Iron Age village. They built their houses with roughly-coursed dry-stone walls of moorland granite, with drains beneath paved floors and hollowed-out stones for grinding corn. Each house had a small courtyard and a back garden. The courtyard gave access to the rooms whose roofs were probably supported by poles set in stone sockets. These villagers were taught to build houses by necessity, since there was little timber or natural shelter on this bleak moorland.

OPPOSITE *Aerial view of the Iron Age village of Chysauster, showing the closely grouped stone houses of the primitive settlement of tin-miners.*

They came here to extract tin from the valley below, its stream providing the local water supply which was the first requirement for any permanent settlement, and the earliest Cornishmen and their successors continued to occupy this industrial village well into the period of Roman occupation.

Its stone walls still stand six feet high, nearly two thousand years after it was deserted, and testify to the skills of the men in handling granite which later and more sophisticated masons considered unworkable. Where did their knowledge come from? The style of the houses is of Mediterranean origin, and no doubt the small dark-haired Celts brought the crafts of their forefathers with them when they came from sunnier climes to these 'tin islands' to ship ore to their customers back home.

This astonishing ghost village has no obvious defences, but nearby is a 'fogou' – a concealed underground chamber of stone, with a roof of stone slabs covered with earth. The purpose of these artificial caves is uncertain, but they probably had a protective function, secreting stores, or perhaps livestock or people when danger threatened. They would also have served as refrigerators, preserving meat and fish on hot summer days in this shadeless region.

As the elders prepared meals in these dark little rooms on winter nights, and families huddled round their fires as fierce winds blew in from the Atlantic, I fancy the children often listened spellbound to their parents' handed-down tales of Greece and Troy, and conjured up in their imaginations the heroes Hector and Achilles, Ajax and Agamemnon, as English children now listen to stories told on television of Robin Hood and King Arthur.

Chysauster lies on the Penwith peninsula, and is best reached by a minor road just beyond Newmill, two and a half miles north of Penzance. The prehistoric village is in the care of the Department of the Environment, and there is a small car park from which a footpath leads to the enclosure a short distance away. SW 473350.

This distant view of Grimspound shows clearly the circular stone enclosure within which the prehistoric community built their dwellings.

Grimspound

Devon

THE NAME is ominous. 'Grim' was an old English name for Woden or Odin. Early Christians identified him with the Devil, to whom they ascribed all building works they could not otherwise explain. Thus they christened this prehistoric compound the 'devil's livestock enclosure'. But it was actually a Bronze Age village, and although we do not know its exact age, its ruins are even older than those at Chysauster in Cornwall.

We missed the nearest approach to the ruins from the roadside, and trudged ankle-deep in heather across the moor with buzzards soaring overhead like vultures waiting for us to expire from exhaustion. We were unsure if we were going the right way, but it turned out to be the best approach, for suddenly we saw before us the circular enclosing wall, surrounding four acres (1.6 hectares) of land, and it was the only man-made feature in the wild and inhospitable landscape.

The enclosure contains two dozen huts or dwellings, built of undressed moorland granite, and well spaced out. The walls do not remain to any significant height, but they show clearly the size and layout of a stone hut in which a family lived long before the Romans came. The huts were circular with a little protected entrance passage to the one room, and were probably roofed with turf or thatch. Some of them had raised platforms, and hearths for winter fires. The others may have been used for storage rather than for living in. There was a paved entrance to the enclosure,

problems of their time as well as they could. They were the first British Do-It-Yourself experts. They could not have grown much in the way of crops on the thin upland soil, but they tended their livestock, protecting it as well as possible from wild beasts and birds of prey, and they almost certainly did some trading in tin, 'streaming' ore from the rock face, while the women made clothes and prepared meals and their children ran about the village.

But it was a hostile environment they lived in, and in the end the community no doubt deserted the village for a more hospitable site on lower ground. The place was empty long before the birth of Christ, and the remains of the village have stood unknown and undisturbed except by the elements and the creatures of the moor through all the ages of our history up to the last century, when they were identified and partly excavated.

Visitors to Dartmoor pass through this lost village today sometimes unaware that they are walking in the footsteps of the earliest people in Britain. They rest to consult a map on a spot where perhaps a woman who never left Dartmoor in her whole lifetime gave birth to her child unaided, three thousand years ago; and a corner where an adder might coil today, basking in the sunshine among warm stones, is maybe the very spot where a man once lay awaiting death after his long labours. We are not so very different from those people, after all. We still build our shelters from the elements in organized groups, as they did, and cherish the family, and share our 'huts' with domestic animals, and dream up imaginary gods and demons who threaten to destroy us.

flanked by large boulders, and a water supply in the form of a stream running through the village.

To my mind, nothing takes away more instantly the forbidding air of threatening mystery and alien culture with which we tend to invest the unknown, than the sheltering entrances to these huts. There is an exciting and comfortingly familiar touch of practical common sense in the construction of these crude dwellings. The doorways, flanked by upright stones like the village gateway, usually face south-west, so as to form an effective wind-break as well as keeping driving rain and snow out of the living room.

These ancestors of ours were not barbaric savages with whom we can have no possible contact, but thinking people content with their lives as simple farmers and facing the

Grimspound is an Ancient Monument in the protection of the Department of the Environment. It lies unsignposted above and east of the unclassified road leaving B3212 southward towards Widecombe-in-the-Moor, and is about three miles north-east of Postbridge. There is very limited parking space by the roadside, and visitors must walk up a stony path, slippery in wet weather, to the enclosure. SX 701809.

Hadrian's Wall

Northumberland

THE MOST dramatic section of Hadrian's northern frontier is the central part where the long serpent of imperial politics snakes its way along the rocky crest of Whin Sill, a volcanic outcrop forming a natural north-facing barrier from the Cumbrian border to a mile or two beyond the Roman fort at Housesteads. The eastern end of this section, three and a half miles of the wall, with the remains of its milecastles and the fort itself, is owned by the National Trust, and is easily the most evocative remaining part of the frontier built to guard the empire against the red-haired Caledonian barbarians to the north.

With typical scorn for the difficulties of the terrain, the Roman engineers planned the wall to run from coast to coast, seventy-three miles long, and their masons quarried and dressed stone at various points along the route to build outer faces with a core of rubble, bonded with clay and mortar, and with drains to run off water. It was about ten feet wide and about fifteen feet high, with fortified gateways along it at regular intervals and two stone observation turrets between each pair of milecastles. At a later date, a series of major forts was built at strategic points to facilitate troop movements, so that soldiers did not have to march two or three miles to the wall from the older forts which lay behind it on Agricola's Stanegate. The wall itself was accompanied by a great ditch on the north side. The entire wall was built in a little over ten years, including the rebuilding in stone of the western section which had been hurriedly built with turf as a stop-gap.

Although the wall was a very considerable feat of building, it was not an impregnable barrier, and cannot have been conceived as such, with so many gates along it. It was more in the nature of a frontier control than a barricade, but it could be heavily armed and defended when the occasion arose. The gateways were like customs posts – imperial

RIGHT *Hadrian's Wall, looking east from the fort at Housesteads.*

Checkpoint Charlies – through which traders, farmers with their livestock, and others with legitimate business on the other side were allowed to pass in either direction. A service road ran more or less parallel with the wall and a short distance behind it. This is known as the *vallum*, and it could serve as a second line of defence if the wall were breached, as well as protecting the wall against attacks from rebels from the south – the local Brigantes were a constant thorn in the side of the occupying forces.

During the course of their occupation the Romans carried out frequent and extensive repairs to the wall, and it seems clear that it was the object of vandalism rather than systematic raids. It is likely that the Brigantes south of the wall caused as much damage as the barbarian tribes of the north with whom they were in league, and from whom the wall effectively separated them. Nearly ten thousand Roman troops were garrisoned along the wall at one time.

Housesteads was not, of course, the Roman name for the fort, which is a little uncertain. 'Borcovicium' is the most frequently used Latin name today, but 'Vercovicium' is now thought to be more likely. The remains of this best-preserved of the garrison forts provide us with the clearest available images of the daily lives of the auxiliaries, recruited no doubt from all parts of the empire, and stationed in this bleak northern climate, most of them far away from their families in southern Europe. Only local girls of easy virtue and an eye for a man in uniform might lend a half-hour of human comfort now and then to those for whom duty and religion were insufficient consolation. Civilian settlements grew up in the vicinity of the garrison forts along the wall, and prostitution must have been one of the services the British natives provided.

The fort was of rectangular plan with a gate in each of its walls, the service road behind the wall running east-west through it, and the wall itself forming its northern boundary. The bolt

The communal lavatory at Housesteads, the best-preserved of the forts along Hadrian's Wall. The parallel channels carried clean water for the soldiers' ablutions.

holes for the doors can still be seen in the impost of the west gate. At the centre of the fort was the *principia*, or administrative headquarters, with the commanding officer's house, granary and hospital nearby, and barracks, workshops and other buildings laid out in orderly fashion around them. Although there were long periods during the fort's three centuries of occupation when it was peaceful, it was destroyed and rebuilt on three occasions, and in the third century a thousand men were stationed here. Cremation or burial of the dead was carried out well away from the fortress precincts and the civilian settlement, in accordance with Roman custom.

Tucked away at the south-eastern corner of the fort is one of the best-preserved and most famous of its buildings – the latrine. Men would have sat on wooden seats with holes, along the walls of this communal lavatory. Stone channels below the seating were flushed by water from a cistern, and clean water ran through narrow channels in front of the seating so that the soldiers could wash their sponges in it. The position of the latrine was chosen at the lowest corner of the fort so that waste water from the whole area could be channelled through it and sewage was carried well away from the buildings.

Kipling suggested that the Roman officers who were in command of the garrison were perhaps posted here as a punishment, and it is a plausible conjecture. There had been plenty of Roman citizens who were not anxious to follow up Julius Caesar's conquest of 55 BC, protesting that Britain was 'beyond the known world'. Who can say what the course of history might have been if Claudius had listened to their counsel?

The Roman Army officers, legionaries and auxiliaries paid dutiful lip-service to the various gods from all parts of Europe and Asia to whom they owed their loyalty. Priority was given to Jupiter and Mithras, the bull-slaying Persian god of light and wisdom, who had a strong appeal for the military mind, and to whom temples were built at several points along the wall, including Housesteads. But there were dedications to many other gods as well, Mars and Hercules, Codicius and Vulcan among them. There is little sign of Christianity having had any hold on the troops manning the wall. Their main off-duty preoccupations were no doubt boasting about their sexual exploits, scratching obscene graffiti on the walls of barrack rooms and latrines, and slandering the cooks. Phallic symbols have been found inscribed here and there along the wall.

Interest in the history and preservation of the wall began with the Elizabethan antiquary William Camden, but it has taken a long time to get the remains protected. Camden was unable to visit Housesteads because of the 'mosstroopers' – feudal clans who made travelling unsafe by their piracy and aggression – for they terrorized the region. Centuries of Christian bigotry regarded this pagan monument only as a source of building stone. It was quarried in the mid-eighteenth century for the Carlisle–Newcastle road, and even during the Second World War its stone was taken away for military use. In 1801 the antiquary William Hutton walked the length of the wall, at the age of seventy-eight, and found at one point a man named Tulip building a house with the wall's stones, and tearfully implored him not to destroy any more of the finest testament to our Roman heritage.

It is extremely sobering to stand here among the rubble of antiquity's most powerful, proud and glorious empire, itself conquered, for all its might, after only a brief moment in earth's history.

Hadrian's Wall crosses the country from Newcastle upon Tyne to Bowness on the Solway Firth. The section in the National Trust's care runs north-eastward from near the inn called Twice Brewed on B6318, and includes the fort at Housesteads, NY 790688. The fort and museum at the site are in the guardianship of the Department of the Environment. There are car parks beside the wall near Twice Brewed and beside the road near Housesteads, to which one must walk a quarter of a mile.

Hardknott Fort

Cumbria

TO THE NINTH circle of his 'Inferno' Dante consigned traitors, whose souls were embedded in a frozen lake of ice. To the imagination of a medieval Florentine poet this was apparently a worse torment than being boiled in pitch or roasted by flames. And no doubt any suntanned Roman natives who were unfortunate enough to be stationed here on Hardknott Pass, in this bleak and forbidding outpost of empire, might equally have thought Hades a city much like Hardknott. Some ancient Greeks had believed that the

Part of the Roman fort at Hardknott Pass, spectacularly sited high up in the Cumbrian fells.

souls of the dead went to the far north where the sun never shone, and others believed the damned were driven there by savage hounds.

The multi-headed dog Cerberus guarding the approaches to hell is replaced here by the most daunting road in England – a tortuous ascent of one-in-three gradients and hairpin bends from the east. When you reach the top of the pass you begin a gradual descent towards Eskdale, and soon on your right you reach the remains of the stone fortress built by the governor Agricola on a triangular plateau, with gates in each of its four walls and dramatic drops on two sides. It had a parade ground, centrally heated quarters, baths and granaries. But what was it for?

Agricola's military objective, before he was recalled to Rome, had been to subdue the whole island, and he may have intended to invade Ireland, too. He established a port on the coast at Glannaventa (now Ravenglass), either for defensive purposes against Caledonian attacks by sea, or for offensive purposes against the Gaels and Picts of Hibernia. And to link the port with inland military networks he or one of his successors during Trajan's reign built, with characteristic Roman audacity, a road straight across the mountains, with a fort at each end and one in the middle.

The middle one was called Mediobogdum, and was nearly nine hundred feet up in the Cumbrian fells, remote and impregnable. Possibly the governor over-estimated the will and organizing ability of Rome's Celtic enemies. Nothing can have taken the imperial troops by surprise here, except perhaps the June thunder, symbolic of the Christian world that was soon to overtake them –

Blackness at half-past eight, the night's precursor,
Clouds like falling masonry and lightning's lavish
Annunciation, the sword of the mad archangel
　Flashed from the scabbard.

That may have startled them now and then, but no native raiding party can have been a threat to this formidable stronghold.

Substantial remains of the walls, partly restored after centuries of plunder by local farmers, show the layout of this military establishment which – though it has been derelict for almost two thousand years – remains as graphic evidence of that Roman thoroughness, discipline and efficiency which gave us the foundations of our civilization. Five hundred men may have been stationed here at one time.

Outside the fort itself, the parade ground was levelled out of the solid rock, and a bath-house was built with the usual *frigidarium* alongside the warm and hot baths. If any proof were needed that the progress of civilization has made us soft, imagine the Roman legionaries, for whom regular bathing was almost a ritual, plunging into a cold bath up here on this wild and windlashed mountain-top in a freezing northern winter.

I doubt if human nature has changed so much in two thousand years that the awful realities of an army on a foreign tour of duty were any different then. No doubt Roman officers kept their men busy and maintained harsh discipline, and perhaps the cold baths cooled their sexual ardour, for no local girls can have hung around the barrack guardroom here to bring relief and warm respite to the soldiers' long and lonely nights far from home. But the hot baths undoubtedly provided a steamy veil behind which consenting auxiliaries could follow their inclinations. Somewhere in the valleys below there must be stones in barn or farmhouse walls on which idle Roman soldiers scratched obscene graffiti to amuse themselves. Such were the by-products of the grandeur that was Rome.

Hardknott Fort stands on the north side of the road between Ambleside and Ravenglass. The approach from the east, via Wrynose and Hardknott Passes, is not to be recommended to nervous drivers or temperamental vehicles. The western approach is easier. You can park near the foot of the pass after crossing the cattle grid and walk to the ruins. There is parking space beside the road near the fort for those who drive there. NY 219014.

Letocetum

Staffordshire

IT IS ONLY the distance of time that marks the remaining fragments of the Roman site at Wall as something of more than passing interest. If they were not protected by a fence and guarded by a ticket office, we would pass without pausing, thinking them the foundations of a building demolished last week by property developers erecting a new supermarket. But the clue is in Wall's position on Watling Street. This was a posting station where a traveller on one of the principal highways of Roman Britain could have a night's rest and change horses. He might be an imperial messenger, travelling on the same road all the way from Londinium to Deva (Chester), via Verulamium and Viroconium.

It appears, in fact, that Wall may have been a town of some size once, originating at an early stage of the Roman occupation as a garrison for the Fourteenth Legion. Excavation goes on here, and no doubt we have much to learn about the place. Coins from the reign of Tiberius have been found here, and a Roman cemetery has been discovered nearby.

The visible remains comprise a public bath-house (naturally) and a building known as the 'villa', though the latter may have been a hostel. The bath-house is one of the most complete remaining in Britain, though it has undergone much structural alteration in its time, and Lichfield has profited from its stone. Village stories of workmen breaking up a statue of Minerva to repair a drain tell us all too clearly why we can no longer see the twelve-foot-high walls that the antiquary William Stukeley described in the eighteenth century. How were they to know that the figure of a woman dressed like a man was one of the foremost Roman deities, who was always represented with a helmet and shield because she protected soldiers in wartime? And would they have cared if they *had* known?

What we can see here among the half-

revealed foundations covered by the archaeologists' tarpaulins is the layout of bath rooms, with their plumbing and hypocausts, where naked Romans lay on tables to be massaged with perfumed ointments by slaves, while the British natives outside scoffed (under their breaths, of course) at these foreign

FURNACE

pansies with such a partiality for communal purification, who washed themselves with sponges on sticks after using the latrine. The British, Tacitus tells us, were easily seduced by Roman manners and customs into the slavery of imitation. But only up to a point, one feels.

The ruins of Letocetum are in the village of Wall just off A5 two miles south-west of Lichfield. They are owned by the National Trust but in the guardianship of the Department of the Environment, and there is a small museum at the site. Park in the village street. SK 099067.

Part of the furnace and hypocaust revealed by excavation at Letocetum, a Roman garrison and later posting station.

29

Segontium

Gwynedd

COMPARED WITH the Roman domestic refinements of Chedworth, the engineering achievements of Hadrian's Wall, and the civilizing influences of Bath, the low remaining walls of the auxiliary fort at Segontium may not seem to offer much to the visitor's imagination. But here at what is now Caernarfon is the clearly laid-out site of what is by any standards an impressively large complex, built to accommodate a garrison of a thousand men at the western entrance to the Menai Straits.

Coastal fortification in Wales was aimed mainly at protecting the empire from Irish raiders, and the first timber fort here was rebuilt in the second century using red sandstone brought from Cheshire. It was the first of several rebuildings, and aqueducts and road repairs were also being made in the area

Segontium. Remains of the extensive auxiliary fort built to guard the entrance to the Menai Straits. The buildings included barracks, granaries, workshops, stables, a bath-house and an underground strong-room.

Roman troops after other forts in the region, such as Chester, had been abandoned, and undoubtedly protection from piracy of the copper brought across to the mainland from Anglesey was one strong reason for the military presence, for the Romans used copper, as an ingredient of bronze, on a large scale throughout the vast empire.

Imperial occupation of Segontium ended in AD 383, when the Roman general Magnus Maximus masterminded a campaign to seize Europe, having declared himself Emperor of Britain. It is said that he took across the Channel thirty thousand soldiers and a hundred thousand natives, none of whom ever came back. Welsh legend calls him Maxen Wledig, a folk hero, and relates him somewhat obscurely to Constantine, and to a line of Welsh kings. The Welsh called this place *Caer Custenit*, the City of Constantine, and believed the Emperor to have lived here once. (As Gibbon remarks, 'The prudent reader may not perhaps be satisfied with such Welch evidence.')

Maximus married Elen, a beautiful native princess, who became known as 'Queen Helen of the Hosts' because she marched with her husband's legions, but he did not long survive his usurpation of the imperial purple, being put to death by Theodosius in 388.

Evacuation of Segontium left it to decline into ruin and local plundering of its stone. In the course of time the site became buried beneath the new town of Caernarfon which grew up around Edward I's great fortress, built, as Defoe put it, to 'curb and reduce the wild people of the mountains'. There it lay hidden for centuries, until the 1920s when Mortimer Wheeler unearthed and interpreted what remained.

at about the time of the first stone reconstruction. The size and regular review of the fort at Segontium indicates an importance to the Romans greater than that of a mere defensive outpost against intermittent raids across Oceanus Hibernicus, or against rebellion among the local Ordovician natives. The Romans had an economic reason for taking good care of this corner of their empire: they mined copper in the area.

Segontium continued to be occupied by

The ruins of Segontium are on the south-eastern outskirts of Caernarfon on A4085. They are National Trust property in the guardianship of the Welsh Office, and there is a museum on the site containing finds from the excavation. Cars can be parked in the road outside. SH 485625.

Stonehenge

Wiltshire

NOWHERE ELSE in Britain – indeed, hardly anywhere else in Europe – does the whisper of prehistory send such a shiver of apprehension up the spine. What power over men's minds drove Neolithic men to such mighty efforts in erecting these great megaliths?

Scientific study of ancient sites and monuments has swept away so much mystery in this century that the lingering spirits of those distant ancestors might seem to have been banished altogether in many places. But Stonehenge is an exceptional case. We know where they got the stones; we have a pretty good idea how they transported them over long distances; we can confidently demonstrate how they hoisted them into their upright positions. But there is one puzzle the scientists cannot solve, and that the most important of all – *why*? It is the unanswered question that renders Stonehenge fascinating and forbidding at the same time, for we are in the presence of the unknown – we cannot comprehend the nature of the men who built this thing, which is at once sophisticated and barbaric.

Stonehenge has nothing to do with Druids, as is commonly believed. It was there on Salisbury Plain a thousand years before the first Druids came to Britain. This fact does not relieve our apprehension, however, but rather increases it, for at least we know a little bit about the Druids. We can relate to them, if only slightly, through the threads of ritual and common beliefs running through all religion. The oak and the mistletoe are not more baffling sacred objects than holy water or the eucharist, and the Christian symbol of torture and death is not less sinister than the Celtic wickerwork instrument of sacrifice. But with Stonehenge we grope in the dark, and that is more unsettling than unpalatable fact.

Not that Stonehenge is without its light relief. Geoffrey of Monmouth repeated the old legend that the magician Merlin had spirited the whole monument over from Ireland, and that 'not a stone is there that lacketh in virtue of witchcraft'. A seventeenth-century author speculated that it was the tomb of Boudicca, and it has even been pinpointed as the burial place of Uther Pendragon, King Arthur's father.

There is no space here to go into great detail about the known history and architecture of Stonehenge, but a brief summary is necessary. The outer perimeter of the site consists of a circular ditch with a bank of chalk built up inside it, and inside them is a ring of pits (now filled in) known as the Aubrey Holes, as it was John Aubrey who discovered them. Many of those excavated have been found to contain burnt human bones. It is believed that these three concentric circles were made around 2200 BC, and were followed about five hundred years later by the erection of an inner double circle of bluestones, which were brought here from Pembrokeshire. Some of them weigh four tons. The men whose work these later circles represent were probably the Beaker people, who may have been sun-worshippers, since the axis of their circle – marked by an entrance at one side and a pit at the other – pointed to the rising sun on the summer solstice.

The early Bronze Age brought fresh building works to Stonehenge, when the bluestone circles were removed to make way for colossal trilithons of sarsen stone, arranged in an outer circle and an inner horseshoe, whose axis also points towards the rising sun on the longest day of the year. The huge grey sarsen stones were dragged from the Marlborough Downs, fifteen miles or more to the north. Many were laboriously shaped into curved lintels to form a continuous architrave round the outer circle, and secured in position by mortise and tenon joints. This circle entitles Stonehenge to the status of architecture and qualifies its present condition as a ruin, as distinct from those more primitive circles of standing stones found in various parts of Britain.

Further elaboration went on up to about 1300 BC, so that the known period of

Stonehenge's building and use was longer than that of any great English cathedral; yet we do not know what it was for, and it refuses to give up its secrets. No echoes bounce off its stones when you call out; you are surrounded by the stubborn silence of antiquity, and some power urges you to speak in hushed tones. George Borrow felt compelled to remove his hat and make obeisance on the ground, and in *Tess of the d'Urbervilles* Thomas Hardy laid his heroine on the so-called Altar Stone here, in the manner of Greek tragedy, before her sacrifice to the idea of Justice. This building may have been a sanctuary, or it may have been an observatory, but whatever its purpose, it was a place of great importance to the people who began it nearly a thousand years before Tutankhamun was King of Egypt. It must have been the focus of all the most powerful beliefs of the tribes of men, women and children living in southern Britain. My own strong conviction is that this building was a temple for worship at a period of human history when religion and astronomy were virtually the same thing.

There seem to be definite links between the Stonehenge builders and the civilization of Mycenae in Greece. Carvings of a dagger and axe-heads on the stones are similar to tools and weapons found in the shaft graves of Mycenae, which were within circles and, in one case, contained the remains of children. The architecture of Stonehenge itself suggests the influence of Mycenae, where the great Agamemnon is supposed to have lived. There is an old tradition that heroes from Troy founded Britain and France, and although Stonehenge was complete well before Troy is believed to have fallen, the possibility that the legend has some basis of truth is perhaps one of the most fascinating things about Stonehenge to the romantic. If the grandson of

A bird's-eye view of Stonehenge in which the whole complex is clearly visible: the ring of Aubrey Holes, now filled with cement, is just inside the circular ditch, and the Heel Stone is on the right, close to the roadside. This view is looking roughly north-west.

OVERLEAF *Morning sunlight on Stonehenge.*

33

Carvings of axes and a hilted dagger on the sarsen stones were only discovered in 1953 among more modern graffiti. The style of the dagger points to a direct link with Mycenaean Greece.

Aeneas *did* land with his Trojan companions at Totnes, it may have been in the wake of earlier travellers from urban Mediterranean centres, who brought their skills to these islands and gave the English the foundations of a civilization different from the military efficiency of the Roman Empire, but possibly of greater influence on the history and culture of the people than has hitherto been realized.

Stonehenge remains a dramatic witness to the fact that sophisticated builders were at work in Britain soon after the pyramids were erected in Egypt, and like those great monuments it has been subjected to irreverent attack over the centuries. Many of its stones have been broken up and carted away for building or for making roads, and visitors have chipped off fragments as souvenirs – to say nothing of its occasional defacement by vandals. This has resulted in one of the greatest disasters of all – a protective barrier which now prevents visitors from mingling with the stones, which is the only way to savour their power and glory. It also has a backcloth of more mundane scenery in the shape of an army camp. But it stands, despite all indignities, as the most ancient and the most awesome of all the ruins of England and Wales, and its haunting mysteries will probably continue to exercise the minds of archaeologists, anthropologists and pure romantics for many centuries to come.

Stonehenge, which is in the care of the Department of the Environment, stands two miles west of Amesbury near the junction of A303 and A344. There is a large car park at the site. SU 123422.

Verulamium

Hertfordshire

ONLY THE RAIN of centuries, surely, could have washed the blood and tears from the stones of Verulamium, the ancient town beside which St Albans grew up. As one stands among the ruins of the Roman *municipium*, in the peaceful outskirts of the modern city, one sees only the remnants of lost civilization – well-built walls, hypocaust, theatre and so on – and it is easy to imagine that it was in the far north, on the boundaries of empire, where all the warfare occurred. But this is a place of massacre, where the little River Ver turned crimson with the blood of both Romans and Britons.

When Julius Caesar made his second expedition to Britain in 54 BC, he marched on the tribal stronghold of the Catuvellauni and attacked it from two sides, overpowering the natives and forcing their war-lord to come to terms with the invaders. This *oppidum* or tribal capital, 'strategically placed among woods and marshland', as Caesar himself described it, may have been at Wheathampstead, not far away, but we know from coins that after Caesar's departure the Catuvellauni moved their headquarters to Prae Wood near St Albans, where the Roman *municipium* of Verulamium was to supersede the British tribe's chief settlement, called by Sir Mortimer Wheeler a 'prehistoric metropolis'.

Under the governorship of Aulus Plautius the city grew on rising ground beside the river and the new military road which we know as Watling Street. It was laid out and built with characteristic Roman precision, with a drainage system and timber-framed houses within its protective earthworks. But it was doomed to destruction. When the Iceni under the wounded lioness Boudicca stormed Verulamium from the east, they burnt the city and slaughtered its inhabitants without discrimination – women and children as well as men had their throats cut or were hanged, burned

or crucified, according to Tacitus. We need not doubt that the Roman reprisals that drove Boudicca to suicide were any less savage, and the smouldering ashes of Verulamium lay for over a decade before a new city began to take shape here.

The public buildings – forum, baths, gateways, theatre, temples, etc. – were built of stone, but houses and shops were built of cheaper materials – wood, clay and bricks. Timber-framed buildings always present a fire risk, and Verulamium suffered a serious fire around AD 155, after which the city was largely re-planned and new houses were built of flint with tiled roofs, the wealthier residents decorating their rooms with frescoes and mosaics. The town was surrounded by a wall with an impressive gateway over the road leading in from London: the two carriageways at the centre, with pedestrian passages on either side, were flanked by large battlemented towers. Building materials found here have included marble from Carrara in Italy and limestone from Purbeck in Dorset.

Undoubtedly most interesting among the ruins of Verulamium is the open-air theatre, for it is the only one of its kind in Britain. A Roman theatre, where mimes and recitations were probably performed, was different from an amphitheatre, where gladiators fought and other blood sports were conducted. A theatre was usually D-shaped with raked seating arranged in a semicircle looking down on the raised stage. There is no evidence to suggest that this form of entertainment was popular in Britain, however, and the theatre at Verulamium was constructed in nearly circular form, with both stage and arena, so that it could be used as a theatre and as an amphitheatre. Its proximity to a Romano-British temple suggests that it may have been used for religious ceremonies as well, but we do not know if more sinister Roman 'entertainments', such as public executions and fights between men and animals, took place here. It would be surprising if they did not. We inherited a great deal from the Romans which we could well have done without.

The theatre at Verulamium. The column has been restored. It stood at the back of the stage, in front of which part of the arena can be seen. Spectators had a clear view of both stage and arena.

It was in about AD 303 that Alban, a citizen of Verulamium, was executed outside the city walls for harbouring a Christian priest. He thus gave his name to the modern city, where the great cathedral tower was built of material from the ruined Roman town. After the departure of the Romans from Britain, Verulamium, by now generally called Verlamacestir, according to Bede, continued to be inhabited for some time, but gradually fell into decay as the new city grew up across the river. The theatre became a rubbish dump, while the ancient walls and houses were quarried for their building materials.

The echoes I hear from these walls are not hymns to Dionysus and Minerva, nor the secret invocations of Christian converts, but the screams of innocent women and children who were among the earliest victims in Britain of political unwisdom.

Verulamium lies on the west side of St Albans, on the south bank of the river and spreading out on either side of A414 Hemel Hempstead road. There is a museum on the site, near St Michael's church, containing many finds and exhibits from the Roman town. The theatre's National Grid reference is TL 134075. It is in private ownership, but open to the public.

Viroconium Cornoviorum

Shropshire

IN AD 129–30 an enlarged precinct and city hall at Viroconium were dedicated to the Emperor Hadrian in a superbly inscribed sandstone tablet thirteen feet long, erected over a portico at the entrance. It read in translation: 'To the Emperor Caesar Trajanus Hadrianus Augustus, Father of his Country, the Community of the Cornovii erected this building.' The new structures were part of the planned improvements resulting from the emperor's visit seven years earlier, and the expanded city, which had begun as a legionary garrison, became the fourth largest in the British Isles and the civic capital of the Cornovii, who had inhabited this part of Britain long before the Romans came.

It has lain in ruins for 1500 years, but its remains, though little enough for the layman to see, can stir the imagination. The city covered 180 acres (70 hectares) astride the road we call Watling Street, 120 miles north-west of Verulamium. It had a planned system of streets with shops along the *via principalis*, many fine town houses where tribal magnates lived, and large public baths. One of the magnates' wives owned a fine silver mirror, circular in shape with a handle formed like two vines tied together in a reef knot. The silver may have come from mines on the Stiperstones to the west where the Romans also obtained lead for their water conduits.

But in a part of England where timber was more readily available than stone, fire was a constant threat, and around AD 155 the relatively new forum and basilica were burnt down. They were promptly rebuilt on a more ambitious scale than before, but in AD 287 another great fire occurred, and this time the will to rebuild the city was not there. Possibly these fires were the results of raids by Celtic brigands, who frequently supplemented the surprise of ambush with the surprise of armed attack in the manner that was to make the Welsh borderland an uneasy area for

The 'Old Work' at Viroconium. This piece of Roman masonry was part of a gymnasium wall. The public baths were close to it, in a city centre dedicated to the Emperor Hadrian.

centuries to come. In one of the hypocausts here, archaeologists found the remains of an old man and two women who had evidently crawled in to hide, and were perhaps afraid to come out again.

The only fragment of Viroconium still standing to a substantial height is a 25-foot block of masonry long known locally as the 'Old Work'. It was built of stone with courses of Roman brick, in the rebuilding after the first fire, and it seems to have formed the south wall of a large gymnasium alongside the public baths. Why a city of such size and distinction should have been established in such an unpromising area for Roman civilization is a mystery. And it is a measure of the early decline of Viroconium Cornoviorum that even before the imperial departure from Britain the basilica had been built over with sub-Roman timber buildings, which probably lasted until the Cornovii moved their headquarters to the Severn-ringed site of modern Shrewsbury.

The derelict city became a stone quarry for builders from far and wide, and it was the great civil engineer Thomas Telford (1757–1834), then employed in Shrewsbury by Sir William Pulteney, who first carried out inexpert but pioneering archaeological work here. He also prevented further desecration by farmers who were in the habit of digging up

stone foundations from beneath their fields in order to repair their barns and sheds. 'They know where there are Ruins underneath', Telford wrote, 'by the Corn being scorched in dry weather, so that when they wish to Dig for Stones they put down a mark on the place until the Corn is off the ground, when on removing the Soil they are sure of finding something or another.' Two centuries later we use observation of crop marks from the air to identify the foundations of antiquity below ground level, and congratulate ourselves on this 'discovery' by modern science!

A medieval cemetery and ridge-and-furrow fields which gradually covered the old city have now given way to exposed walls and foundations which were long ago a noisy hubbub of cosmopolitan activity. Soldiers would have marched along streets where market traders shouted to potential customers, children played, blacksmiths worked at their anvils and potters at their wheels.

Viroconium lies close to the modern village of Wroxeter, just south of A5 between Shrewsbury and Telford. The site is in the care of the Department of the Environment. There is a car park and small museum at the site. Other finds, including the reconstructed dedicatory inscription and the silver mirror mentioned above, are in Rowley's House Museum in Shrewsbury. SJ 565085.

Wayland's Smithy

Oxfordshire

THIS HAUNTING presence from the distant past is a long barrow – a Neolithic burial chamber which was once roofed with stone slabs and entirely buried within an earth mound. It was excavated in the nineteenth century, but its hidden secrets were intimated long before that in the name given to it in local folklore – Wayland Smith's Cave. It is probably a thousand years older than the oldest parts of Stonehenge, its entrance flanked by ten-foot-high sarsen stones which Stone Age men dragged across the Marlborough Downs.

Wayland's Smithy stands beside the ancient track now known as the Ridgeway, and only a

Wayland's Smithy. A Neolithic burial chamber once believed to contain the magic forge of the Norse god Wayland. The huge sarsen stones flank the entrance to a gallery grave built c.3700 BC.

mile from the most famous prehistoric carving on the chalk hills of southern England, the Uffington White Horse. What could be more natural than that awe-struck Anglo-Saxons should pick up the Viking myth of Wayland or Volund, the fabulous smith, and attach it to this hidden chamber, for Wayland himself was said to be the owner of a white horse, and the legend grew that any traveller whose horse had cast a shoe need only leave the animal and a coin at the entrance to the 'cave' for the horse to be shod by the smith's magic by the time its owner came back for it.

Wayland was the Teutonic equivalent of the Greek Hephaestus and the Roman Vulcan, gods of fire and furnaces. Norse legend has it that he was the son of the giant Wade and the lover of a sun-maiden called Allwise, but was crippled by King Nidud for stealing his gold. Wayland's hamstrings were severed, and he was always represented as being lame. He was marooned on an island, but escaped by making wings from birds' feathers, with which he flew away, having taken revenge on the king by killing his sons and making goblets from their skulls and jewels from their eyes. Thereafter he applied himself to making wondrous ornaments and weapons at his anvil. In the epic poem 'Beowulf' the hero goes into battle against the fiend Grendel in a coat of mail from the forge of Wayland, bearing a sword to bring him victory –

> a Giant-sword from former days, formidable
> were its edges,
> a warrior's admiration. This wonder of its kind
> was yet so enormous that no other man
> would be equal to bearing it in battle-play –
> it was a Giant's forge that had fashioned it so
> well.

This brings to mind, of course, King Arthur's 'Excalibur'. The links between Christian heroes, prehistoric men and pagan gods are strong and well forged, and Wayland's Smithy is one of them. The Church tried hard to suppress pagan myths, but the collective unconscious retained them and transferred their best attributes to its own folklore.

Legend apart, however, the so-called Wayland's Smithy is interesting enough in the established facts about it to qualify as one of the most fascinating prehistoric ruins in Britain. It was originally built as a gallery grave for fourteen people around 3700 BC, and consisted of a stone-floored mortuary hut with a wooden roof like a ridge-tent. Later this was replaced by a stone tomb in the shape, ironically enough, of a cruciform church, with a passage and two side chambers. It contained eight bodies, from which the heads had been separated.

Of the six huge sarsens which once framed its entrance, four remain – an imposing façade which indicates clearly the ritual importance that burial of the dead had for the folk who mourned their departed here. The barrow itself is now enclosed within a grove of trees which does little to help the visitor feel the presence of Stone Age spirits – it reminds one more of Druids. Whether the dead were mourned as friends or relatives of the more exalted members of the community, we cannot tell, but it is remarkable that the ruins of a tomb built more than five thousand years ago have retained such an enduring place in the English imagination.

Wayland's Smithy is an ancient monument in the care of the Department of the Environment. It is a mile north-east of Ashbury (near Swindon) and is reached from B4000 along a signposted road leading to the Ridgeway long-distance footpath, where one must leave the car and walk about a third of a mile to the ruin. SU 281854.

Ecclesiastical Ruins:
HALLOWED STONES

- Lindisfarne Priory
- Lanercost Priory
- Egglestone Abbey
- Mount Grace Priory
- Jervaulx Abbey
- Rievaulx Abbey
- Furness Abbey
- Bolton Priory
- Fountains Abbey
- Kirkham Priory
- Whalley Abbey
- Kirkstall Abbey
- Thornton Abbey
- Calceby Church
- Valle Crucis Abbey
- Pickworth Church
- Wenlock Priory
- Bawsey Church
- Crowland Abbey
- Castle Acre Priory
- Coventry Cathedral
- Ramsey Abbey
- Abbey-Cwm-Hir
- Lower Brockhampton Chapel
- Walberswick Church
- Hailes Abbey
- Clophill Church
- Tintern Abbey
- Ayot St Lawrence Church
- Glastonbury Abbey
- Bayham Abbey
- Netley Abbey
- Knowlton Church

AFTER THE military and civil engineering achievements of the Romans came the religious buildings of Christian England; and of those that have been reduced to ruin, most – though by no means all – are accounted for by Henry VIII's suppression of the monasteries. This act was, of course, one of the most outrageous misuses of kingly power in the history of England, but the holy men and women of the abbeys, priories and nunneries to a great extent brought the Dissolution upon themselves by their scandalous neglect of their vows. They had received short shrift long before from William Langland, who was among the first, with John Wycliffe, to state publicly that there was something rotten in the state of Rome, and in 'The Vision of Piers Plowman' he gives us a picture of a nunnery rather different from what we might imagine when standing among the quiet ruins of the cloisters:

> Sister Joan was a bastard.
> Sister Clarice was a knight's daughter;
> Sister Pernell a priest's wench, not fit to be a
>   Prioress;
> She bore a child in cherry-time: all the chapter
>   knew it.
> They challenged her with it at election-day –
> 'Liar', cries one. 'Liar, liar', cries the other.
> Each hit the other under the cheek bone.
> Had they had knives, by Christ, each had killed
>   the other.

Although the charges brought by Henry's commissioners were frequently exaggerated and sometimes invented, there is no doubt that monstrous corruption had infected the religious houses, and Henry needed no other excuse to visit his wrath upon the Church and turn its wealth in England to his own account.

The ruined abbeys did not have to await the arrival of the Romantic Movement before their charms were appreciated. Both Shakespeare and John Webster had referred to them within eighty years of the Dissolution, and Webster anticipated the Romantics when he put some lines into the mouth of Antonio in *The Duchess of Malfi*:

> I do love these ancient ruins.
> We never tread upon them but we set
> Our foot upon some reverend history:
> And, questionless, here in this open court,
> Which now lies naked to the injuries
> Of stormy weather, some men lie interr'd
> Lov'd the church so well, and gave so largely to't,
> They thought it should have canopied their bones
> Till doomsday . . .

Many of the old abbeys can be seen in paintings and engravings, and even in early photographs, with their decaying walls rising from grassy floors and clad in ivy. It is a matter of great sadness that we can no longer see them as the Romantics saw them, untouched by the hand of over-zealous restorer or conservationist. The tidying up of so many ruins, whilst revealing their foundations and architectural design, has inevitably destroyed much of their romance.

The little cabin or kiosk where you pay your entrance fee and get your ticket from a machine like those at a cinema box-office does nothing to sustain the sense of awe you would feel on coming to the place by chance, silent and deserted, with no sign of disturbance by man or beast for four centuries. But waste-paper baskets, displays of literature and well-meaning signposts are the price we must pay for preservation of these treasures in an age of easy accessibility and deplorable vandalism.

In some ways, this fact lends a special charm to those tiny ruins one occasionally finds which no one feels impelled to protect. I have a vivid memory of walking down a quiet lane to the little ruined church at Bix Bottom, in Oxfordshire, and hearing a murmur, as I approached, which I fancied was the ghost of some long-dead incumbent preaching the gospel to a congregation of sparrows. It turned out to be the beehives of the local apiarist occupying the former churchyard, but it was no less haunting an experience for that. I have included a few of these almost-forgotten little churches in contrast to the rich and powerful abbeys which everyone expects to find here. They are sometimes harder to track down and are often on private land, but their discovery is nearly always rewarding, and their forlorn remains more poignant than the ruins of places so much more magnificent and awe-inspiring.

It was the great abbey churches which appealed to the Romantics, of course. Tintern inspired poets more than painters; Fountains *vice versa*. But whereas a tiny castle is less awesome than a great one, simply because it is the very size and scale of the thing that impresses us most, it is not the same with churches. The great abbeys may haunt us with their melancholy beauty, their mouldering towers and edifices harbouring bats and screech-owls and their cloisters ghostly with moon-cast shadows. But even the most humble of decaying churches affects our senses, inducing involuntary reverence which, though it may be a preconditioned reaction, we cannot escape. We may not feel the presence of God in this materialistic age, but the enduring superstitions of mankind impart a kind of sanctity.

Abbey-Cwm-Hir

Powys

ONLY A FEW overgrown and scarcely visible bits of stone wall remain above ground as evidence that any building ever stood in this riverside meadow deep in the Welsh country-side, in what used to be Radnorshire, and one needs a vivid imagination to see Cistercian monks filing solemnly into a great abbey church here for matins. Leland told the story with his usual conciseness in the sixteenth century:

Comehere an abbay of White Monkes stondith betwixt ii great hilles in Melennith in a botom wher rennith a little broke. No chirch in Wales is seene of such length as the fundation of walles there begon doth show; but the third part of this worke was never finisched. Al the howse was spoilid and defacid be Owen Glindour.

Lest we are misled by Leland's spelling, 'Comehere' or *Cwm hir* means 'long valley'. The abbey is said to have been founded here in 1147. But can we believe that these few scattered stones on the ground were actually part of the greatest church in Wales at one time? Well, it stood in ten acres (4.4 hectares) of ground bounded by the Clywedog Brook and had extensive fish-ponds which can still be traced, and an eighty-yard-long nave in its church. And when Llywelyn ap Gruffydd, the last native Prince of Wales, was killed in 1282 it was to this church that his body is believed to have been brought for burial. If it had not been reduced to rubble, it might have become a shrine as important to the Welsh as West-minster Abbey is to the English.

Surely Owain Glyndwr would have been kinder to the place if his ancestor, to whose

Abbey-cwm-hir. Nothing but a few fragments of masonry and scattered stones remain to show the site of what was once the greatest church in Wales.

fame he owed a great part of his own success as a leader of the Welsh, was really buried here? Glyndwr was descended from Llywelyn and styled himself 'Prince of Wales' when he raised an army against England. He was not solely responsible for the abbey's ruin, in any case, as Henry III had ordered its partial destruction in revenge for the alleged treachery of the monks, but Glyndwr completed the job in 1401, and only slight restoration was carried out before the Dissolution, after which practically all its stone was carted away to be used in other buildings – in particular the church at Llanidloes.

This abandoned place of worship, where neither nave nor chapter house, cloister nor dormitory, remain even in part to start our imaginations wandering, is eloquent only in the site itself – a characteristic Cistercian habitation, low, remote and well-watered.

The remains are in the village named Abbeycwmhir, surrounded by woods on a minor road north-east of Rhayader. They lie in a field between road and stream, and are reached by a path from the village street, where cars can be parked. SO 057712.

Ayot St Lawrence Church

Hertfordshire

IN 1948 the long-ruined fourteenth-century church of Ayot St Lawrence was given a new pair of wrought-iron gates at the churchyard entrance from the village street, and the occupant of the old rectory, who was invited to unveil them, told the gathered villagers: 'This is His house, this is His gate, and this is His way.' Nothing unusual about that, one might think, except that the speaker was Ayot's most famous resident, the ninety-two-year-old sage George Bernard Shaw, not exactly noted for such orthodox Christian sentiments.

Ayot St Lawrence had become used to the

unpredictable by that time, however, for the man who had brought the church to its ruinous condition was the eighteenth-century lord of the manor, Sir Lionel Lyde, whose classical tastes led him to build a new church in the Greek style to improve the view from his new house. He had alleged that the old church was already in a ruinous state and began to demolish it without ecclesiastical consent, but the bishop intervened and prevented its further despoliation (the church windows once contained fine medieval stained glass) after being calmed somewhat by a good dinner and the promise of the new church.

In the old days, on Good Friday, the church bell had been traditionally tolled thirty-three times to mark the years of Christ's life, and the village fair had been held in the High Street, opposite the church, on the second Sunday of August, but a Victorian rector had succeeded in suppressing that.

The old church was never rebuilt, and has remained a picturesque ruin at the village centre, with ivy clambering up its flint walls and battlemented tower. There is no roof over its nave and no longer any glass in its windows. Its churchyard contains overgrown and illegible gravestones of generations of

The old church at Ayot St Lawrence, unused since about 1780, when the lord of the manor was only prevented from demolishing it completely by the urgent intervention of the bishop.

villagers, and the birds are its only congregation. Beneath the tower is the tomb of a fifteenth-century knight and his lady, who no doubt once worshipped in this building like the generations of local people buried outside, and whose remains have been abandoned along with this hollow shell.

Ayot St Lawrence lies three miles north-west of Welwyn Garden City, between M1 and A1(M), and is best reached from A6129 at Wheathampstead or B656 at Codicote. The ruin is not approachable but can be well seen from the village street. TL 195169.

Bawsey Church

Norfolk

YOU CAN SEE this church clearly from the main roads just east of King's Lynn. Its wrecked stone tower stands above the surrounding landscape like the tattered flag of a beleaguered army, and if you approach it from the south, along a farm track, you find it isolated except for derelict farm buildings which you pass on the way. The church clearly belonged to one of Norfolk's lost medieval villages. But was it Bawsey?

Richard Muir, in *The Lost Villages of Britain*, has a photograph of the church and a seventeenth-century map of Mintlyn, and he says this is Mintlyn church, but I suggest that Dr Muir's map and photograph do not match. No use looking for Mintlyn in the guide book, gazetteer or average map: it is not there, and for good reason – there is no such place. The village has long since disappeared. Sir Nikolaus Pevsner, in his *Buildings of England* volume on north-west Norfolk, includes this church and another one nearby under Bawsey, a little way east, and though I am a layman in these matters, my guess is that the church we are discussing here belonged to Bawsey, while the church in Dr Muir's map of Mintlyn has been reduced to hardly visible

fragments near the course of the old railway line, one mile south. It was dedicated to St Michael.

Bawsey is also listed as a deserted medieval village, and it appears to have shifted its centre of population to the Norwich road. Zig-zag decoration remains in a broken arch of the church's doorway through which small congregations used to pass, and the voices of many parsons no doubt echoed round these walls of roughly coursed rubble as they delivered their interminable sermons. The poor villagers, whose community may have been reduced by the Black Death, gradually migrated to more amenable sites, leaving their ancient church of St James, with its Norman tower showing traces of Saxon work, as the only sign above ground of the original settlement. There it remains, high and dry, at the edge of a cornfield.

The church stands on raised ground between A149 and B1145 just east of King's Lynn. No public right of way is marked on the Ordnance Survey map, but there are several access routes, and intending visitors should merely take care to avoid trespassing or causing damage to farm property. TF 662208.

Bawsey church. The ruins stand in isolation at the edge of a cornfield.

Bayham Abbey

East Sussex

THE CISTERCIAN ABBEYS, which shunned publicity while they were alive, get all the best notices now they are dead, so abbeys of the lesser orders, such as this Premonstratensian one, tend to be relatively little known.

Bayham, as Pevsner says, is 'the most impressive monastic ruin of Sussex'.

The Premonstratensians were not as wealthy nor latterly as strict as the Cistercians, but they favoured the same kind of secluded and low-lying situation and the same general approach to building, so that Bayham was like a Cistercian abbey in miniature, and its ruins occupy a damp meadow by the River Teise. It

Part of the remains of Bayham Abbey, looking towards the east end of the Premonstratensian abbey church, built in sandstone at the end of the thirteenth century.

was built of local sandstone in the early years of the thirteenth century, when the first abbot and canons came here from two ailing establishments not far away, and it was adopted as a daughter house of Prémontré in northern France, from which the order took its name.

Bayham was among the earlier victims of suppression, when Cardinal Wolsey used its moderate wealth to finance his colleges at Oxford and Ipswich. He thought to bribe the abbot into acquiescence by finding him another abbacy, but made no provision for the canons, who joined the outraged populace in a riot and reoccupied the abbey. But this medieval sit-in was of no avail, and the abbey church and monastic buildings were soon in ruins.

The walls of the east end of the abbey church, rebuilt at the end of the thirteenth century to extend the presbytery, remain to a substantial height, along with parts of the cloister, and make a picturesque scene in the broad wooded valley of the river that forms the boundary between Kent and Sussex at this point.

The relative seclusion of the remains protected them from too much further despoliation until, in the late eighteenth century, they won the attention of the Romantic Movement. They were eventually made the focal point, as at Fountains, of a man-made landscape to enhance the view from a mock-Tudor mansion, the abbey's gatehouse being turned into a summerhouse by the lake, which had been created by damming the stream.

The owners of the estate during this metamorphosis were a family with the unromantic name of Pratt and the more becoming title of Earls Camden, who received advice from Humphry Repton on the landscape, admiration of the house from Horace Walpole, and some belabouring from William Cobbett for their wealth.

Bayham Abbey is in the guardianship of the Department of the Environment. It stands four miles east of Tunbridge Wells just off the north side of B2169. There is a car park at the site. TQ 651366.

Bolton Priory

North Yorkshire

BOLTON PRIORY is an example of a common phenomenon in North Yorkshire – a ruin in a highly picturesque landscape beside a stream or river. It is frequently referred to as Bolton Abbey, but that is merely by courtesy or conceit of one of its owners during the Romantic period, when many a priory was 'upgraded'; and from this affectation the adjacent village takes its spurious name.

In fact, Bolton is rather weighed down by romance. Legend has it that the priory was founded by Alicia de Romille in her grief at the loss of her son, popularly called the Boy of Egremond, who was drowned in the River Wharfe. Actually, the priory was originally founded at Embsay, near Skipton, by her parents William de Meschines and Cecilia de Romille, and was transferred to Bolton by Alicia in 1154, when her son was certainly still alive. But Wordsworth, who could always be depended upon to pounce on a sentimental local tale and turn it into a national romance, gave credence to the false account in his poem 'The Force of Prayer'. And he saddled Bolton with another popular fable in 'The White Doe of Rylstone', which versifies a local tale that a white doe used to attend the grave of Emily Norton, its former owner, in the priory churchyard during divine service.

The priory hardly needs these poetic myths, since its situation alone is romantic enough to ensure its continuing fame. There is not a more beautifully situated ruin in England or Wales unless it be Tintern or Rievaulx. Ruskin vividly described its idyllic surroundings in *Modern Painters*, and Turner and Landseer were among the many artists who painted it, set among hills and moorland beside the Wharfe.

Bolton was an Augustinian establishment for a prior and fifteen canons, who served parish churches in the locality, provided alms and hospitality, and supervised the priory's trading interests in wool, lead and iron. The

Bolton Priory. The ruins of the priory church set in the beautiful surroundings of Wharfedale.

priory also received much cheese and butter from its scattered farms. As its prosperity increased its buildings rose on fairly simple lines until the climax of the church's west front, in the mid-thirteenth century, with its Early English arcading and lancet windows.

In the sixteenth century the prior, Richard Moone, began the building of an ornate tower at the west end, which obscures the earlier west front and would have replaced it altogether if completed. 'In the yer of our Lord MVCXX', stated an inscription which clearly meant 1520 (MDXX), 'R. ⌒ begaun this fondachyon on qwho sowl God have marce. Amen.' But in the year of our Lord 1539 Prior Moone surrendered the property to the Crown and the tower was left unfinished. The annual value of the priory was reckoned at £222 3s 4d. Three years later, Henry VIII sold it to the Earl of Cumberland for £2490 1s 1d!

The nave of the church was kept in repair as the local parish church, but the choir and transept were allowed to fall into ruin and the monastic buildings were almost totally obliterated in the quarrying of their material for other building. The gatehouse was incorporated into a mansion, Bolton Hall, which now belongs to the Duke of Devonshire.

The ruin itself is not spectacular by Yorkshire standards, but combined with its superb surroundings, it makes as fine a ruin-in-a landscape as was ever painted by Claude or Ruysdael.

The ruins are beside the village of Bolton Abbey, off A59 five miles east of Skipton. There is a large car park at the village centre from which one crosses the road to enter the priory grounds. SE 075542.

Calceby Church

Lincolnshire

THE ENDING of the name 'Calceby' betrays the fact that the village was founded by the Danes

in the ninth or tenth century, but when it was deserted we cannot tell. The sparse remains of its church, dedicated to St Andrew, stand on the high point of a field, where it once looked down on the cottages of those who came to worship here. Now it affords a little welcome shade for cattle on hot days. All that is left is some pale masonry, mainly chalk, once part of the tower and the nave's north wall, with the arch of the plain Norman tower just about intact among it, but threatening to succumb to a sharp gust of wind.

We do not know what brought the village to its end, but Lincolnshire has a large number of lost village sites and was one of the worst sufferers from the Black Death, which may well have accounted for this church's fate. Perhaps because of its long coastline, the county was especially vulnerable to the dread disease, carried by rats from vessels on the

There are precious few remains of the former church of St Andrew at Calceby, one of Lincolnshire's deserted medieval villages, which may have been a victim of the Black Death.

North Sea; and Calceby was on the eastern edge of the Wolds, not far from the coast.

'The plague', wrote a local chronicler, 'slew Jew, Christian and Saracen alike; it carried off confessor and penitent together. In many places not even a fifth part of the people were left alive. It filled the whole world with terror. So great an epidemic has never been seen or heard of before this time, for it is believed that even the waters of the flood which happened in the days of Noah did not carry off so vast a multitude.'

In his review of Ranke's *History of the Popes*, Lord Macaulay remarked that the Roman Catholic Church 'may still exist in undiminished vigour when some traveller from New Zealand shall, in the midst of a vast solitude, take his stand on a broken arch of London Bridge to sketch the ruins of St Paul's'. No doubt that seemed as unimaginable in 1840 as the idea of total destruction would have seemed to the villagers of Calceby in 1347, but today, it is not unduly far-fetched to postulate a visitor from Botswana standing on a broken arch of St Paul's to photograph the ruins of London. Perhaps the forlorn remains of Calceby's church should be preserved as a symbol and a warning.

The church is off A16 two miles north-west of Ulceby Cross. The ruin is on private farmland, but can be seen quite clearly from the roadside. TF386757.

Castle Acre Priory

Norfolk

THE VILLAGE NAME suggests that this entry should appear in the next chapter, but the priory has withstood time rather better than the castle and is, in fact, the most important Cluniac remnant in England, and the most impressive ruin of any sort in East Anglia.

Its early story is largely one of 'ifs' and 'buts'. The castle was built, in all probability,

by William de Warenne, whose wife Gundreda *may* have been a daughter or stepdaughter of the Conqueror. De Warenne was made Earl of Surrey, but whether it was he or his son, the second earl, who founded the priory is uncertain. It was without doubt the first earl and countess who introduced the Cluniac order into England, having visited the great abbey at Cluny in Burgundy. They established the priory of St Pancras at Lewes in Sussex, where Gundreda was apparently buried in 1085. The earl died four years later and seems also to have been buried there, despite a story that both their coffins were found in the River Nar by nineteenth-century workmen and thrown back again like under-

Flint and dressed stone form the impressive ruins of Castle Acre Priory: looking across the cloister to the arcaded south-west tower of the priory church.

sized fish. Their coffins are also said to have been uncovered at Lewes when the priory there was being demolished to make way for the town's new railway line.

If the countess died at Castle Acre, as is sometimes asserted, and both she and the earl were taken to Lewes for burial, this would indicate that the priory at Castle Acre was either not founded by 1089 or was, at any rate, very little advanced in its building. So whoever founded it, we should credit William the second earl with its progress and rich endowment; it seems likely that he founded the priory as a memorial to his parents in 1090.

There was none of the architectural restraint here that was later to characterize the great Cistercian houses. The Cluniacs were famous for their church services, the elaborate *Opus Dei*, rather than for practical matters like sheep-breeding. The west front of the priory church still stands almost to its full height, and its Norman doorway, with four orders of columns and intricate moulding, is set in three rows of rich wall arcading, flanked by smaller doorways with more arcades above them. Over the main doorway a large Gothic window was inserted in the fifteenth century, destroying some of the arcading of the original façade. This earlier work is in brown sandstone, and must be partly the work of a serf named Ulmar, a stonemason who was donated to the priory, 'along with his garden', by the lord of the manor.

Behind this imposing front, only fragments of the church remain. It had an aisled nave and a central tower supported on four huge stone-cased piers. But after passing the west façade, there is little ashlar stonework to be seen; what remains is a vast conglomeration of shattered arches and ragged walls and soaring towers of flint, the only easily available local material.

The ruins cover about 36 acres (14.5 hectares) of land, and when one wanders round the fragments of the large church and the extensive monastic buildings, it is hard to believe that this establishment was intended only for a prior and twenty-six monks. It is true enough that the place became wealthy, with much land scattered around East Anglia as well as some in Yorkshire, and with five watermills among its properties. But the size of the reredorter, or *necessarium*, built over the river to a length of 90 feet, induces a bizarre vision of all the monks entering it in solemn procession to use it simultaneously.

The affairs of the priory seem to have been somewhat fraught during the years of its ascendancy, though its benefactors included kings of England and rich local families. The Cluniacs were frequently criticized for their wealth and ostentation. The first two King Henrys endowed it, but the first three Edwards taxed it heavily, when some fifty thousand pounds a year were being sent abroad by 'alien' monasteries in rendering tribute to their parent houses across the Channel. During Edward i's reign the monastery was actually fortified against one Benedict, who had been appointed prior in place of William of Shoreham. But 'possession is nine-tenths of the law' and the retainers of the then lord of the manor came to the aid of the prior and monks in keeping the new man out.

The monastery drew large numbers of pilgrims to see its 'divers relics of saints', most valuable of which, and most gruesome, was claimed and believed to be the arm of St Philip, worth ten shillings a year in admission fees, such was the gullibility – or at any rate the morbid curiosity – of the pious. But discipline in the monastery had foundered on the rocks of affluence, and some monks were chastised by the prior in 1351 after being arrested under royal warrant for spurning their habit and conducting themselves improperly.

In 1537 the priory was surrendered to Henry viii's commissioners by the last prior, Thomas Malling, and the buildings soon became a quarry for all the masons in the neighbourhood. The property was granted by the king to Thomas Howard, Duke of Norfolk, but Queen Elizabeth gave it to Thomas

Henry VIII's demolition gang and subsequent plunderers of building stone have left much of the priory looking like a wierd but almost natural formation of pillars of flint.

Gresham after Norfolk's execution. It then passed to the Cecils and finally to the Coke family, during whose ownership parts of the west range, once the prior's lodging, were converted into a dwelling house.

The priory stands at the edge of the village which itself lies within the vast outer bailey of the castle, on the ancient Peddars Way – which prehistoric and Roman men walked, as well as medieval monks and pilgrims. It is almost impossible to imagine now what these desecrated buildings must have been like at the height of their glory, but in their extent it is easy to see the importance of the monastery to the ordinary people, who obtained spiritual well-being and the rudiments of an education from the monks.

Castle Acre is four miles north of Swaffham off the west side of A1065. The priory ruins are on the south-west side of the village, and are in the care of the Department of the Environment. There is a car park near the Tudor gatehouse. TF 814148.

Clophill Church

Bedfordshire

SIR NIKOLAUS PEVSNER describes it as 'a strange building', referring of course to its architecture, but Clophill's old church of St Mary is strange in more ways than one.

It stands, separated from its little graveyard, on a hilltop, well outside the village, and is built of brown ironstone rubble, with a square tower and a nave which has only two windows, in opposite walls. Also well away from the present village is a motte-and-bailey earthwork known as Cainhoe Castle, but this is a mile away from the old church. Did they both once belong to the same village, or to two different ones? Many Bedfordshire villages are scattered to such an extent that they have names for their separate parts, and 'Church End' is common. Perhaps this ruin stood at the church end of the original Clophill village with the castle at the other.

Local legend has it that the old village was devastated by the Black Death. The loss of medieval villages is attributed rather too freely to the pestilence, but it may be the simple truth in Clophill's case. The county

The ruined ironstone church at Clophill.

had been among the most prosperous in England early in the fourteenth century, but Bedford itself is known to have been set back 150 years by its economic losses as the trading centre for the agricultural villages around it.

Crops would have been left to rot in the fields for lack of manpower to harvest them, and by the time the ghastly epidemic had passed, and all the dead were buried, there were probably too few villagers left to keep Clophill's population going. Subsequent housing was built on the main road, where such villagers as were left could take some advantage of passing trade.

They continued to use the old church until the nineteenth century, for its chancel was rebuilt as late as 1819, but then they got a new one, more conveniently situated, and old St Mary's was allowed to fall into its present forsaken condition.

The ruins of Clophill church stand in a field beside a rough track leading north from A507 at the eastern extremity of the present village. It is possible to drive up to it, but intending visitors are perhaps better advised to drive up the Haynes road (by the new church) and walk to the ruin by the footpath. TL 092388.

Coventry Cathedral

West Midlands

THIS RUIN was brought about not by the Dissolution of the Monasteries, nor by any internal strife. I remember vividly, though I was only a child, the night when Coventry Cathedral, and so much of the old city with it, was reduced to ashes. I saw the sky glowing with the flames from fifteen miles away.

It was only in 1918 that Coventry had been made a cathedral city, and its chief parish church, dedicated to St Michael, became the cathedral. It was one of England's largest parish churches. Its steeple – soaring to nearly three hundred feet – had moved Ruskin to remark that 'the same laws of chemical change which reduce the granites of Dartmoor to porcelain clay bind the sand of Coventry into stone which can be built halfway to the sky.'

The church had stood here since the late fourteenth century, when the master masons of Coventry had set to work to give the place a building worthy of what was then the fourth largest city in England – only London, Bristol and York exceeding it. It was already an important manufacturing centre, and as its steeple rose, its prosperity grew. The church was built of New Red sandstone in the Perpendicular style of the period, among half-timbered buildings where the city's cloth and cutlery makers carried on their trades. It had a huge nave, battlemented walls, crocketed gables and pinnacles, flying buttresses, and an unusual polygonal apse in the chancel. When it was consecrated as a cathedral it was over five hundred years old, the glorious centre-piece of the place to which eleven thousand legendary virgins had come long ago from Cologne with gifts of as many virtues for all succeeding generations of Coventry women.

On the moonlit night of 14 November 1940, the Nazi Luftwaffe commenced its new night-time offensive against Britain, and Coventry was its first target. Hundreds of tons of bombs rained down on the city, and the cathedral received a direct hit. By the morning, St Michael's Cathedral was a smouldering shell; sixty years of dedicated work by medieval masons, sculptors and carpenters were reduced to rubble in a single night. But the citizens of Coventry gradually awoke to the fact, with that wonder of disbelief which quickly speaks of miracles, that the cathedral's crowning glory, the octagonal tower surmounted by its banded spire (exceeded in height only by Salisbury and Norwich), remained intact.

Sir Basil Spence's new cathedral slowly took shape next to the blackened ruins of the old. He made imaginative use of the former chancel as a precinct, where a cross made from charred timbers stands as a permanent reminder of what happened here, while the empty windows still contain bits of jagged stained glass and twisted lead, warped and distorted by the heat of that terrible night.

The ruin still evokes an awful memory in all English men and women over fifty, and I suppose that all ruins, except the smallest and most isolated, once brought memories of unbelievable destruction to the minds of those who saw them in after years, and made them wonder if the world would ever be the same again.

Coventry Cathedral stands at the centre of the city between Michael's Avenue and Bayley Lane. There are several car parks within easy walking distance. SP 334791.

Crowland Abbey

Lincolnshire

CROWLAND or Croyland Abbey seems to have been attended by catastrophe right from the beginning, having been repeatedly destroyed by earthquake, Danish raiders or serious fires throughout its long history. Nothing at all remains of its monastic buildings –

Perpendicular tracery remains in the glassless windows at the east end of Coventry Cathedral, bombed to smouldering ruins in November 1940.

only the north aisle of the abbey church, now used as the parish church, and the ruins of the nave. And the Dissolution did not end the story of disaster here, for the nave actually survived that trauma until 1720, when its roof collapsed. Even its name has been lost. Some say it was Croixland, the land of the cross; others that it was Crowland, the land of crows; others that it was the land of mud, from the Latin *Crudam terram*!

Despite all this somewhat demeaning uncertainty and physical insecurity, Crowland (as the modern village is called), was once a wealthy and splendid establishment, and some hint of its former glory can still be seen in its ruins.

It was a Benedictine foundation, established by Ethelbald, King of Mercia, in honour of Saint Guthlac, who is said to have settled here on what was then an island in the Fens, having arrived by boat across the swamps to seek refuge from the world and from the shrieking demons and spirits which tormented him. If there is such a thing as 'total allergy', Guthlac had all the symptoms. If not, he was out of his mind.

At any rate, the monastery grew and flourished, despite its proneness to disaster, until it became a renowned centre of learning, and the richest monastic foundation in Lincolnshire, with a fine library and a reputation for hospitality, although it never housed more than about forty monks. It grew wheat and oats on its extensive domains, and bred cattle

as well as sheep, making cheese and butter from the cows' milk and feeding the lay brothers and hired labourers uncommonly well with its own dairy produce.

The abbey's final rebuilding may have been financed partly by the sale of indulgences, but it was certainly built on a magnificent scale, as the west end of the nave shows, with its tiers of stone figures flanking and surmounting the huge empty window over the doorway. This west front, Early English below and Perpendicular in the upper stages, is still impressive, notwithstanding the dizzying effect of its alarming vertical alignment, being wider at the top than at the bottom. Some of the abbey's statues have been lost, while others stand on the ground leaning against the ruined walls like refugees resigned to a long wait for repatriation. One of them, believed to represent Christ, stands on Crowland's unique triangular stone bridge which once spanned three streams and is now high and dry at the village centre.

Local legend has it that the outlaw Hereward the Wake was brought here for burial, but everything purporting to have happened at this ill-fated place must be regarded with a degree of scepticism, for it has been the subject of spurious history as well as curious stories, such as the alleged intercourse between the 'devils of Crowland' and the monks. Nevertheless, as well as fires, slaughter of monks by the Danes, and the earthquake of 1118 – after which the abbey was rebuilt in stone quarried under licence at Barnack – the monastery suffered from the devastation of the Black Death, which left a large number of its estates unmanned. Certainly horrors of one sort or another seem to have been visited with a vengeance upon this unhappy place, as if the delusions Guthlac brought with him were actually prophetic symbols, from which all his prayer and supplication failed to preserve it.

The small town or village of Crowland is beside A1073 between Peterborough and Spalding. The church cannot be missed, and there is a small car park close to the churchyard. TF 241149.

Egglestone Abbey

Durham

SIR WALTER SCOTT used this ruin as the scene of the final tragedy in his poem 'Rokeby', but in spite of that romantic association the abbey remains a relatively little-known place. It is unusual among monastic settlements in that it stands on a small hilltop, close to the River Tees.

It was founded towards the end of the twelfth century by Ralph de Malton for Premonstratensian canons, and built of honey-coloured limestone on a site that was then more heavily wooded than it is now. Here the canons went about their business and their study in peace and isolation for three and a half centuries, until the Dissolution. The abbey was never in the first league in terms of size or wealth, and its story is not punctuated by the scandals and disasters we find so often elsewhere.

It was in 1540 that the abbey was surrendered to the king's commissioners, and it was acquired a few years later by Robert

Egglestone Abbey. This view shows the ruins of a house built from the east range of the abbey's monastic buildings after the Dissolution.

Strelley, who converted part of the east range of monastic buildings into a Tudor house. This, like the abbey church and the rest of the buildings, now stands in ruins, and even to the layman looks incongruous, with its mullioned windows, domestic stairs and passages and several fireplaces and chimneys, as if it really ought to be in the last chapter of this book. But the lord of the manor's great hall was the monks' refectory, and instead of sundials and statues for his garden ornaments he had the tomb-chests of the abbey's cemetery.

Little else remains of the monastic build- ings, but of the church itself some walls of the nave and chancel still stand to a fair height, with a variety of Gothic windows. The vener- able fabric makes a melancholy sight, and the eerie silence of the place at dusk calls up white phantoms of holy men, subject to severe discipline in the early days of their order, gliding noiselessly about the shadowy cloister.

Egglestone Abbey stands a mile and a half south-east of Barnard Castle, on a minor road off B6277. It is in the care of the Department of the Environment, and there is a car park at the site. NZ 062151.

Fountains Abbey

North Yorkshire

FOUNTAINS is indisputably the aristocrat of British ruins. Of all the building remains mentioned in this volume, probably only Stonehenge and Hadrian's Wall exceed its fame beyond these shores. It had unpromising beginnings, for the Cistercians who built it were enjoined to adopt architecture of stark simplicity, avoiding extravagance and ornamentation, while the site itself was a 'lonely and forbidding spot' in the wild and rocky valley of the River Skell, 'fit rather to be the lair of wild beasts than the home of human beings'. How has it come, then, to be the most celebrated and – to my mind – the most beautiful of all the treasures of Britain's heritage? The answers emerge from its long history.

The abbey was founded in 1132 by zealous Benedictine monks who were unhappy with the state of things at St Mary's Abbey in York, where they felt that the strict rules of their order had been too far relaxed. Abbot Bernard of Clairvaux, the champion of Cistercian reform, sent them encouraging messages from France, and Archbishop Thurstan granted them land in Skelldale where they built their first shelter of timber in the wilderness, in accordance with the Cistercian principle of withdrawal from human intercourse. It was an uninhabited place 'remote from all the world'.

The abbey's name comes from the Latin *Sancta Maria de Fontanis* – St Mary of the Springs – for all Cistercian churches were dedicated to the Virgin Mary, and the River Skell got its name from the Anglo-Saxon for the springs which rise here.

Building in stone began around 1135, in Romanesque style with hints of Gothic, using pale sandstone quarried locally. Its delicate shades – brown and grey, pink and fawn – enhance the architectural qualities of the buildings, and are completely in harmony with the surrounding landscape.

The abbey church followed the Cistercian rule of plain unadorned building, with thick circular piers, Norman capitals and round arches, although pointed arches were also used, the Cistercians being responsible for the introduction of Gothic into England. But in 1147 much of the abbey was burnt down. This came about through a little ungodly fracas between the third abbot and the Archbishop of York. Pope Eugenius III came down on the side of the abbot, for the Pontiff was also a Cistercian, and the archbishop's knights went off on a vengeful rampage to Fountains.

Subsequent abbots carried out extensive repairs and new building, which culminated in the new east transept of the church known as the Chapel of Nine Altars, one of the building masterpieces of the period. This 'glorious consummation', with its immensely high slender pillars, lancet windows and arcades on every side, is one of Europe's architectural treasures, even in its ruined state. The octagonal piers, with their decorated capitals, formerly had shafts of black spotted marble from quarries in Nidderdale. All this was a radical departure from the Cistercian taste for austerity, and it is clear that increasing wealth had had its usual corrupting influence, even on zealous monks.

Fountains was enriched by gifts from popes and princes; it owned extensive lands on which it kept sheep, cattle, horses and swine, and grew corn; it had fisheries and game reserves, quarries and lead mines; and it profited from the donations of wealthy personages who wanted to be buried there. From being a wild place with only the trees for shelter and their leaves and fruit for food, it had come in four hundred years to be the richest Cistercian house in Britain. Along with other local monasteries, its production and export of wool had helped to bring back population and prosperity to medieval Yorkshire after the long period of barrenness and poverty following the Conqueror's 'harrying of the North'. The abbots spent lavishly, and by the time of the Dissolution all Cistercian restraint had been thrown to the winds, with the building of the tall tower by Abbot Huby. The Cistercians had always forbidden steeples and towers, which were held to be useless extravagances inspired only by vanity.

Henry VIII's commissioners furnished Thomas Cromwell with a catalogue of trumped-up charges to justify the royal grabbing of this rich prize. The abbot was accused of theft, sacrilege, perjury and the keeping of whores, but the commissioners had no hesitation in recommending Cromwell to encourage simony and accept a bribe of six hundred marks from one Marmaduke, 'the wysyste monke within Inglonde', who duly replaced the discredited abbot. Marmaduke's wisdom, presumably, consisted in his bribery of the commissioners as well as Cromwell. Soon afterwards, the abbey was suppressed.

The valuable lead, glass and furnishings were confiscated by the Crown, and the property then passed through a succession of hands, some of the monastic buildings being demolished to provide stone for the nearby mansion, Fountains Hall. But before the abbey was too far gone in decay, it had what was – for us at any rate – a piece of rare good fortune which put the final seal on its future as the most magnificent ruin in England.

In 1768, the property came into the possession of William Aislabie, owner of the adjacent estate of Studley Royal Park. This estate had been laid out over a period of twenty years by his father John Aislabie, the disgraced but wealthy Chancellor of the Exchequer at the time of the South Sea Bubble scandal. The year of William's acquisition of

Fountains Abbey from the air. The plans of most Cistercian monasteries were similar to this layout, with the monastic buildings extending south from the church.

Fountains is significant. It was a decade after Burke's definition of the 'sublime', and wealthy landowners were busy building fake ruins in expensively laid-out grounds, in their pursuit of the 'ideal landscape'. Aislabie, on the other hand, took the real ruins of Fountains Abbey and audaciously developed the grounds around them, turning the ruins and the terrain into the most spectacular and romantic of picturesque landscapes, soon celebrated by poets and artists galore.

Apart from the lofty and majestic ruins of the abbey church itself, one of the most exciting remains is the undercroft or *cellarium* below the monks' dormitory. It runs three hundred feet southward from the west end of the church, along the west side of the cloister, and across to the opposite bank of the river. It is divided down the centre by a line of nineteen columns, sprouting – without capitals – into completely intact quadripartite vaulting. The arches at the church end are rounded, those at the other end pointed, and the earlier part may pre-date the fire. The drainage and water supply of the abbey involved elaborate tunnelling and re-routing of the river, and these works can also still be seen.

So far from being 'remote from all the world', Fountains now attracts visitors in their millions. The best approach is unquestionably from the north-east, walking from Studley Park by the banks of the Skell, and coming suddenly on the most seductive distant view of the ruined abbey – one of the mightiest ecclesiastical institutions of medieval Europe and a place of matchless beauty.

Fountains Abbey is three miles south-west of Ripon, and lies on the north bank of the River Skell. It is reached by minor roads off B6265 and is well signposted. Studley Royal Park is the property of the National Trust and the ruins themselves are maintained by the Department of the Environment. There is a large car park at the site. SE 275683.

The cellarium at Fountains Abbey, adjoining the nave of the church.

Looking across the monastic quarters and chapter house to the presbytery of the church and Huby's tower.

66

Furness Abbey

Cumbria

STRIKING red sandstone lends this magnificent ruin a tone of northern worldliness which instantly diminishes any impression of medieval sanctity, and although it is relatively quiet, on the outskirts of Barrow-in-Furness, its position on this dreary industrial peninsula of what was formerly north Lancashire, overlooking Morecambe Bay, seems hardly conducive to the remembrance of things past. As so often, however, the visitor has only to be surrounded by its Norman arches and the columns of the chapter house for the world to be eclipsed by the architectural splendour of this great and powerful monastery.

The realization that it was a Cistercian house makes one aware that this place was once a wilderness, despite all the railways, dockyards and belching foundry chimneys that surround it now. But the monks themselves exploited the deposits of iron ore and building stone, and the flamboyant stonework in their buildings persuades us that, after all, they *were* rather worldly, and did not for long follow the strict rules of their order. A mere glance at the richly carved Perpendicular canopies of the *sedilia* and *piscina* in the presbytery of the abbey church is enough to show that by the fifteenth century the abbot and monks had totally cast aside the Cistercian principle of plain architecture and austere living conditions. It was only human nature, for it is surely a measure of man's homage to the gods that he should shout his genius to the heavens rather than hide it under a bushel.

The monastery had been founded as a Savignac establishment by Count Stephen of Mortain, later King of England, in 1123 at a site near Preston, and the monks moved to Furness four years later. In 1147, the orders of Savigny and Citeaux amalgamated, and the monks swapped their grey cowls for the white Cistercian habit as their buildings took shape in the Valley of Deadly Nightshade.

The chapter house of Furness Abbey.

In this northern part of England, the abbey had to withstand aggressive attention from Scottish raiders who made no distinction between religious and secular targets in their ravaging of the borderland, and so far from turning the other cheek, the monks of Furness raised an army which fought at Flodden. They also erected a watchtower to warn the neighbourhood of the enemy's approach, and rebuilt the rectangular castle keep on Piel Island, from where the monastery exported its wool in ships built in its own dockyard. In 1322 the then abbot paid a ransom to Robert the Bruce to preserve the monastery from arson and plunder.

This troubling insecurity was accompanied, however, by expansion and increasing wealth, and the abbots of Furness came to exercise a

feudal lordship over vast territories of north-west England, with other lands in Ireland and on the Isle of Man. All of the Furness district was under the abbey's rule, along with much of the central Lake District and parts of Yorkshire. In 1209 the abbey purchased Borrowdale for £156 13s 4d from Alice de Romille, who had endowed Bolton and given land to Fountains some years before. The monks administered their land there from the place now known as Grange – *grangia nostra de Boroudale.* Later they acquired fourteen thousand acres of upper Eskdale. The manor of Hawkshead also became part of the abbey's empire, and its wealth grew to such an extent from iron-founding, sheep farming and the exporting of wool that at the time of the Dissolution Furness was second only to

Fountains as the most prosperous and power-ful Cistercian monastery in the kingdom. Kings of England and Popes of Rome had secured the foundation and granted it rare privileges throughout its four hundred years of existence. Several daughter-houses were established from it, most notable of which was Byland Abbey in Yorkshire.

It was famed for its lavish hospitality. The abbot entertained important guests in his lodging, and the monastery's local tenants had weekly gifts of bread and ale, while their children were taught grammar and singing by the monks. Tenants who owned a plough could dine at the abbey, accompanied by a guest, once a week during the winter and spring months. Meat and drink were always available to those who needed them, but

Ornate stone canopies over the sedilia and piscina in the presbytery at Furness show the degree to which the Cistercians had abandoned their traditional austerity by the fifteenth century.

pilgrims were sometimes drowned in their attempts to reach the abbey across the treacherous sands of Morecambe Bay, which they would often prefer to risk rather than take the extremely long route round dry land. The abbey employed a guide to take people across safely, saying that 'every Christian should be stricken with pity' at the loss of life that occurred here.

It is hardly surprising that there was great local and internal outrage at the threatened suppression of the monastery. No doubt the abbot, Roger Pyle, was urgently implored to join the Pilgrimage of Grace, that great northern rising of both ecclesiastical and secular leaders in protest against Henry VIII's proposed suppression of the monasteries. It began in Lincolnshire in 1536 and spread throughout the north. The powerful wished to defend the north from greater royal power, and the poor wished to prevent enclosure of their land for pasture, while the monks simply wanted to keep their way of life. But as for Abbot Roger, he was summoned to Whalley Abbey in April 1537 to appear before the king's representatives headed by the Earl of Sussex, and there he submitted meekly, declaring 'I, Roger abbot of the monasterie of Furnes, knowyng the mysorder and evyll liff both unto God and our prynce of the bredren of the said monasterie, in dischargyng of my conscience doo frely and hollie surrender, giff and grant into the kynges highnes, and to his heyres and assignes for evermore, all suche interest and titill as I had, have, or may have, of and in the said monasterie of Furnes, and of and in the landes, renttes, possessions, revenous, servyces ...'

This declaration was made, added the abbot, 'frely of my selff and without any inforcement'. But this is all too familiar a formula. Less than a month before Abbot Roger's summons to Whalley, the abbot of the latter, with two of his monks, had been hanged in front of the gatehouse there for their part in the Pilgrimage of Grace. Their bodies were still dangling from the ropes to greet the weary abbot of Furness on his arrival, and two of his own brethren had been clapped into gaol at Lancaster. After such intimidation, there was no need for bribery. The abbot was compensated, if that is the word, with the curacy of Dalton, worth a mere forty pounds a year, and the monastery that was given by King Stephen in 1127 to 'remain firm and inviolate for ever' passed in 1537 to Henry VIII 'for evermore'.

The monastery was brought down, some say partly by fire when molten lead fell from the roof and damaged the fabric. It passed into the possession of Thomas Cromwell, Henry's chief henchman in the suppression of the monasteries, and then through the hands of various families until 1923, when it came into the care of the Office of Works.

If the belladonna which gave the little valley its name once grew among the stone walls and beside the stream used by the monks for plumbing purposes, it can hardly do so now in the tidied-up public park atmosphere in which the ruins stand. But there is still sufficient romance in these solid piles of masonry to stir the imagination and even, here and there, genuine beauty, as when one passes from the cloister, with its splendid Transitional arches, through the vaulted vestibule and into the thirteenth-century chapter house. Its clustered pillars are still standing, missing their capitals but erect like classical columns in some Mediterranean temple, and it still has its twin lancet windows with finely carved *paterae* between their heads. In this fine chamber the practical monks of Furness regularly met after matins to discuss their day's business. It was a rib-vaulted medieval boardroom, and the abbots presided over the meetings like chairmen of the board, with the profit motive high on their agenda, for all their outward appearance of holiness. The buildings of Furness are a witness to their success.

The ruins stand on the northern outskirts of Barrow-in-Furness on a signposted lane leading east from A590. There is a large car park at the site, which is in the care of the Department of the Environment. SD 218717.

OPPOSITE *Furness Abbey. Looking across the cloister from the south, towards the chapter house and transepts of the church.*

Glastonbury Abbey

Somerset

THERE COULD hardly be a greater contrast in ecclesiastical style and story than between the abbeys of Furness and Glastonbury. The solid red sandstone buildings of the north are here replaced by golden limestone, and the worldly affairs of the Cistercian monks of Lancashire give way to a multitude of romantic legends and the most sacred associations of any monastery in Britain. Dismiss the absurd tales of Joseph of Arimathea coming here with the Holy Grail, and of King Arthur being brought here for burial, along with all the other wonders and miracles, and the place still stands head and shoulders above all other monastic foundations as the cradle of Christianity in England.

A church stood here before either Anglo-Saxons or Danes invaded Britain's shores, on what was then an island, at least in winter, when the shallow sea lapped across the low-lying Somerset Levels and gave the land a glassy appearance from which the place name derives. The island readily lent itself later to identification, here in the midst of cider country, with the legendary Isle of Avalon – the place of apples. Tennyson called it:

The island valley of Avilion,
Where falls not hail, or rain, or any snow,
Nor ever wind blows loudly, but it lies
Deep-meadowed, happy, fair with orchard lawns
And bowery hollows crowned with summer sea.

Well, nowadays Glastonbury is a busy town where rain falls and wind blows as regularly as anywhere else, and the streets are fair with double yellow lines and crowned with television aerials. The ruins being situated close to the town centre, the abbey is not, alas, the ideal place for quiet contemplation and romantic daydreams. Nevertheless, Glastonbury Abbey is surrounded by myths which provided a star attraction for credulous pilgrims, and it is as well to remember these myths before we consider the mere facts.

Joseph of Arimathea is supposed to have landed at Glastonbury after being sent by St Philip with eleven companions (a mystical number) to carry the glad tidings to the wild island of Britain. It was even said by some that Mary, Martha and Lazarus were of the company. Joseph buried the chalice used by Christ at the Last Supper beneath Glastonbury Tor, whence sprang the Chalice Well. Joseph also allegedly leaned on his staff on a nearby hill, and it took root and formed the famous Glastonbury Thorn, which blossomed at Christmas every year until it was cut down by a Puritan soldier, who either blinded himself or cut off his own leg in the process. The winter flowering of this hawthorn is not regarded as especially miraculous by horticulturalists, who recognize it as *Crataegus monogyna biflora*, but many others have been impressed by it, a cutting having been sent from here for Woodrow Wilson's tomb.

King Arthur was brought hither in hope of healing his wounds in the mineral waters of the sacred spring, but he died and was laid to rest here in Avalon with his queen, Guinevere. Their remains are said to have been seen in the twelfth century when Henry II ordered a search to be made so that their bones could be given a more honoured place in the abbey. Arthur's skeleton was said to be of giant size – as befits a national hero – and Guinevere's still had its flaxen hair. Among other notable burials claimed for Glastonbury were King Edgar, Edmund Ironside, Helen the mother of Constantine the Great, Joseph of Arimathea, St Patrick, St David and St Dunstan, to name but a few.

So much for the fiction, which sounds like a commercial for the Roman church, likely to bring in even more profit than the sale of indulgences. The truth is that Glastonbury was not only of ancient foundation, but that it was the only monastic establishment we know of which survived the Saxon devastation and served both British and English Christianity in their infancy without a break. Its charter can be traced with certainty back to the eighth century, and its greatest abbot was Dunstan –

A section of the elaborate stone carving round the south doorway of St Mary's Chapel at Glastonbury.

he who pinched the Devil's nose with red-hot tongs, and who became Archbishop of Canterbury before the Normans came.

But in 1184 a fire destroyed most of the buildings, and what we see now are the remnants of the rebuilding that followed that calamity. It was all carried out in Doulting limestone, the Lady Chapel at the west end of the church being the first part to be rebuilt, apparently on the orders of Henry II, for its site was that of Joseph's legendary shrine, and it is still known as St Joseph's Chapel as well as St Mary's. Its style was Transitional, with much Romanesque detail. It is the finest remaining part of the great new abbey church, which was of enormous length and is now but a petrified skeleton, only its transept walls remaining to any impressive height. Nothing of the monastic buildings remains but foundations, except for the famous Abbot's Kitchen, which is not a ruin.

By the beginning of the sixteenth century the Benedictine monastery not only had the longest church in England, but was also the richest in the country next to Westminster. Its mitred abbots had held the rank of earl, and were superior to all others until those of St Albans were given precedence by Nicholas Breakspear, Pope Adrian IV, in 1154.

The abbey owned many manors, especially in the Somerset Levels, and it follows that the abbey was more concerned with arable and dairy farming than with sheep and wool. It grew large crops of oats which went into the ale consumed by the servants and labourers, and beans which would have formed the staple diet of the villeins. The abbey owned rich plate, jewels and sacred vessels, and its fish ponds were stocked with pike, bream, perch and roach. The abbot was said to have a retinue of at least a hundred whenever he travelled abroad.

LEFT AND
FAR LEFT
*The remains of the
crossing tower and
presbytery of the
abbey church at
Glastonbury.*

The covetous Henry VIII was hardly likely to let this prize elude his grasp. 'The house', his commissioners reported, 'is greate, goodly, and so pryncely as we have not sene the lyke.' But the abbot, Richard Whiting, was eighty years old, and he stubbornly refused to surrender the monastery. He secreted the abbey's plate to prevent it falling into the king's hands, but Cromwell's agents made out that he had stolen it for his own profit, and the old man's fate was sealed. Arrested and charged with treason, he awaited the mockery of a trial, for Cromwell had already noted: 'Item: the Abbot of Glaston to be tried at Glaston, and also executed there.' On 15 November 1539 the white-haired old abbot was drawn on a hurdle to the top of Glastonbury Tor, where he was hung, drawn and quartered, his head being stuck on a pole above the abbey's gate and his quartered corpse displayed in four cities as a warning of what the king was prepared to do to uncooperative subjects, however aged. By any standards, it was one of Cromwell's blackest deeds.

The abbey itself suffered similar mutilation at the hands of the monarch and its successive owners, who tore it apart for its building material, and it is a scant ruin compared with those of many other great monastic establishments of England, impressing rather by its pathos than its spectacle. Its stones were quarried for making the road to Wells, and the imaginative may trace the noble dust of Arthur supporting traffic on the A39. But Glastonbury holds its place of honour among England's ruined abbeys – partly, it is true, because of the wealth of legend cultivated by medieval monks who would have made first-rate advertising agents – but also because it represents a giant historical step, as the first great church of a nation turning from paganism to Christianity.

Glastonbury lies on A39 between Wells and Bridgewater. The abbey ruins are at the centre of the town, and there is a car park close by. The ruins are in the care of the Department of the Environment. ST 502387.

Hailes Abbey

Gloucestershire

BY THE TIME this monastery was built in the mid-thirteenth century, the Cistercians had already abandoned their customary austerity, and although very little of it remains standing, there is enough of Hailes left to show that the builders were seduced by the easy workability of the fine-grained Cotswold limestone which still glows in the sunlight like old gold.

Only parts of the cloister walls remain to any height, but fragments and relics in the adjacent museum and *in situ* show fine Early English ornament in the carving of columns and bosses. What we have lost in terms of romanticism in this century by excavation, removal of undergrowth and tidying-up operations, we have gained in terms of clarity and impressiveness by revealing the scale and ambitiousness of the buildings. The fame of Hailes over three centuries before the Dissolution, however, was due to a relic that is not to be seen in the museum or anywhere else.

The abbey was originally founded in 1246 by Richard, Earl of Cornwall, as a thanksgiving for his safe deliverance from shipwreck off the Isles of Scilly, and it cost him ten thousand marks to build. Twenty monks and ten lay brothers came from Beaulieu in Hampshire, and the church was consecrated five years later in the presence of Henry III and his queen, Eleanor of Provence, but within twenty years, the abbey suffered a disastrous fire. Richard of Cornwall, by this time uncrowned king of the Holy Roman Empire, came to the rescue and rebuilt the abbey, but he died shortly afterwards and was buried here with his wife, Sanchia of Provence.

Meanwhile, their son Edmund, who inherited the earldom of Cornwall, had given to the abbey a small crystal phial containing what was said to be blood from the body of Christ, and lest any heretic should entertain doubts about the authenticity of this coagulated souvenir, it had been certified as genuine by the Patriarch of Jerusalem, no less, who was

Pope Urban IV by the time the holy relic reached England.

The relic made Hailes a famous place of pilgrimage, the faithful flocking like sheep to its shrine in a quinquelateral apse with chapels radiating from it at the east end of the church. Not surprisingly, when the monastery buildings needed repair, funds came readily from Rome, and the fame of Hailes earned it a mention by Chaucer, who includes in the Pardoner's Tale the oath –

By goddes precious herte, and by his nayles,
And by the blode of Crist, that is in Hayles . . .

When the quarrel between Henry VIII and the Church of Rome blew up, however, a commission was appointed to report on the treasure. Its members included Hugh Latimer, Bishop of Worcester, who was soon to perish at the stake under Mary Tudor, and who had remarked that people believed that the sight of the blood 'with their bodily eye doth certify them and putteth them out of doubt that they be in clean life, and in state of salvation without spot of sin'. He and his colleagues now declared bluntly that the gory relic was 'an unctuowse gumme colouryd', and shortly afterwards it was publicly destroyed by John Hilsey, Bishop of Rochester, who said it was nothing more than clarified honey coloured with saffron.

But we should not scoff too easily at the credulity of medieval monks and pilgrims. Most of us believe what we want to believe, and modern materialists can as easily be fooled as mystics of the Middle Ages.

We may ignore the exaltation of Hailes and admire it for what the visible evidence shows us. It was the last major foundation in the Cotswolds and one of the few Cistercian houses there, despite the order's predilection for sheep-rearing and wool trading. The peasants in the locality must have wondered what was going on when men began to clear the ground and teams of horses hauled cartloads of stone here from local quarries to start the building of this great abbey. It was a bleak and secluded place then, such as the Cistercians normally chose, where they could live their simple lives in God's service without distraction from local communities.

It was a place of beauty they built here, however, fit for angels to walk in, and a worthy repository for the sacred treasure which the abbot and monks believed themselves specially honoured to possess. The holy men reverently exploited their extensive estates and gave thanks to God for his goodness, while lay brothers worked the land and tended the sheep. The abbey prospered from the reign of the third Henry to that of the eighth, until the day in 1539 when the abbot gave up the properties to the king's agents and received the customary pension.

The abbey lands and buildings at Hailes, valued at £357 a year, were granted to Sir Thomas Seymour of nearby Sudeley Castle, and they passed from him to the Tracy family, a large mansion having been built on the site meanwhile. This house has entirely disappeared, and the monastery buildings, which

became easy prey for everyone in the locality requiring building stone, gradually sank beneath weeds and grass, with hardly one stone left standing on another, until excavation and preservation began at the end of the nineteenth century.

The graceful remaining arches of mellow limestone are not awe-inspiring like great Cistercian ruins elsewhere; they induce a feeling of serenity. Sheep graze the neighbouring meadows today as they have done through all the centuries since the king and queen of England came here, with thirteen bishops, many lords and ladies, and three hundred knights, to witness the consecration of the new church and be entertained by Richard of Cornwall.

Hailes Abbey lies two miles north-east of Winchcombe and one mile east of A46 on a well-signposted minor road. It is owned by the National Trust and managed by the Department of the Environment. There is a car park opposite the entrance. SP 049301.

LEFT *Hailes Abbey – a fragment of the cloister walls. The three larger arches led into the chapter house vestibule.*

OVERLEAF *The glowing Cotswold stone arcading of Hailes Abbey.*

Jervaulx Abbey

North Yorkshire

ALTHOUGH it is less celebrated, and certainly less spectacular, than its imposing fellow-Yorkshiremen of Rievaulx and Fountains, Jervaulx is among the most romantic half-dozen ruins in England and Wales. Its remains are not grand or extensive, but it is to the great credit of its owners that it has not been subjected to the vacuum-cleaning, clearing and levelling which has so often turned ruins into open-air museums. At Jervaulx carved stones and broken columns lie on the ground, half-hidden by grass and weeds, where they fell centuries ago, and one feels a magical closeness to the time when this holy place was tragically destroyed.

It was a Cistercian foundation, like so many of its neighbours in these parts, but did not come into being until a quarter of a century after Fountains and Rievaulx and was, as it were, a satellite of Byland Abbey. The monks moved here from Fors, where the land was barren, and their flocks were ravaged by wolves. The new monastery was built on the characteristic Cistercian ground plan in the valley of the River Ure, whence comes its name (which is pronounced Yervo, although Yorkshiremen often call it 'Jarvis').

The local people had much affection for the monks of Jervaulx. In time the abbey became wealthy, and was widely famed for the fine horses it bred, and for the splendid cheese it made from ewes' milk, subsequently known as Wensleydale. Besides, the Cistercians were always charitable to the poor. So when this part of the country got wind of the peril in which the monasteries found themselves early in the sixteenth century, the people were incensed at the threat to the old religion. They had much to thank the abbey for, and did not want to see it suppressed, let alone destroyed. However, the abbot, Adam Sedbar, was a man of peace who would, if the occasion arose, surrender the abbey without a fight rather than join that great northern rebellion which became known as the Pilgrimage of Grace. Some of the local populace formed themselves into an angry deputation and turned up at the abbey gates demanding to see the abbot, whom they were now calling a traitor. The abbot had prudently gone into hiding, but the crowd, with that ludicrous lack of logic that distinguishes the herd instinct, threatened to burn down the abbey if he did not come to them, and did actually set fire to some of the buildings they were so anxious to preserve.

When Adam Sedbar appeared before them, some made blunt threats against his life if he did not stand against the king's injustice. If there was one thing more frightening than the wrath of Henry VIII, it was a Yorkshire mob, so the abbot was forced to join the Pilgrimage of Grace against his better judgement. For this he was seized by the king's men and thrown into the Tower of London, whence he was shortly taken to Tyburn and hanged for his trouble, along with many others.

The demolition of Jervaulx was done thoroughly and with alacrity. Little remains of the great 270-foot-long abbey church, and the monastic buildings of mellow limestone lie shattered and mutilated like flotsam washed up on the shore from some great wreck. Ivy, shrubs and trees protect them from the elements, and wild flowers bring a touch of cheerfulness to their melancholy foundations.

Only the minimum of modern protection intrudes on these ruins to distance visitors from the days of 1537, before the buildings were first set upon by the king's demolition gang, and what we have here, instead of the awesome vaults and arcades of lofty churches such as at Tintern and Rievaulx, are isolated details which stir the imagination through flashes of recognition rather than through breathtaking architecture. Here we might step over the illegible tombstone of someone long forgotten and untraceable, who knew the abbey when it was a thriving concern, and no doubt saw the white brothers from time to time moving silently about their business, and requested in his will that he might be buried

Jervaulx Abbey. Tumbled remains in one of England's most romantic ruins, looking as if they have hardly been touched since the abbey was destroyed by Thomas Cromwell's henchmen in the sixteenth century.

among them, for there he felt sure he would be able to lie in peace for all eternity. Or we might notice some finely carved block of limestone which still bears the mark of the mason who worked at it here more than eight hundred years ago.

Jervaulx in its incomparable setting is a place of meditation rather than triumphant assertion – it is the Delius of ruins rather than the Beethoven or Brahms. A crowd of visitors

destroys its unique atmosphere, and one needs it to oneself. Go in the winter, or by moonlight, and savour its haunting magic alone.

Jervaulx stands on the north side of A6108, halfway between Leyburn and Masham. There is a car park on the opposite side of the road from the entrance, and a short walk across a field to the 'paradise garden'. SE 172858.

Kirkham Priory

North Yorkshire

'WE PERFORMED some madnesses there in the way of forfeits, picnics, rustic games, inspection of ancient monasteries at midnight, when the moon was shining, that would have gone to your heart...'

This is the still-youthful Charles Dickens, touring Yorkshire while finishing *Martin Chuzzlewit*, and one of the 'ancient monasteries' was Kirkham Priory, set beside the River Derwent in beautiful country thick with woods. There is not a great deal of it left, but what there is should not be missed.

Kirkham was a house of Augustinian canons, founded around 1125 by Walter l'Espec, a wealthy judge and landowner in these parts who later gave the Cistercians the land for Rievaulx Abbey. According to legend, he endowed the priory as a mark of his grief at the loss of his son, who had been killed in a fall when his horse was startled by a wild boar.

The buildings in which the earliest canons lived and worshipped, between doing their good works, began to be replaced in the thirteenth century in a complete rebuilding programme which was never finished, perhaps because they ran out of money to finance the work. But some of what they did achieve remains to delight the eye of the beholder, beginning, before one even enters the precincts, with the façade of the gatehouse. This has a wide Gothic arch in a crocketed gable, flanked with sculptures of St George and the dragon, and David and Goliath, as well as heraldic shields. Above the gable are more shields and sculpture, smaller gables and two windows with Decorated tracery.

As one passes through the gatehouse, the scattered blocks of masonry draw the eye in all directions, with an arch here, a doorway there; but especially notable is the arcaded *lavatorium* where the canons washed their hands before meals.

At the Dissolution, Prior John Kyldwyche

and seventeen canons surrendered the buildings to the king's commissioners. The priory's annual income was estimated at £269 5s 9d. Four centuries before, Walter l'Espec, lord of

Part of the impressive remains of Kirkham Priory. This Augustinian establishment was founded by a wealthy landlord in the twelfth century.

the manor of Helmsley, had intended that Christ should be heir to much of his land and title, but the king saw fit to rob God of his inheritance.

The priory, which is in the care of the Department of the Environment, is in the village of Kirkham beside the road to Westow, reached from the east side of A64 five miles south-west of Malton. SE 740658.

Kirkstall Abbey, a gaunt northern ruin of Carboniferous sandstone, is among the best-preserved Cistercian abbeys in England. The first monks came from Fountains around 1153. All the window and doorway arches in this view across the cloister are round, but there are also many pointed arches in the structure of the abbey church and monastic buildings.

Kirkstall Abbey

West Yorkshire

AS KIRKSTALL was a Cistercian establishment, we may guess that when it was founded it was not within shouting distance of Leeds. And sure enough, we find the place referred to in the twelfth century as a 'solitary vale'. Thomas Girtin's well-known watercolour shows the abbey still isolated in rural surroundings as late as 1800. Oddly enough, though, the abbey was partly to blame for the growth of the city that now engulfs it, for it was the monks here who began the working of iron which contributed to the establishment of industry in Airedale.

It was in 1153 or thereabouts that the monastery was founded on the banks of the river as a daughter-house of Fountains. It was a second attempt for the monks who came here, for about five years earlier they had set up house at Barnoldswick and fallen foul of the locals by demolishing their parish church. It seems that the monks were not too happy, either, with the inhospitable climate of the Pennines, so they shut up shop, as it were, and came to Kirkstall instead, where their abbey was built at the expense of Henry de Lacy, lord of the manor of Pontefract.

Architectural specialists are inclined to say that the remains of Kirkstall are second only to Fountains in interest, and it is true that the abbey church is the most complete and un-altered Cistercian ruin in England. It stands to a greater height than those at Fountains or

Rievaulx, with one side of its crossing tower intact, though it looks alarmingly insecure, as if a gale would bring it crashing down around our heads. But the dour grey Millstone grit and Carboniferous sandstone, of which the abbey is built, combined with the customary severity of Cistercian architecture, gives it a northern ruggedness which its position beside a suburban main road does nothing to soften. Indeed the road separates the monastery buildings from their original gatehouse, which now serves as a museum. So the imagination is hard pressed to visualize silent monks dressed in white, eating their one daily vegetarian meal between manual labour and prayer and making their own clothes, as had been enjoined upon them by Bernard of Clairvaux.

One cannot fail to respond to the work of the Norman masons, however, who rose to the necessity of erecting a church of nobility but without flamboyance. The plan is basically the same as that of Fountains, with the monastic buildings spreading out to the south side of the church. The aisled nave of eight bays is 150 feet in length, and its huge solid piers consist of clustered shafts rising to pointed arches, though the arches of doors and windows are round. The west entrance into the church is a fine and uncharacteristically rich doorway of five orders. The quadripartite vaulting of the aisles survives, and in each transept three separate chapels retain their barrel-vaulted roofs.

The other buildings are easily traced, with chapter house and parlour on the east side of the cloister, and kitchen, warming house and refectory on the south side, with various courts and traces of the infirmary and the abbot's lodge beyond. The latter was added in the thirteenth century and is an indication that the monks got fed up with their austere life-style rather earlier than is usual among the Cistercians, for the abbot was expected to live as his monks did, among them; not to have a three-storey house with privacy, fireplaces and other comforts. This bit of class distinction and self-indulgence was the thin end of the wedge, no doubt, that led in due course to

the establishment of a flesh kitchen, and a *misericord* where the monks could eat meat. They had presumably succumbed to envy and gluttony, two of the seven deadly sins, and added butchery and who knows what other civilized practices to their other skills as wool-traders and iron-founders. St Bernard must have turned in his grave. A combination of Cistercian hypocrisy, stand-offishness and high-handed intercourse with local communities must have got the monks a bad name early on, for the twelfth-century judge Walter Mapas, on taking his oath to do equal justice to everyone, made an exception of Jews and Cistercians, and William Langland foretold the wages of sin a century and a half before the Dissolution in 'The Vision of Piers Plowman':

But there shall come a king, and he shall shrive
  you all,
And beat you as the Bible saith, for breaking of
  your Rule.

The king not only shrove the monks but also plundered their abbeys, and Kirkstall is fortunate to have been spared as much as it has.

The abbey is owned by Leeds Corporation and lies in a formal park beside the A65 Skipton Road about two miles north-west of the city centre. SE 261360.

Knowlton Church

Dorset

THIS SMALL Norman church of flint, with its square fourteenth-century tower of banded flint and stone, stands alone at the centre of a prehistoric circle on Cranborne Chase, surrounded by a ditch and bank. The circle is one of three henge earthworks known as the Knowlton Rings, dating from the Bronze Age, and there are several round barrows in the vicinity. No one knows the purpose of the circles, and indeed, one might well wonder at the purpose of the church, for the village which it once served has entirely disappeared. Had its people become uneasy in such close proximity to lingering pagan mysteries? The village's name seems clearly enough to have been derived from the prehistoric mounds around it – Knoll Town – and it is not far from the enigmatic Dorset Cursus, that six-mile-long ceremonial avenue or astronomical sight-line dating from the New Stone Age.

The early Christian missionaries in England were always ready to commandeer the sites of pagan religion, following Pope Gregory's wise instruction to Augustine to absorb rather than destroy places of idolatry and 'devil-worship'. It is probable that more churches than we realize were built on the sacred sites of pre-Christian England, thereby aiming to acquire some of the strength of association already existing between place and people.

What went on in this circle, before the church was built in the twelfth century, we have no idea, but the place has gathered much legend about it and is said to be haunted, and it was near here in 1685 that the rebel Duke of Monmouth was dragged trembling from a ditch, disguised as a shepherd. The church has not been used since 1647. It had three bells originally, but one of them was stolen, ending up – so the story goes – in the River Stour beneath White Mill Bridge, whence all attempts to recover it failed, as the ropes always snapped inexplicably. 'All the devils in Hell', a local verse said, 'could never pull up Knowlton bell.'

As for hauntings, Jacquetta Hawkes owns up to being startled by a barn owl there in broad daylight, but in the service of this book I recently spent a night there and saw no ghosts. The only thing that disturbed my sleep was the sound of cattle moving about in a nearby field. At least, I think that's what it was.

The church is in the care of the Department of the Environment, and stands beside a minor road off west side of B3078 one mile south of Wimborne St Giles. There is very limited parking space at the roadside. SU 024103.

RIGHT *The church of unknown dedication at Knowlton stands at the centre of a prehistoric earthwork, and has been deserted since 1647. It is a place of unsolved mysteries.*

Lanercost Priory

Cumbria

THE GEOGRAPHICAL position of this red ruin is mainly responsible for the wondrous variety of its associations in fact and fable. Romans, Scots and Vikings, as well as English, have left their assorted marks on its history, while its fine situation in quiet countryside in the valley of the River Irthing, close to Hadrian's Wall, gives another dimension to its romantic character.

Lanercost was founded at an uncertain date in the twelfth century by Robert de Vaux,

baron of Gilsland, for Augustinian canons, and dedicated to St Mary Magdalene. One tradition has it that de Vaux founded the monastery in expiation of his murder of the previous lord of Gilsland, but there is no evidence for that supposition. At any rate, when he died he was buried in the church which had by that time been built of local sandstone and material from the nearby Roman wall.

De Vaux's kinsman, Sir Roland de Vaux, also buried here, was the chivalrous hero of Scott's romantic poem 'The Bridal of Trier-main', which links the fabulous Castle Rock referred to in my introduction not only with

The impressive sandstone ruins of Lanercost.

King Arthur and the Knights of the Round Table but also with the fairies which Viking influence left to become an integral part of Cumbrian folklore. Even as late as 1885, the vicar of Lanercost could write seriously of hauntings by fairies in this district, and report that a local man had been dragged from his horse by fairies and was only saved from being thrust through a door in a fairy hill by the lucky circumstance that he had a page from an old Bible in his pocket.

The priory was raided on several occasions by the Scots, and in 1296 it was badly damaged by fire when troops under the Earl of Buchan raided what was then Cumberland. The prior's lodging was a pele tower – one of those square tower-houses built in the northern counties to defend their occupants against forays across the border – and Edward I stayed here during his campaigns against the Scots. The priory had become poor by the fifteenth century, and after the Dissolution, when its canons were executed for participation in the Pilgrimage of Grace, it was allowed to fall into ruin by its new owners, the Dacre family of Naworth Castle. Much of its stone, particularly of the monastic quarters, was carted away for use elsewhere, and in this way Roman material from the great wall found its way into yet more modern buildings.

The western range was converted into a mansion by Sir Thomas Dacre, whose tomb is in that part of the priory church which was subsequently restored and now serves the parish. This is the nave of the old church. The choir and transepts are open to the sky, but their solid northern stonework of regular courses rises to lofty heights, with Early English arches and arcades looking as if they will stand for ever.

Lanercost is at a junction of minor roads two and a half miles north-east of Brampton, and is reached from A69 or B6318. The ruined parts of the priory are in the care of the Department of the Environment. There is a car park in front of the parish church entrance. NY 555637.

Lindisfarne Priory

Northumberland

MORE THAN twelve hundred years ago the venerable and informative Bede described Lindisfarne, which, 'as the tide flows and ebbs twice a day, is enclosed by the waves of the sea like an island; and again, twice in the day, when the shore is left dry, becomes contiguous to the land.' The sea still cuts off Lindisfarne twice a day. Even fifty years ago, a writer could tell us that 'the way is so long and the danger of being overtaken by the tide is so great that, in addition to a line of stakes placed in the sands, to guide strangers, there are two or more boxes, fixed upon piles, into which those who are unfortunate enough to be overtaken by the rising tide may take refuge until the ebb.' The boxes are still there, but now there is a surfaced roadway, and instead of the sandalled imprints of monks' and pilgrims' feet, the tide daily washes away the tyre marks of tourists' motor cars.

Glastonbury alone can lay claim to being a more sacred place in Christian England than the ancient monastery here, where the Lindisfarne Gospels came from and where St Cuthbert was bishop. Celtic monks came to convert the kingdom of Northumbria to Christianity in the seventh century, and on this land called by the Anglo-Saxons Lindisfarne they founded a monastery which shone like a beacon of learning across the narrow sands that separate it from the mainland at high tide.

The Normans called the place Holy Island, and they built a Benedictine priory on the site formerly occupied by the monastery, which had been destroyed by the Danes. It is the priory, occupied at first by a colony of monks from Whitby Abbey, whose remains we see here now, and this in itself is a splendid ruin – a fine piece of Romanesque architecture exposed to the scourging wind and the lashing sea but still standing to a substantial height. One does not have to be a Christian to feel a profound respect for this spot, even though

the monks who inhabited the priory were scarcely of the same holiness as those of the earlier monastery.

The priory church was built early in the twelfth century of dark red sandstone, and had features resembling those of Durham Cathedral, built a little earlier and England's greatest masterpiece of Romanesque architecture. In particular the massive piers incised with geometric patterns are reminiscent of Durham. The highly ornamented remaining rib of the crossing tower, bridging two great masses of masonry, is affectionately known as the Rainbow Arch.

The Benedictine monks lived out their lives here in relative peace and wealth until the Dissolution, although the threat of raids by the Scots forced them to build some defensive features into their monastic buildings. Their wealthy estates were on the mainland, and they supplied the priory with venison, geese, pork, cheese and a store of strong ale and wine 'for the solace of the brethren'. But the monks were evidently too busy gorging themselves and dressing in fine vestments of coloured silk to make any spiritual or cultural contribution to society, and standing in this spot it is inevitable that our imaginations go back to those earlier buildings, of which nothing remains.

Cuthbert, who performed many miracles of healing, it is said, lived here with his monks and dressed in a habit made of undyed sheeps' wool until he retired to solitude on the island of Farne, where he died. 'No one, before God's servant Cuthbert', Bede says, 'had ever dared to inhabit this island alone, on account of the evil spirits which reside there: but when this servant of Christ came, armed with the helmet of salvation, the shield of faith, and the sword of the Spirit, which is the word of God, all the fiery darts of the wicked were extinguished ...'

It was not long after the death of Saint Cuthbert, whose body was laid to rest here, that another bishop of Lindisfarne, living on a more frugal diet than those who came after him, began the famous gospels which are now

LEFT *An 1830 engraving by W. Tombleson of a dramatic view of Holy Island drawn by J.M.W. Turner.*

Lindisfarne Priory. The so-called 'Rainbow Arch' of the famous Holy Island priory church forms a bridge between two masses of masonry in the crossing tower. Romanesque incised patterns are still visible on the piers.

RIGHT *The east end of the neglected little chapel at Lower Brockhampton, now in the care of the National Trust.*

in the British Museum and have made the island known throughout the western world. He was Eadfrith and 'he at the first wrote this book for God and St Cuthbert and for all the saints in common that are in the island'. This illuminated manuscript, in rich colours and superb design, is one of the great works of art of the so-called Dark Ages. With what skill and patience the maker of this book spent his years in contriving the intricate and harmonious designs and writings on his 258 pages of vellum!

In 793, the Anglo-Saxon Chronicle tells us, 'terrible portents appeared in Northumbria, and miserably afflicted the inhabitants: these were exceptional flashes of lightning, and fiery dragons were seen flying in the air, and soon followed a great famine, and after that in the same year the harrying of the heathen miserably destroyed God's church in Lindisfarne by raping and slaughter.' The Danish raids drove the surviving monks away, and they took the body of St Cuthbert and the Gospels with them. Legend has it that they accidentally dropped the book into the sea as they tried to cross to Ireland, but it was miraculously recovered without damage.

Various miracles were also attributed to St Cuthbert's body, which duly came to rest in

Durham Cathedral. But the local fishermen had their own story to tell, which was that on dark and stormy nights the spirit of St Cuthbert could be heard, in lulls between the waves crashing on the shore, forging beads for the faithful, using pieces of rock as his hammer and anvil. Moreover, the beads could be found scattered on the shore when the storm had abated and daylight came.

The fact that the 'beads' were the rounded fossils of tiny sea creatures does not detract from the relevance of this legend as indicating the continuing presence of the gentle and revered saint in the minds of local people in quite recent times, and if our materialistic age discourages belief in such romantic ideas, nevertheless one cannot help, as Sir Nikolaus Pevsner has put it, 'a feeling of awe, as one treads the ground of Holy Island'.

Holy Island is reached from the village of Beal, a mile east of A1, by a causeway which can be crossed except for about five hours around high tide. Tide tables are displayed at the approaches from both ends. The priory ruins are in the care of the Department of the Environment. NU 127418.

Lower Brockhampton Chapel

Hereford & Worcester

THIS TINY chapel stands hidden in a farmyard, near the former manor house which draws many visitors. They admire the half-timbered house, the gatehouse standing astride the moat, and perhaps the herons usually to be seen loitering not far away. But they often miss the chapel, which was here first.

This is not one of the grand, imposing ecclesiastical ruins whose sacred history speaks to us from every stone. On the contrary, it is a small, bare and simple rectangular shell, with only its gabled east wall standing to its original height (and that is not saying much). It was built with thick walls of pinkish

tufaceous limestone, and had lancet windows in its chancel. Now it has no roof, no monuments, no ornament except the early Perpendicular tracery of its east window. It stands open to the elements, and to the farmyard animals through its single doorway in the south wall. Its only furnishing is a plain stone font, and it is hard to feel any special reverence for this place. One might even be tempted to wonder if the preservation of such a forlorn and insignificant wreck is not carrying conservation a little too far.

Yet here centuries ago the lord of the manor came from the neighbouring house to confess his sins and receive the sacraments, and there is perhaps someone alive in England today whose distant ancestor cried in the priest's arms as he was baptized at this font, while the morning sun cast a narrow shaft of light across the chapel floor. It has its place in the religious history of England, far removed from the wealthy monasteries and the great churches, for many small ruined churches more truly represent the social history of the country than larger ones still in use. This simple chapel is hidden in its secret valley which civilizing influences were slow to reach, but rustic gossips no doubt told tales which reached the ears of the local ecclesiastical court, and got their neighbours into trouble for not attending church on Sunday or for more serious country matters. Their neighbours sat on wooden benches and stifled yawns at the endless admonitions of the country clerk in holy orders, who doubtless kept, if not a wife, at least a hearth girl, who 'kindled his fire but extinguished his virtue', for the country clergy were not, on the whole, immune to worldly influences.

Lower Brockhampton is two miles east of Bromyard, and is reached by a long narrow road, signposted from A44, through farmland and the grounds of Brockhampton Park. You reach a small parking area opposite the manor house, and must then ask permission to go through the adjacent farmyard to the chapel, which is owned by the National Trust. SO 682550.

Mount Grace Priory

North Yorkshire

THIS RUIN is the best remaining example in England of a Carthusian priory or Charterhouse. The Carthusians were of very different persuasion from the other monastic orders of western Christianity. They were extreme in their austerity, embracing not only the rule of silence, but of almost total isolation. Hence their buildings were unique in having, instead of the communal quarters of other monasteries, individual cells round a large cloister. The brothers (*conversii*) were supposed to eat only coarse bread and vegetables, and wear a black cassock and black cloak over a hair shirt.

Mount Grace is a convenient modern appellation for what was properly called the House of the Assumption of the Most Blessed Virgin and St Nicholas of Mount Grace at Ingleby. It was founded in 1398 by Thomas de Holand, Duke of Surrey, who was related to Richard II and was later executed for his opposition to Henry IV, being brought here for burial twelve years after his death.

It is in the nature of the Carthusian order that, until the Dissolution, the history of its houses was uneventful. Each monk, as well as the prior, lived in seclusion in a stone-built cell, cut off not only from the world but from one another, like hermits. Eating, sleeping, studying and praying alone, these men of curious dedication met only at church services and on special feast days when they dined together.

There were twenty-four cells round two courts at Mount Grace, with the priory church between the courts or cloisters. Each cell was virtually a two-storey cottage, with a lobby, living room, study and oratory on the ground floor, and a garden with a garderobe or privy at the bottom. Beside the door to each cell was a hatch with an elbow bend in it, where the monk's meals were placed by a servitor with no chance of the two men catching sight of each other. Each cell had a

Mount Grace Priory. The ruins of the priory church.

piped water supply, with a tap in a recess in the lobby wall; and in the great cloister, on the outside wall of the prior's cell (which had the class distinction of a wall fireplace) was a laver where the monks washed their hands before their infrequent entry to the refectory.

In these surroundings men passed away their lives in what they perceived, in their wisdom, as useful pursuits, with the small plain priory church and its square tower literally the centre of their world. If there was anything that could remotely be construed as luxury in their bleak lives, it was space. They cultivated their gardens and tortured their bodies for the sake of their souls. Here at the edge of the North Yorkshire moors, with nothing but their faith to sustain their morale and with poor diets lacking in fats and vitamins to sustain their bodies through bitterly cold winters, many of them must have died of hypothermia, though they had never heard of it, at ages we now consider still relatively young.

By the time the Dissolution came the priory was surprisingly prosperous, its annual value being estimated at £323 2s 10½d. One of the monks and a lay brother had the wit to flee for Scotland, but were captured and imprisoned. The prior, John Wilson, was interrogated about his suspected involvement in the Pilgrimage of Grace, but was cleared.

Part of the range to the west of the church was converted into a dwelling by the Lascelles family who owned the wood-enclosed site in the seventeenth century. This house is still occupied, but the church's crossing tower of mellow limestone, with its battlemented parapet and pinnacles like Fountains in miniature, now presides over the bare remnants of a monastery that must have had the same eerie quality of silence, when it was occupied, that we readily associate with its ruin.

Mount Grace Priory is signposted off A19 one mile north-west of Osmotherley. It is a National Trust property in the guardianship of the Department of the Environment, and there is a car park at the site. SE 449985.

Netley Abbey

Hampshire

AT THE TURN of the century it was still possible to say of Netley Abbey that 'its fragments, many of them sculptured with armorial bearings and other devices, lie scattered in heaps over the floor'. Horace Walpole, in 1755, wrote: 'The ruins are vast, and retain fragments of beautiful fretted roof, pendent in the air, with all variety of Gothic patterns of windows, wrapped round and round with ivy.'

Now both the ivy and the scattered heaps of stone have gone, sacrificed to the 'Keep Britain Tidy' doctrine from which ruins alone should perhaps have been granted exemption. Yet Netley remains a tranquil and beautiful place, despite ill-treatment by Henry VIII and more recent vandals. Trees push upward from among its pale walls and cast dappled shadows on its ancient stonework. Its situation on the east bank of Southampton Water seems to lend it a fine distinction among the ruined abbeys of southern England, which are not, on the whole, as specially favoured as those in the north.

Netley Abbey was a Cistercian establishment, however, so this must have been a wild and remote spot in the thirteenth century, when monks came from Beaulieu to colonize a monastery adopted, if not actually founded, by Henry III. Leland ascribes its foundation to Peter Roche, Bishop of Winchester, who died in 1238, but most guide books give the date of the abbey's foundation as 1239. No doubt building work started then. At any rate, in 1251 the king assumed patronage of the abbey and endowed it liberally with lands and other gifts.

As a latecomer among Cistercian foundations (more than a century after Rievaulx), when the austerity of the order had given way to a little self-indulgence, and with a royal patron who was a champion of the Gothic art and architecture the Cistercians themselves had introduced into England, the monastery

Gothic arches in the beautiful abbey church of Netley.

might have been expected to have a rosy future as well as seductively beautiful quarters. But although its Early English abbey church was of surpassing majesty, the monastery never equalled Beaulieu in importance and did not long enjoy prosperity.

Already by 1338 it was in financial difficulties, and had petitioned the Crown for relief on the ground that its position on the coast forced it to provide hospitality for large numbers of mariners who were constantly coming and going. Indeed this liability persisted until the Dissolution, for the king's commissioners praised the abbey as being 'To the Kinges Subjects and Strangers travelinge the same Sees great Reliefe and Comforte'. The abbey maintained a lighthouse for the comfort of the king's subjects on the water, but the sailors got some of their relief on dry land by stealing the abbey's sheep, and the monastery was reduced to such poverty that its library contained only one book, Cicero's *Treatise on Rhetoric* – a volume singularly unfitted, one might think, to sustain an abbot and half a dozen monks through such trials and tribulations.

At its suppression, the abbey was granted to Sir William Paulet, Comptroller of the Royal

Netley Abbey. Most of the abbey was put to domestic use after the Dissolution. This view shows part of the eastern range of former monastic buildings.

Household, who converted the ruins into a residence, built of brick, with its great hall in the nave of the former church! Much brickwork, faced with stone, can still be seen remaining from this time among the monastic stonework. The property then passed through various hands until about 1704, when the then owner, Sir Berkeley Lucy, sold the ruins to a Southampton builder named Taylor, who proposed to dismantle them for the sake of the materials, beginning with the abbey church. Popular report has it that before embarking on his demolition work, Taylor had a dream in which a phantom monk warned him against proceeding with the job, but he ignored this and went ahead with his men. While he was working at the foot of a wall all the tracery of the great west window suddenly fell out and crushed him to death. This could hardly be seen otherwise, even in the Age of Reason, than as an Act of God, and the work of demolition was promptly abandoned.

Some years afterwards a recess in one of the walls was found to contain the skeleton of a woman, and this discovery gave rise to one of Rev. Richard Barham's 'Ingoldsby Legends' in which he ended by deploring the vandalism to which the ruins had by his time become subject, the place having become a sort of tea-garden in the ownership of the Chamberlaine family:

'Dear me!' I exclaim'd, 'what a place to be in!'
And I said to the person who drove my 'shay'
(A very intelligent man, by the way),
'This, all things considered, is rather too gay!

It don't suit my humour, – so take me away!
Dancing! and drinking! – cigar and song!
If not profanation, it's "coming it strong",
And I really consider it all very wrong. –
– Pray, to whom does this property now belong?'
– He paused and said, scratching his head,
'Why I really *do* think he's a little to blame,
But I can't say I knows the Gentleman's name!'

'Well – well!' quoth I, as I heaved a sigh,
And a tear-drop fell from my twinkling eye,
'My vastly good man, as I scarcely doubt
That some day or other you'll find it out,
   Should he come your way,
   Or ride in your "shay"
As perhaps he may, be so good as to say
That a Visitor, whom you drove over one day,
Was exceedingly angry, and very much
   scandalized,
Finding these beautiful ruins so Vandalized,
And thus of their owner to speak began,
   As he ordered you home in haste,
   "NO DOUBT HE'S A VERY RESPECTABLE MAN,
   But – *I can't say much for his taste*".'

In view of this, we should be more than grateful to the then Office of Works for rescuing the ruins from further despoliation, even if the view the Romantics had of it has been lost for ever; at least we have intact that spectacular east window in the church, which is the glory of Netley's remains, and was probably made by Henry III's own master mason whose work is to be seen in Westminster Abbey.

Netley now trembles within an inch of Southampton's spreading tentacles on the south-east side of the city, and is reached by minor roads from A3025 or B3397. The ruins are in the care of the Department of the Environment and there is a car park at the site. SU 453089.

Pickworth Church

Leicestershire

I HAVE WALKED several times across the sloping and bumpy field to this little-known ruin in the former county of Rutland, and continue to find it more poignant than many a more famous ruin elsewhere. It is all that remains of a medieval village whose stone foundations still lie beneath the grass and prevent farmers from ploughing the land. This solitary Gothic arch was once the doorway of the village church, which had a spire visible for miles around.

It is nearly five hundred years since any villager walked through it into church for divine service, but it has remained there long after all around it has collapsed and disappeared. Some say that Pickworth was a casualty of the Wars of the Roses. There is a wood called Bloody Oaks beside the Great North Road, not far away, and in 1470 Yorkists and Lancastrians joined battle here in what became known as the Battle of Losecoat Field. According to legend, the Lancastrian soldiers, fleeing from a sound drubbing by the Yorkists, shed their tunics to avoid being recognized. It is generally assumed that the rebel troops destroyed the church and the village, for by 1491 Pickworth was recorded as having no parishioners. No one is sure, however, and it may be that the Black Death had already devastated the area so that the troops merely went on a rampage through what was already a ghost village.

In any case, by 1731 the church was in such a state of ruin that the local people thought fit to demolish the remaining steeple to use the stone for other building work and, from that point onward, the arch stood alone. Eventually, the deserted village began to grow again, but at a little distance from the former site, which the locals christened 'the old foundations'. Local lore says that a man hanged himself from this arch once, and that if you come here at midnight you can see him still swinging there.

The remaining fragment of the village church at Pickworth. Parishioners used to pass under this arch to enter their church for divine service. Now it is the only evidence above ground level of the village that once stood around it.

In 1817 a poor young peasant came to the resurrected community to work as a lime-burner, while trying to save a pound out of his scanty wages to get a prospectus printed for some poems he had written. John Clare had come to Rutland to work for Wilders of Casterton, who owned several lime-kilns in the area. It was on one of his long walks here that he first saw his future wife, known to his readers as 'Sweet Patty of the Vale'.

Clare wrote later that the ground where he worked at Pickworth was 'full of foundations and human bones', so it must have been close to this old arch, where the churchyard had once been, and he wrote an 'Elegy on the ruins at Pickworth'. I have not enough space to quote the poem in full, but the following verses indicate its melancholy tone:

Ye scenes of desolation spread around,
  Prosperity to you did once belong;
And, doubtless, where these brambles claim the
  ground,
    The glass once flowed to hail the ranting song.

There's not a rood of land demands our toil,
  There's not a foot of ground we daily tread,
But gains increase from time's devouring spoil,
  But holds some fragment of the human dead.

Since first these ruins fell, how chang'd the
  scene!
    What busy, bustling mortals, now unknown,
Have come and gone, as tho' there naught had
  been,
    Since first oblivion call'd the spot her own.

The arch's stonework, with its carved capitals, seems an appropriate memorial, not only to the fifteenth-century village which was destroyed, but also to the nineteenth-century poet and peasant who likewise defied oblivion and left a finely-wrought part of himself above ground when he descended into delusion and death.

Pickworth is close to Leicestershire's border with Lincolnshire, at a country crossroads six miles north-west of Stamford. The ruin is beside the road leading west to the A1. The land is private property, but the arch can be seen clearly from the roadside. SK 992139.

Ramsey Abbey

Cambridgeshire

FORMERLY in Huntingdonshire, Ramsey was an ancient foundation of considerable size and importance, with about eighty monks in medieval times and extensive estates in the Fens, and in Norfolk, Bedfordshire and elsewhere in eastern England. Its feudal manors and tenants owned over four hundred plough-teams of oxen, and its revenues were higher than those of any other monastic establishment in the Fens. Its abbots were mitred, and the abbey was celebrated for its learning and for its fine library, which contained in particular a notable collection of Hebrew books, bought by the abbey when Edward I expelled the Jews from England in 1290 and confiscated their property.

So may we expect substantial remains to feed our imaginations of this great Benedictine abbey in the days of its glory? Alas, no. The church and monastic buildings have vanished into thin air, like ghosts at cock-crow. All that remains visible to the public is a small part of the abbey's original gatehouse beside the green at the centre of this small market town. But this in itself, though fragmentary, is splendid enough to justify the inclusion of Ramsey Abbey in this section.

The abbey was founded on an island in the marshes, called Ram's Island, in AD 969 by Ailwine, an East Anglian nobleman, whose thirteenth-century monument of Purbeck marble is still to be seen in the gatehouse. The abbey was built of stone quarried at Barnack under licence from Peterborough, in return for which privilege Ramsey supplied four thousand eels during Lent each year.

Already, by the time of the Norman Conquest, the abbey had established a school which had a wide reputation, while some of its monks became noted later as scholars of Hebrew. The abbey's estates grew large crops of wheat, oats and barley and kept flocks of sheep and herds of cattle on its Fenland pastures. It had a small dependent priory at St

The wealth of this great Benedictine monastery is evident in the ornamental stonework of its remains.

Part of the former gatehouse of Ramsey Abbey.

Ives, where in about 1415 it built the stone bridge still to be seen over the River Ouse, with its little chapel in the middle.

The gatehouse itself was built around 1500, and is an ornate piece of Decorated architecture, with a two-light oriel window over its doorway, panelled buttresses and richly carved friezes all round. The gatehouse was originally much larger and grander, as befitted an abbey of such wealth and splendour, but at the Dissolution the greater part of it was dismantled and taken to Hinchingbrooke by the Cromwells, who also acquired the nunnery there.

As for the rest of the abbey, it was gradually broken up, its stones being used in local churches and Cambridge colleges, until the Cromwells built a mansion out of the remains, which became a grammar school in 1937.

Ramsey is at the junction of B1040 and B1096 eight miles north of Huntingdon. The gatehouse stands at the corner of Abbey Green near the parish church, and is owned by the National Trust. TL 285852.

Rievaulx Abbey

North Yorkshire

THE SOARING piers and majestic arches of Rievaulx Abbey rise from the valley floor of Ryedale into such a picturesque ruin-in-a-landscape that we are forced to wonder whether the sensuous magic of the place worked as effectively on twelfth-century saints as it does on twentieth-century sinners. And when we find that the ground space of the site was so restricted that the alignment of the nave is north-south instead of the traditional east-west, we know for certain that the situation had a very strong appeal for the medieval holy men. In fact, however, the Cistercian monks described this place as one of 'horror and waste solitude'. True to form, it was the solitude that appealed to them, the church's axis being forced on them by the confines of a heavily wooded valley. Yorkshire's desolate landscape, not yet recovered from the devastation wrought by William the Conqueror, presented ideal sites to the Cistercians, who wanted no intercourse with local inhabitants to cloud the purity of their remote and self-reliant existence.

Rievaulx, with its early Gothic arches, is one of the most priceless treasures of England's heritage, even in its fallen state, although – we are led to suppose – in the days before the Dissolution, men were less responsive to architectural beauty. Certainly any aesthetic merits the building had were provided for the greater glory of God, not for the hedonistic appreciation of man. Indeed, the Cistercians were noted for the austerity of their architecture as well as their living standards, and their best known and most influential medieval figure, Abbot Bernard of Clairvaux, made a famous attack on the decorative church sculpture of other orders:

What profit is there in these ridiculous monsters, in that marvellous and deformed comeliness, that comely deformity? To what purpose are those unclean apes, those fierce lions, those monstrous centaurs, those half-men, those striped tigers, those fighting knights, those hunters winding their horns? ... We are more tempted to read in the marble than in our service books and to spend the whole day in wondering at these things than in meditating the law of God. For God's sake, if men are not ashamed of these follies, why at least do they not shrink from the expense?

When we consider that so many of the finest monastic ruins in Britain – Rievaulx, Fountains, Tintern – were Cistercian houses, it is difficult to argue with the principle of simplicity, even if we cannot go along with the reasoning.

It was very soon after St Bernard's strictures appeared that Walter l'Espec, lord of the manor of Helmsley, granted some land in the Rye valley to the abbot and twelve monks who became the nucleus of the first large Cistercian establishment in England. The Norman lord, a bearded warrior whose voice was 'like the sound of a trumpet', entered the abbey as a novice himself, in advanced age, and died here in silence after making his peace with the Almighty. The date of the abbey's foundation was 1131, and within thirty years the third abbot, Ailred, was apparently presiding over a hundred and forty monks and some five hundred lay brothers in a spacious monastic settlement with extensive agricultural interests, though how the place could have accommodated so many is a mystery. The lay brethren were the poor and illiterate whom the Cistercians habitually sheltered in return for their labour.

The buildings were erected in sandstone quarried near the site and at Bilsdale, a little to the north, and the church and principal living quarters were completed in a remarkably short time. The nave is older than any Cistercian nave remaining in France. The aisles were separated from the nave in early Cistercian churches by stone walls between the huge square piers, but at Rievaulx these were removed in the fourteenth century. By that time a choir and presbytery had been added to the southern end of the church which were scarcely in accord with the principle of plain architecture enjoined upon the earlier brethren, having stone-ribbed vaults and arcading, some Gothic ornament, and flying buttresses, the floor being paved with glazed tiles in green and yellow patterns. Such relative ostentation was a symptom of the corruption that brings down ecclesiastical empires as well as secular ones, for as the monasteries

RIGHT *Looking across Rievaulx' chancel from the east. It was originally paved with green and yellow glazed tiles. The building of this extension to the original church put the abbey heavily in debt – and its architecture was far removed in style from the simplicity enjoined upon the Cistercians – but it left to us some of the most beautiful Gothic buildings in Britain.*

FAR RIGHT *Rievaulx Abbey. This view, looking across the ruins of some of the monastic buildings on the south side, shows the south transept and chancel of the abbey church.*

grew increasingly wealthy, so they abandoned their allegiance to austerity, and the numbers of the faithful decreased. And even its isolation could not protect Rievaulx from Scottish raids and the devastation of the Black Death, the abbot being among those who succumbed to the dread plague in 1349. By the time of the Dissolution, there were only twenty-two monks left at Rievaulx. The property was granted to the Earl of Rutland, and a village grew up near the site with houses built of stone plundered from the monastery buildings. It is only because of the relative isolation of Rievaulx that so much of the decayed monastery building is left to us. Its stone would certainly have been carted away in great quantities if it had been nearer to a larger or growing population.

The chapter house, with its rounded apse, is among the most easily distinguishable of the buildings, though none of its walls remains intact. It was rectangular at first, in accordance with Cistercian custom, the apse being added later. Here in the monastery's early years its abbots were buried, and gravestones of thirteenth- and fourteenth-century abbots can still be seen, together with uninscribed graves and the shrine of the first abbot, William, who had been secretary to Bernard of Clairvaux and died in 1148.

It is to the medieval centuries of prosperity that we return in imagination, seeing the brethren bustle about their business, summoned by bells to matins, keeping silence in the cloister, intoning their prayers in the church, studying in the library, tending their sheep in the fields and revitalizing their circulation before the two great fires of the warming house in the bitter northern winters.

Six hundred years on, William Cowper was tempted to make his home here so that he could gaze at the ruins for the rest of his life. And after him came Wordsworth. His sister Dorothy recorded in her journal in 1802 that she 'went down to look at the Ruins – thrushes were singing, cattle feeding among green grown hillocks about the Ruins … I could have stayed in this solemn quiet spot till

evening without a thought of moving, but William was waiting for me, so in a quarter of an hour I went away.' The abbey featured in Scott's *Ivanhoe* and also in the paintings of the Romantic artists.

All this, of course, was after Burke's discovery of the sublime, and by the Wordsworths' time, the Duncombe family of Duncombe Park had built the so-called Rievaulx Terrace in the course of landscaping their vast grounds. From this high viewpoint we can gaze upon the abbey ruins – the forlorn but still magnificent work of twelfth-century masons – which form part of the picturesque Rye valley landscape stretched out below.

The abbey, which is in the care of the Department of the Environment, is in the village of Rievaulx, two and a half miles north-west of Helmsley off B1257, and is within the North York Moors National Park. There is a car park at the site. No visitor should miss the view from Rievaulx Terrace, which is in the ownership of the National Trust. SE 576849.

Thornton Abbey

Humberside

THORNTON, formerly in Lincolnshire, was originally an Augustinian priory founded in 1139 by William le Gros, and the first prior and monks came from Kirkham. It was elevated to abbey status after only a short time, having become wealthy and influential. In 1541 the monastery welcomed Henry VIII, with his current queen Jane Seymour and their retinue, and entertained them during a break on their return journey to London from the north. In recognition of this hospitality, the abbey was treated leniently at the Dissolution, but this did not save it from being reduced at last to ruin: relatively few walls of its once extensive buildings now remain standing, the octagonal chapter house, built between 1282 and 1308, being the most impressive fragment of the former abbey.

The imposing gatehouse of Thornton Abbey, approached by a stone bridge across a wide defensive ditch.

The huge gatehouse at the entrance to the monastery, reached by a bridge across a wide ditch, is a fourteenth-century addition for which licence to crenellate was granted in 1382, when Abbot Thomas completed this building in brick and stone, apparently to defend the abbey against piratical raids from the Humber. Among the surviving sculpture on its front elevation are figures of the Virgin, St John the Baptist and St Augustine, but several statues have disappeared.

Can it have been Thomas de Greetham, the fourteenth abbot and builder of this gatehouse, who was buried alive here for some unspecified crime that would have brought 'scandal to the Church' if the record had not been obliterated? In the eighteenth century, according to unreliable evidence, a human skeleton was found walled up among these ruins, sitting at a table with a book and candle on it. This method of capital punishment was widely employed on the Continent at one time, often for sexual offences, and although it was never common in England, it was not entirely unknown, especially in monasteries, as at Netley. Perhaps the abbot entertained women of ill repute in his new gatehouse. The evidence suggests that nuns who had fallen from grace were more liable to suffer this terrible death penalty than men, and we need not be surprised at that.

The abbey was totally suppressed in the reign of Elizabeth, and its stone was plundered for building local farmhouses and the like until such time as what little remained came under the protection of a seventeenth-century owner, Sir Vincent Skinner. He lived in a house converted from the ruins and took some interest in the abbey's history, but according to report, his house 'fell quite down to the bare ground without any visible cause'.

The remains of Thornton Abbey are in the care of the Department of the Environment. They stand within sight of the oil refineries of the Humber, a mile and a half east of the village of Thornton Curtis, on a minor road leaving A1077 there. There is a small parking area in front of the approach to the abbey gatehouse. TA 116190.

Tintern Abbey

Gwent

SO WE COME to another great climax in monastery building in Britain. At first sight it may be disappointing, for our sense of expectation is not fed here as it is at Fountains Abbey. We come upon it suddenly beside the road, and as the northern side of its dark Welsh stonework does not get the sunlight, it looks gaunt and a trifle forbidding. But this atmosphere quickly evaporates on closer acquaintance, and we see Cistercian restraint somewhat relaxed in a mighty piece of religious architecture which has drawn gasps of admiration from Romantic poets and painters since Wordsworth and Turner.

In their day there was no road beside it; visitors came by boat, and old engravings and paintings and early photographs show us how different, and how much more romantic, it looked then. Here is a description of Tintern from 1801:

Nature has added her ornaments to the decorations of art; some of the windows are wholly obscured, others partially shaded with tufts of ivy, or edged with lighter foliage; the tendrils creep along the walls, wind round the pillars, wreath the capitals, or hanging down in clusters obscure the space beneath . . .

Sculptured stones then lay where they had fallen long ago, and cottages stood within the monastery precincts.

Over the years government departments stripped the ivy, demolished the cottages, removed all the fallen stones and levelled the ground, and since the walls of Tintern's abbey church are more or less intact, with only the roof and crossing tower missing, there has even been a suggestion, from time to time, as with Fountains, that the building could easily be restored. This, of course, would destroy its romance utterly.

In fact the Rev. William Gilpin, an early champion of the 'ideal landscape', went so far as to suggest that a few well-aimed taps with a

mallet might improve the picturesque qualities of the abbey's too-perfect gable-ends!

Tintern was among the first of the great Cistercian establishments in Britain. It was founded a year before Rievaulx, in heavily wooded country beside the Wye, by Walter de Clare, and one would thus expect its architecture to be of the same austere beauty as its Yorkshire sister. However, the small original church here was almost entirely rebuilt in the thirteenth century, by which time the monastery was wealthy and evidently ambitious. It

Tintern Abbey in a fine drawing by Turner.

had begun conventionally enough, in this lonely and narrow rock-bound river valley. But from 1220 onwards, new buildings began to rise. The church itself was begun in 1270, and took over thirty years to complete, with its Early English style merging into early Decorated, as is seen most effectively from the east end of the church, looking through the clustered columns and soaring arches towards the great west window, with its marvellous tracery intact.

Partly because of the practical problems of drainage into the river, the monastic buildings were erected on the north side of the church rather than the south, as was more usual with Cistercian monasteries. It is a fascinating exercise to walk among the walls and trace the layout of chapter house and cloister, abbot's hall and monks' frater, and the infirmary at the east end of the site, where sick and aged monks were looked after as well as those who were in for the annual blood-letting.

Much of Tintern's history is lost to us because its records, which passed to the Earl of Worcester after the Dissolution, were destroyed when Raglan Castle was besieged and many of its contents burnt in the Civil War. But even if the monastery had to contribute its whole wool production for one year towards paying the £100,000 ransom demanded for Richard the Lionheart only sixty years after its foundation, it had clearly progressed rapidly from being a poor settlement in the wilderness to a working establishment which had cleared the forest around it and developed sheep farming, employing lay brothers to carry out the manual labour.

Soon after the great rebuilding, Edward II sought shelter here for two nights before his ghastly death at Berkeley Castle, and in return for their hospitality he granted the monks fishing rights on a nearby stretch of the Wye. Some years after that the number of lay brothers at the monastery was drastically reduced, and this must signify the intervention of the Black Death in monastic affairs. We have no records of the period, but the abbey – in spite of its isolated situation 'remote from

the traffic of men' – cannot have escaped the catastrophe, as the dread plague swept across the Severn valley early in 1349. The infirmary must then have been a frightening place, as monks went down with the symptoms and their brothers put their lives at risk in caring for them. After that terrible year, those who were left had to cope with all the work themselves, and the abbey doubtless became poorer in spite of its wealthy patrons. When Abbot Richard Wyche surrendered the property to the king's commissioners in 1536, its annual value was reckoned at £192.

The site was granted to the Earl of Worcester, but not before the king's plumbers had moved in to strip the lead from the roof and remove the bells from the crossing tower. After that, Tintern's remoteness protected it to some extent from plunder, although some of its stone was used in local houses, and gradually vegetation crept back to engulf the monastery buildings, which had suffered much more than the church itself.

Alas, opening hours do not extend to dawn or dusk. We are not allowed today the privilege that eighteenth- and nineteenth-century visitors enjoyed, of wandering round the moonlit cloister, listening for the faint echoes of monks dining frugally to the accompaniment of one of their brethren intoning the words of the scriptures; or seeing their shadowy figures with hooded heads reverently bent as they filed into church through the beautiful processional doorway from the cloister; or in periods of permitted relief from their vows of silence discussing matters of moment in the parlour. Broad daylight tends to dissolve such fleeting images except in the church itself, whose awesome completeness fuels the imagination more readily and allows the ruin to be transformed magically from mere broken walls into living history.

Tintern Abbey stands beside A466 five miles north of Chepstow. It is in the care of the Department of the Environment, and there is a car park at the site. SO 532998.

The west entrance to the abbey church at Tintern.

RIGHT *Turner did this romantic watercolour of the ruins at Tintern in 1794.*

FAR RIGHT *The north side of the abbey church at Tintern.*

Valle Crucis Abbey

Clwyd

ABOVE LLANGOLLEN, beside the road to Ruthin, stands an isolated column known as Eliseg's Pillar. It is one of the oldest monoliths in Wales, and is thought by some to have been a cross when first erected. Others have said that it was a column brought here, perhaps, from Roman Viroconium. It now looks more like a phallic symbol – a nice irony, since those who destroyed its original shape were fanatical Puritans, who took it to be a religious relic. Its now-illegible inscriptions included a tantalizing but unreliable reference to Magnus Maximus, whom we encountered at Segontium. It was actually put here a thousand years ago as a monument to a prince of Powys, and whatever its original form may have been, it gave the valley its popular name, Valle Crucis – the Valley of the Cross. Between the erection of the pillar and the suppression of the monastery, this unquiet valley saw a great deal of frenzied and impious activity.

The founder of the abbey was Madoc ap Gruffyd Maelor, the lord of Castell Dinas Bran, the ruins of which stand on the lofty hilltop overlooking Llangollen. He was the head of a powerful local ruling family which could trace its descent from that same prince of Powys who is commemorated by Eliseg's Pillar, and who may have lived in an earlier castle on the hill. Maelor had spent his life in warfare and plunder, and now in 1201, to ease his conscience, he spent some of his ill-gotten gains on founding the abbey of Valle Crucis. It was built beside a small tributary of the River Dee in this steep-sided and narrow valley, in Early English style, without ornament except for carved capitals, and on a smaller scale than the great Cistercian abbeys of England. Maelor himself was buried here in course of time.

Meanwhile, his son Gryffydd ap Madoc Maelor had married a foreigner, Emma, the daughter of Lord Audley. A chip off the old block, Gryffydd threw in his lot with the winning side, aiding Henry III in his programme of subjugating the Welsh, and keeping clear of his outraged countrymen in his hilltop fortress until he, too, found his final resting place in the abbey precincts. By that time, however, the abbey had suffered a disastrous fire.

Much rebuilding was carried out around the middle of the thirteenth century, and this work included the upper part of the west front, built in ashlar instead of random rubble like the earlier work, and including the great symmetrical window of six lights arranged in pairs within a round arch. In the following century the gable and its fine rose window were renewed, and an inscription in Latin announced that 'Abbot Adam carried out this work; may he rest in peace. Amen.'

At this time also the chapter house was rebuilt, with its vaulted aisles and Decorated windows, and this remains largely intact – one of the best Cistercian chapter houses in the country. At the beginning of the present century there was still glass in its windows, but then there were also ash trees growing among the forsaken foundations and ivy covering the crumbling fabric: a much more romantic prospect than the grey stone ruins present now, with a ghastly caravan site alongside – far worse than the farmhouse that once occupied part of the eastern range of monastic buildings. The farm itself represented a decline, for after the Dissolution the property with its surrounding land was granted to Sir William Pickering. A dwelling house was made out of the eastern range, and a fireplace was put in, with a chimney breast faced with one of the abbey's old grave slabs.

When George Borrow came here he was not impressed. The church was 'roofless, and had nothing remarkable about it, save the western window, which we had seen from without.' Clearly he did not sense the spirit of this remarkable place. The white monks who came here in the thirteenth century, anticipating their customary life of withdrawal, were in for a rude awakening it seems, and years of

The nave and west wall of Valle Crucis. Note the fine rose window.

fighting a losing battle must have sapped their will, gradually leading them to join those they could not beat and enjoy a little of the good life.

In the fifteenth century the Welsh bard Guttyn Owain praised the hospitality of the Cistercian abbey. He had evidently dined on four courses of meat, served in dishes of silver and washed down with claret, at a table presided over by an abbot who wore rings on his fingers. The poet also mentions expensive sculptured images in the choir of the church, which was lit by enormous lancet windows. This mode of living was a far cry from the asceticism of earlier Cistercians, and was soon to be ended abruptly by order of Henry VIII.

Several thirteenth-century grave slabs are among the most interesting remains of Valle Crucis, which had a large burial ground. Most of them have been moved from their original sites, and their inscriptions are lost, but they show elaborate carvings of foliage, weapons, dragons and Celtic crosses. And in the crossing of the church is a niche with a weatherworn image of a man in armour bearing a shield. It is a memorial to the lord of a nearby manor, Ievan ap Adda, who died early in the fourteenth century and whose bones came to rest here among those of the abbots who had been his neighbouring landowners.

Valle Crucis Abbey lies on the east side of A542 Ruthin road, two miles north-west of Llangollen, and is in the care of the Welsh Office. There is limited parking space near the entrance. SJ 203443.

Walberswick Church

Suffolk

DANIEL DEFOE, discussing in the eighteenth century the decline of Dunwich as a port, quoted a local verse he found current on the coast here:

> Swoul and Dunwich, and Walderswick,
> All go in at one lousie creek.

Swoul was Southwold, and the 'lousie creek' was the mouth of the River Blyth, which was being closed up by the formation of a sand barrier. Walberswick had profited at the expense of its declining neighbours, and was at one time a thriving fishing port with a large church, built in the fifteenth century by local masons Richard Russell and Adam Powle, who were paid forty shillings and a barrel of herrings a year for their work. The church was dedicated in 1493 to St Andrew the fisherman, and its noble tower was one of the two things for which Walberswick was most noted in the region, the other being the loud voices of its menfolk, who were ironically called the 'Walberswig Whisperers'.

An assortment of natural and social changes gradually brought about the decline of Walberswick, however. Shifting sands and coastal defences interfered with the fishing industry, and anyway the consumption of fish was reduced by Protestant eating habits in Tudor times and afterwards. An outbreak of arson followed early in the seventeenth century, during the witch craze, and three people were executed for setting fire to about forty houses in Walberswick. But it was Cromwell's zealous lieutenants who began the destruction of the town's church, when windows, tombs, ornaments and images were smashed at the direction of Dr William Dowsing in 1643.

Half a century afterwards, the town had declined to such a degree that the church was far too big for the remaining population, which had become too poor to restore it, and the villagers petitioned for its reduction. Three-quarters of the building was taken down, leaving only the tower, the porch and the nave's south aisle to serve henceforth as the parish church.

Joined to these parts now are the scant and broken flint and stone walls and arches of the former proud building, with flushwork in the diagonal buttresses. The church is almost isolated from the remaining community, now

Walberswick. The flint and stone ruins of the village church, built by local masons in the fifteenth century and partly demolished two hundred years later when the population had become too small to support it.

a residential village which has long attracted artists following in the footsteps of Wilson Steer, who did much of his best work in and around Walberswick.

This is not a grand and imposing ruin, by any standards, but it remains as a worthy representative of my proposition that there is no such thing as a ruin – however small and insignificant – which doesn't have an interesting story to tell.

Walberswick lies on the south bank of an artificially constructed channel for the River Blyth, and can only be reached by road from Blythburgh, two and a half miles west, via B1387. One comes to the church on the left hand side of the road. TM 490749.

Wenlock Priory

Shropshire

THERE ARE only two important remains of Cluniac priories in England. Castle Acre is one and this is the other, standing beside the little market town of Much Wenlock. It is an enchanting place much decayed, like the leaves that drift across its green floor. To many eyes, it is a little too fragmented to qualify as picturesque, but it has several fascinating details wonderfully intact. I have visited it often, and enjoy its serenity and the subtle weathered shades of its surviving walls, built of the pale limestone quarried on Wenlock Edge.

The original building here was a nunnery founded by the Mercian princess St Milburga in about AD 680, but this was destroyed by the Danes in the ninth century, and was then re-founded by Leofric, Earl of Mercia – some say at the instigation of his wife, Lady Godiva. After the Conquest, at any rate, Roger de Montgomery, Earl of Shrewsbury and one of the great Marcher lords, established it as a priory of the Benedictine Cluniacs, and friars came here from La Charité-sur-Loire. The kings of England penalized the priory for its allegiance to a foreign power during the French wars, and in 1395 the priory severed its connection with France.

Little of the earliest buildings survives, for much reconstruction went on in the centuries after its foundation. The great church, with its long, aisled nave and fine transepts, was built in the first half of the thirteenth century, and a good deal of the south transept still stands, 70 feet high, and it has been said to be 'excelled by few medieval buildings'.

It is the priory's roofless chapter house, however, which compels the attention of the modern visitor. One enters it via three decorated Norman arches to find superb stone-carving of the late twelfth century in the form of interlaced wall arcading. A small doorway in the south-east corner has a stone lintel on which dragons are carved.

Another piece of fine Norman sculpture is on the stone basin of the *lavatorium* in the cloister. This building was of octagonal shape with a double arcade round it – a lavish wash-house – and the only part that survives bears a panel showing Christ calling the Apostles from their fishing. The four Apostles are in two boats, and two of them are using oars while another takes Christ's hand as they reach the shore.

The annual value of the priory at the Dissolution was four hundred pounds, some of it deriving from iron working, and it is sobering to think of the medieval holy men, who operated two foundries, hammering away at their anvils within striking distance of the now world-famous Ironbridge Gorge.

Much Wenlock lies on A458 Shrewsbury-Bridgnorth road. The ruins are in the care of the Department of the Environment. There is a car park opposite the entrance. SJ 626001.

The entrance to the chapter house of Wenlock Priory, showing interlaced arcading on the walls inside – a fine example of twelfth century stone-carving.

Whalley Abbey

Lancashire

THE RUINS of the Cistercian monastery at Whalley are scanty, and the remains of the abbey church virtually non-existent; its main claim to fame is the fate of the last abbot, John Paslow, who was hanged in front of his own gatehouse for participation in the Pilgrimage of Grace, and apart from that its history is usually forgotten. But Whalley Abbey was much too important a place to be passed over so cursorily, and its old stones reward more patient contemplation.

The site below the whale-backed mass of Pendle Hill was hardly the customary Cistercian habitat, 'remote from all the world', but the monks who came here in 1296 had perforce moved from their original settlement at Standlow, in the Wirral, which was not only barren, but occasionally stood three feet deep

in water when the Mersey rose with the spring tides.

So here they came to build a new monastery, close to a tributary of the Ribble – which was less apt to leave them waterlogged, even though the name Whalley means 'field of wells'. Steadily over the next hundred years the church and abbey buildings rose, while their wealth and influence grew to such an extent that before the Dissolution the abbey's authority covered a tenth of Lancashire. It was famed for its prodigal hospitality. The abbots kept body and soul together with something like two hundred slaughtered animals a year – oxen, calves, sheep, lambs and pigs – not to mention occasional variations of game and poultry. Not for them the self-denying ordinance of a frugal vegetarian diet which had been one of the chief tenets of their order in the beginning.

The abbey's ecclesiastical court, however, saw no hypocrisy in zealously punishing moral offences and in guarding against evil spirits. It recorded at Padiham in 1513 that John Henryson's wife was rumoured to practice fortune-telling and witchcraft; and at Rossendale in 1530 that Thomas Wardyll was 'notorious in the neighbourhood' for not fasting on the fifth Friday in Lent. At Bowland in 1519 it forbade Elizabeth Robinson to enter church when she failed to appear on a charge of threatening a 'black fast' against Edmund Palmer. At Pendle in 1531 it threatened Hugh Whiteacre for begetting children on Margery Cronkshay and Katherine Botheman, but the incorrigible fellow repeated the offences with both women later and, for good measure, with Agnes Towneley as well. Meanwhile, John Cronkshay was made to do public penance for incest and adultery with his cousin's wife, Emma.

Among those who suppressed the Pilgrimage of Grace and profited from the Dissolution was Assheton, lord of the local manor, who bought the monastery for a little over two thousand pounds and knocked it down in order to build himself a house from its venerable stones. The house still stands among the

Nothing remains to any great height of the former powerful abbey of Whalley, which once ruled much of Lancashire with an ecclesiastical rod of iron.

ruins, but a curse was put on the Asshetons, and it is a nice irony that there seems to have been an unholy alliance against the family between the spirits of the expelled monks and the notorious Lancashire witches, who were believed to hold their covens on Pendle Hill. Richard Assheton was supposed to be among the victims of the twenty-one who were sentenced to death in 1612 for bewitching local people 'by devilish practices and hellish means'.

It is not surprising that in this most superstitious corner of England, some believe the monks still glide about the moonlit cloister, and others say you can still see Abbot Paslow swinging on his death-rope below the gatehouse. As for the abbey, it too is still present in spirit, for not only do its well-kept ruins stand here in haunting beauty, but its stolen stones are ever-present witnesses in many buildings in the village.

Whalley lies just off A666 between Blackburn and Clitheroe. The abbey ruins, close to the parish church, belong to Blackburn Diocese, which uses the Assheton mansion as a Conference and Retreat House. Cars can be parked in the road in front of the gatehouse. SD 730356.

Military Ruins: THE MIGHTY FALLEN

WHILE THE ABBEYS of England and Wales were being built in secluded sites in the valleys, the castles were being raised in dominating might on the hilltops. And as the ruin of so many abbeys must be charged to the account of Henry VIII, the ruin of many castles was the work of Oliver Cromwell, for a great number of them were either in royal ownership or were loyal to the monarch and were defended for Charles I in the Civil War.

Most of the great castles whose ruins are now famous tourist attractions date from the Norman and Plantagenet periods. Castles of the Saxon and early Norman builders were usually of timber, so nothing of them remains; what we do see are the much stronger fortifications of stone which replaced them. The building of mighty castles stimulated the invention of more powerful weapons and siege-engines, and the more powerful the armaments, so the greater the challenge of building impregnable castles became. Thus the later a castle was built, as a rule, the bigger was its keep, the higher its curtain walls, the wider and deeper its moat. That this medieval arms race ended in victory for the attackers' weapons is only too evident from the huge number of ruined castles all over the country. Only a very small number of them can be included here, as some five to six hundred castles were built in stone between the Norman Conquest and the Battle of Bosworth in 1485. Unlike the medieval monasteries, of course, many of these castles, such as Windsor, Berkeley, Arundel and the Tower of London, are not ruined at all and remain in use.

When the Tudor dynasty brought more centralized and settled government to the realm and the feudal system fell by the wayside, the practice of castle building ceased to all intents and purposes, since most non-royal castles had been built by powerful feudal landlords as bastions from which to rule their domains and defend themselves from attack by hostile barons.

To those for whom ruined castles are an emotive echo of the life and death drama of battle, Britain has a rich heritage. But the romantic view of castles ignores the reality of life behind these battlements and drawbridges. 'What a dignity', Dorothy Wordsworth wrote, 'does the form of an ancient castle or tower confer upon a precipitous woody or craggy eminence!' Well, yes, when it has been finally vanquished by time and its mouldering fabric seems to have become a part of the natural landscape. But this is what Gertrude Bell called the child-like delight we all take in 'the dungeons and battlements of a fortress' more than 'in any other relic of antiquity'. We may shiver with apprehension as we descend into a damp and dark dungeon, but then we climb the spiral staircase and look out from the high tower as king of the castle, and romance floods our imaginations.

All this, of course, is the candyfloss of castle imagery, and the true ruin-lover will also see in these brooding ruins, rearing up from their rocky foundations, a necessary evil; for the old saying 'An Englishman's home is his castle' arises from the building of these invincible fortresses in an age when no man could feel entirely safe unless incarcerated behind thick stone walls which usually excluded light and air as well as enemy missiles.

The armoured apparitions we might imagine glowering from these lofty battlements curdle the blood and impart to military ruins entirely different sentiments from those we entertain about fallen abbeys, churches and mansions. Our thrill at the erstwhile mightiness of castles may be tempered by unconscious relief at their present impotence.

Ashby Castle

Leicestershire

THIS CASTLE was built in stone by Richard III's Lord Chamberlain, William Lord Hastings, late in the fifteenth century, and completed before he fell from grace, unlike the one he was building in brick at Kirby Muxloe, near Leicester, which was abandoned after his death.

The ruins at Ashby-de-la-Zouch are dominated by the so-called Hastings Tower, which still stands to almost its full original height – 90 feet – in spite of the castle's partial demolition in the Civil War by William Bainbrigg, one of Cromwell's generals, acting under instruction from a parliamentary committee in Leicester to 'demolish these goodly towers by undermining'.

It is arguable that, technically, Ashby is a fortified manor house. That is to say, it was not at first built for military purposes. But Lord Hastings' construction of a high curtain wall, as well as the huge tower-house, turned what had already been a fortified house into a formidable defensive structure. The place had previously been owned by the locally powerful Beaumonts and by the Norman overlord after whom the town is named, Alain de Parrhoet la Souche. When it came into the possession of the rich and powerful Lord Hastings, a representative of bastard-feudalism who felt the need for security, he built what amounted to a medieval keep with a portcullis to protect the entrance. The four-storey tower had no windows on the ground floor and spiral staircases led to the upper floors.

Across the courtyard the twelfth-century great hall and service rooms still stood, flanked by a fourteenth-century solar at one end and a kitchen at the other, with a cellar from which an underground passage led to the new tower. The courtyard was enclosed by a chapel, and another block had been built between the tower and the old solar.

None of these elaborate precautions saved Lord Hastings, the protégé of Edward IV and Master of the Mint, Knight of the Garter and Lieutenant of Calais, as well as Lord Chamberlain, when his erstwhile friend Richard, Duke of Gloucester, accused him of treason and ordered his immediate execution. His head was hacked off on Tower Green, on a block of timber awaiting use in building repairs, in Richard's outrageous coup d'état.

It was Friday the thirteenth. Here in Leicestershire the family and friends who had loved him mourned his death. All his lands and titles were restored to the family after the Bosworth battle and Lord Hastings' grandson was later created Earl of Huntingdon.

The third earl had Mary Queen of Scots in his custody here for two nights, and her son James I came to Ashby later with an enormous retinue designed to keep the Hastings wealth and power within acceptable limits. The vast kitchen must have been used to the full to feed the seventy-odd guests who dined and supped daily in this castle for seven weeks. Legend has it that the noted eccentric Lord Stanhope, expected at Ashby during the king's visit, failed to turn up until James ordered his attendance and said: 'I excuse you, for the people say you are mad.' 'I may be mad, my liege Sovereign,' his lordship retorted, 'but I am not half so mad as my Lord Huntingdon here, who suffers himself to be worried by such a pack of bloodhounds.'

Nevertheless, though Huntingdon was impoverished by the lengthy royal visit, Ashby Castle remained one of the stately homes of England until the Civil War, when the Royalist banner flew from the masthead and Charles I came here more than once during his travels. But the war brought an end to the castle's two hundred years of occupation by the Hastings family, and we can only dimly perceive the place in its prime, surrounded by three thousand acres (1,213 hectares) of land split into three great parks, one of which was stocked with fallow deer and another with red deer. On the south side of the Hastings Tower was a large garden called the Wilderness, with a bowling green and ornamental fish-ponds.

What is plain to see, however, is that Lord Hastings' tower was so strongly built that when the Parliamentary agents had used all their gunpowder to blow the place up, and all the dust had settled, the citadel remained surprisingly intact. Romantic interest in the ruins was stimulated by Sir Walter Scott's *Ivanhoe*, which set the famous tournament at Ashby. It is not to be wondered at that so

Ashby Castle. The remains of the Hastings Tower, built by Richard III's unfortunate Lord Chamberlain. Note the ornate fireplace on the upper floor, carved with Hastings devices. This chamber was Lord Hastings' solar.

many visitors have scratched their initials on these ancient walls, fancying their chances of a little share of immortality here when their cemetery headstones have long been forgotten.

Ashby-de-la-Zouch lies on A50 between Leicester and Burton-on-Trent. The castle ruins are on the south side of the town, on A453 Tamworth road. The property is in the care of the Department of the Environment, and there is a small car park at the entrance gate along a short drive from the road. SK 363167.

Barnard Castle

Durham

THE KING who put paid to the owner of Ashby Castle himself came to own Barnard, through his marriage to Anne Neville, daughter of Warwick 'the king-maker'. Richard III made improvements to the castle, which remained Crown property from the Wars of the Roses to the Civil War.

The castle occupies a spectacular site on a

Barnard Castle, standing high above the fast-flowing River Tees.

high cliff above the River Tees, and was originally built by Bernard Balliol, whose father aided William the Conqueror and whose descendants included a king of Scotland and the founder of Balliol College, Oxford. The first castle was probably built of timber but was soon replaced in stone, and covered a large area of what is now the town named after it.

For about three hundred years the castle was the subject of a fierce dispute between its owners and the bishops of Durham, who claimed that the land on which it stood was theirs because it had been ecclesiastical property prior to the Conquest – not what one might call an overwhelming argument – so the castle became a pawn in the political manoeuvring of the period.

In the northern rebellion of 1569, when the Earls of Northumberland and Westmorland took up arms on behalf of the Catholic religion, the castle, under the command of Sir George Bowes, was besieged and starved into surrender. But eventually the rebellion was crushed, and Bowes was responsible for hanging more than sixty of the insurgents at Durham, including a priest and an alderman, as well as many others elsewhere.

The castle's gaunt northern masonry extends to the so-called Brackenbury Tower, used as a prison and named after Sir Robert Brackenbury, who was Lieutenant of the Tower of London under Edward IV and Richard III. The great hall's mullioned window looks down over the bubbling Tees, which for so long formed an effective defence of this well-placed fortification on its eastern side.

The town of Barnard Castle is fifteen miles west of Darlington on A67. The castle is in the care of the Department of the Environment. Admission may be restricted to a limited part of the ruin owing to excavation and repair work, but many of the best views are from the outside, in any case. NZ 049165.

Beaumaris Castle

Gwynedd

BEAUMARIS was one of Edward I's last and mightiest strongholds built to subdue the unruly Welsh. It was not begun until 1295, and the king was dead long before work stopped, but this castle, along with those at Conway, Caernarvon and Harlech, put an end to the Welsh wars for a century. It is one of the more visually attractive of Edward's fortresses, with its towers and turrets of light-coloured stonework reflected in its tree-lined moat. It is said to stand on the site of a palace owned by the ancient kings of North Wales, and it is certainly a choice situation, over-looking the Menai Strait with a fine view of the mountains of Snowdonia beyond.

The ruin's present picturesque qualities should not blind us, however, to its military effectiveness. It commanded sea movement along the northern end of the Strait and land movement over the whole island, and it was Edward himself who named the place Beaumaris (meaning 'beautiful marsh'). Boats were able to dock in the moat, whose waters were fed from the sea, and iron rings in the outer walls were used for mooring these vessels, which could thus bring supplies to the castle when approaches by land were cut off by the enemy.

Furthermore, the castle was built on the concentric principle, with one castle, in effect, inside another. Hostile troops who succeeded in crossing the moat and breaking through the outer curtain wall might have thought they were home and dry until they found them-selves under attack from the higher wall and towers of the inner castle, and they had to set about capturing that, too, from a much more exposed position in the open ground of the outer bailey. The inner castle at Beaumaris had a round tower at each angle of its square

The gateway through the outer curtain wall at Beaumaris. The wooden bridge over the moat replaced an earlier drawbridge. Arrow slits and machicolations provided further defensive strategy, but the castle was never involved in military action.

plan, huge twin-towered gatehouses in the north and south walls, and semicircular towers in the east and west walls; and then there were a dozen smaller towers in the surrounding curtain wall.

In the event, this defensive system was never put to the test, but the castle is a tribute both to Edward's military engineer, James of St George, and to the restless spirit of the Welsh who gave the king cause for such elaborate precautions. If there is no tale of siege and battle to be told of Beaumaris, the story of its building is a worthy substitute, for we know that James of St George was employing more than three thousand men on the building in the early stages, comprising excavators, quarrymen and masons, carpenters and smiths, all protected by a garrison of troops in case of Welsh attacks. This corner of North Wales has surely never seen such a bustle of activity in all the centuries since building at Beaumaris ceased, with the castle incomplete for lack of funds, or lack of interest – perhaps both.

Of course, royal castles had to have accommodation befitting the occasional visit of a monarch, as well as dungeons for their prisoners. Edward and his queen were not disposed to stint on home comforts, even on active duty, so Beaumaris was provided with luxurious state apartments, each with a hall, private chamber and ancillary rooms, including garderobes which discharged into the moat via shoots disguised with grotesque stone faces. One of the less romantic details of medieval castles is that these shafts frequently became clogged, and in 1306 a man had to clean out the garderobe shoots at Beaumaris to allow the passage of excrement and prevent unpleasant smells from rising into the living quarters.

The D-shaped tower on the east side of the inner bailey contained the chapel, with arcaded walls and vaulted ceiling, where an English king and queen and an English Prince of Wales probably prayed to a God whom they naturally assumed to be an Anglophile, for success in overcoming the hostile Welsh. It

This aerial photograph of Beaumaris Castle shows clearly the concentric principle of Edward I's later castles, with the outer curtain wall completely surrounding the more-or-less symmetrical castle proper.

was Cromwell who finally took Beaumaris from its long-time royal ownership, when the castle was surrendered to Parliamentary forces in 1646.

The castle is in the care of the Welsh Office, and lies on the north side of the town of Beaumaris, beside B5109 four and a half miles north-east of Menai Bridge. There is limited parking space in the street outside. SH 608763.

Beeston Castle

Cheshire

THE CASTLE in its heyday perched on the edge of its sandstone cliff like an eagle looking down at the Cheshire plain spread out hundreds of feet below. But despite its apparently impregnable position, it has been taken several times during its seven hundred and fifty years' existence, and twice reduced to ruin. Today you enter at the foot of the hill and climb the slopes past fragments of the outer bailey, and reach the inner ward via a modern footbridge which has replaced the former drawbridge across a deep ditch cut out of the solid rock. Then passing between the semicircular towers of the inner gatehouse you come to the highest part of the castle on its precipice. There is not a great deal left here, but its thick walls of roughly dressed sandstone blocks indicate the great strength its builders intended.

Randulph de Blundeville, Earl of Chester, was its instigator, in 1220. There was never a keep here, for what need was there of a defensive tower on this lofty hilltop? A long curtain wall enclosed the sloping outer bailey, and even if an enemy reached the great ditch it would have a hard time crossing it and scaling the rocky inner defences without being shot on sight. But staying on one's feet up the slopes might have been the greatest challenge, for after a heavy shower the sandy mud here is extremely slippery, as I know to my cost.

*The scant remains of
Beeston Castle stand
high above the
Cheshire plain with a
huge precipice on one
side.*

Perhaps an easier course was taken by a Royalist officer in the Civil War, who is said to have scaled the cliff.

At the beginning of the Tudor period the castle already lay in ruins, having been the site of battle between opposing factions in the struggle between the king and the barons in Simon de Montfort's time, and again in the Wars of the Roses. But it was rebuilt and strengthened, and again changed hands during the Civil War, until finally besieged by Cromwell's troops in 1645. The garrison under Colonel Ballard held out for four months until supplies ran out and he was forced to surrender. Water came from an incredibly deep well cut through the sandstone rock, but for food men had to eat the castle's cats when nothing else was left to give them sustenance.

The Department of the Environment is responsible for the care of Beeston Castle, whose entrance is in the village, just off A49 two and a half miles south of Tarporley. There is a car park opposite the entrance. SJ 538594.

Bodiam Castle

East Sussex

FOR SHEER picturesque qualities, Bodiam hardly has a rival among the castles of England and Wales. It sits sedately, like a great ship at anchor, in the middle of a rectangular pond over which dragonflies perform their dazzling aerobatics on hot summer days. Nowhere is an escape from the realities of the present into dreams of an age of chivalry so fuelled by alluring towers and stone battlements. But one has only to cross the causeway over the moat and pass through the gatehouse to realize at once that the castle is a perfect but hollow shell. Inside, it is like a modern bombsite, and we must hastily adapt our romantic imagery to take account of the devastation within as well as the serenity without.

It was in October 1385 that Richard II gave permission for Sir Edward Dalyngrigge to fortify his manor house at Bodiam as part of the national defence against the French, who had sacked and burnt Rye and Winchelsea some years earlier. 'Know ye that by our special grace', the royal licence stated, 'we have granted and given license on behalf of ourselves and our heirs, so far as in us lies, to our beloved and faithful subject, Edward Dalyngrigge, Knight, that he may strengthen with a wall of stone and lime, and crenellate and may construct and make into a castle his manor house of Bodyham, near the sea, in the county of Sussex, for the defence of the adjacent county, and the resistance to our enemies, and may hold his aforesaid house so strengthened and crenellated and made into a castle for himself and his heirs for ever . . .'

Civil Service English was always verbose and ambiguous! Did the 'adjacent county' mean Kent or Surrey? Besides, Bodiam is not *that* near the sea, though it did command the valley of the navigable River Rother, which the enemy might conceivably use for surprise attacks inland. Sir Edward, in any case, quite reasonably regarded the unusual wording of the licence as *carte blanche*, and instead of fortifying his existing manor house he pulled it down and built a full-scale military castle instead. As it happened, he need not have bothered. The castle's defences were never put to the test by foreign aggression, and it was left to the English themselves to prove, in the Civil War, that this fortification was as susceptible to destructive forces as any other.

Sir Edward had, however, for the times, built a high degree of domestic comfort and convenience into his castle, so that it was far from being a disagreeable place to live; in fact it remained occupied throughout the fifteenth and sixteenth centuries by a succession of owners. One thing that strikes the visitor immediately about the shattered walls of the interior is the number of fireplaces in them. The castle had more than thirty, at a time when the wall fireplace – as opposed to the central hearth – was a relatively recent introduction.

There were also several spiral or newel staircases ascending to the rooms in the upper storeys, ample garderobes, and a huge well in the kitchen tower, with a mouth eight feet across, where the castle's water supply came from a spring which still keeps the well full of water.

The kitchen tower, which had a pigeon-house in the top storey, is at the south-west angle of the castle's curtain walls. Each of the four corners has a circular tower, and a square tower projects from the middle of the south, east and west walls. On the north side is the elaborate gatehouse, with its machicolated towers and spiked portcullis which still give an impression of formidable medieval military architecture. Any aggressor who managed to reach the gatehouse might have boiling oil or pitch poured on him from the parapets of the towers, and if he escaped this ordeal with his life, he might find himself captured and flung into the dungeon in the north-west tower where, as like as not, he would starve to death.

One range of buildings was reserved for the mercenary soldiers whom the lord of the manor was obliged to employ in case of attack, and their quarters were naturally somewhat more primitive than those in which the lord and his family lived in a style becoming their status. *Their* rooms would have had fine oak roofs, tapestries adorning the walls, and no doubt in the dining hall there was a gallery over the screens passage from which minstrels entertained the lord and his family during their meals.

It is easy to be carried away by the magic of Bodiam's exterior and forget that life in the fifteenth century was scarcely civilized by today's standards. The moat itself had more than one purpose. It may have been designed primarily for defence. (The original approach to the gatehouse was not, as now, a straight causeway across the moat, but a right-angled approach from the west bank via a barbican and three drawbridges!) Moats were commonly used as water supplies in the event of fire, which was not infrequent in buildings with much timber in their structures and primitive flues to cope with the huge fires necessary to warm vast and draughty stone halls in winter. They might serve for watering livestock, and were often stocked with fish to supply the lord's table. But they also provided drainage. The castle's garderobes drained into the moat, and there is nothing to suggest that these various functions were considered mutually exclusive.

Nor would the lord's pigeons have made him popular with the tenants on his estates, though they might sometimes use the guano as fertilizer on the poor chalk soil. Three hundred pairs of pigeons, bred for training the lord's falcons and supplying his table with eggs and fresh meat, would consume a goodly proportion of the tenants' crops in the course of each season.

Bodiam has been called 'a castle without a history'. No great events are associated with it – only a slight skirmish during the Wars of the Roses when the Lewknor family who then owned it were threatened with a siege but surrendered without a fight. It would not have been so in Dalyngrigge's day, one feels. Above the north gateway is his coat of arms, with two others, and the head of a unicorn, a medieval symbol of power and virility; while above the postern gate on the south side are the arms and crest of Sir Robert Knollys, placed there by Dalyngrigge as a tribute to the commander he had served with distinction in France. The crest of Knollys is a ram.

Bodiam Castle is a National Trust property. It stands close to the village on minor roads between A229 and A268 three and a half miles south-east of Hawkhurst. There is a large car park and a tea room at the site. TQ 785256.

OPPOSITE *Bodiam Castle, standing majestically in its tree-fringed moat, is from the outside one of Britain's most romantic-looking ruins.*

Brougham Castle

Cumbria

And they that shall be of thee shall build
the old waste places; thou shalt raise up
the foundations of many generations; and
thou shalt be called, The repairer of the
breach, The restorer of paths to dwell in.

The quotation is from Isaiah 58:12, and it was
thought fit to be carved on a slab in this castle
to commemorate the rebuilding by Lady
Anne Clifford in the seventeenth century. She
was the successor of Bess of Hardwick as a
female empire builder, and a descendant of
that bloody Baron Clifford who was known as
'the Butcher' after his cruelty in the Wars of
the Roses. He features largely in
Shakespeare's *Henry VI, Part III*. Like Bess,
Dowager Countess of Shrewsbury, Lady
Anne – Dowager Countess of Pembroke
among her other titles – lived to a great age
and kept her business-like energy to the end.

As well as Brougham, Lady Anne, last of
the Clifford line, owned the castles at Ap-
pleby, Pendragon, Skipton and Brough, and
all of them received her attentions. Her family
had lorded it over much of Cumberland and
Westmorland for four hundred years, and she
had a taste for inscriptions, a feel for history
and a great deal of pride. She called her keep
at Brougham 'Pagan Tower', for the castle
had been built within the ramparts of a
Roman station founded by Agricola, and the
air of the district was thick with legend and
whiffs of prehistory.

Lady Anne lived in the castle from time to
time, and recorded in her memoirs how she
always chose to lie in the room where her
father was born, her mother died, and James I
lodged in August 1617 on his return from his
last visit to Scotland, after which the castle
had fallen into decay. But the repairer of the
breach and restorer of paths to dwell in only
survived her work by fifteen years. And after
her death it soon fell to ruin once again, its
lead being sold, its stone taken for other
buildings in the neighbourhood, and its oak
wainscoting bought up by local people to
enhance their own more humble homes.
Nevertheless, the remains of this sandstone
pile are considerable, much of it dating from
the thirteenth century, when the new Clifford
owners extended the buildings round the

original rectangular keep. It stands impressive and unbowed beside the River Eamont and is a monument to that extraordinary old woman who, unlike Bess of Hardwick, had the saving graces of charity and humour and whose ghost, if it haunts this place, treads lightly.

Brougham Castle stands a little way south-east of Penrith and is reached from a minor road between A66 bypass and B6262. It is in the care of the Department of the Environment. Cars can be parked in the village near the entrance gate. NY 538290.

Caerphilly Castle

Mid-Glamorgan

THERE ARE so many castles in Wales – many of them small and most of them ruined – that I have had to consider very carefully which ones to include and which to leave out, lest the military section of this book should seem like a tribute to Edward I who, as the late Gwyn Thomas put it, 'set an all-time record for killing Welshmen'. But there could never be any question of leaving out Caerphilly. In the first place, it was not one of Edward's; in the second, it is exceeded in size only by the castle at Windsor; in the third, it is one of the outstanding examples in Britain of medieval military architecture.

As you approach it from the town, which perhaps you associate only with a rather pallid cheese, its curtain wall looms up before you, though it does not stand high. It dominates the little town whose houses and shops are humbly gathered round its skirts, although not too close.

The castle was begun in 1268 by Gilbert de Clare, Earl of Gloucester and Hereford and Lord of Glamorgan, one of the most powerful of Marcher lords, to protect his domains against Welsh raiders. It was built on a concentric plan within elaborate water defences, and the curtain wall which flanks 300 yards of the town's Castle Street is actually a dam as well. Its great thickness, with wide platforms along the top, holds back the water of two streams to form a lake, in the middle of which sits the main body of the castle – an impregnable island. The water level round it is maintained by sluices, and its liquid defences are solidly reinforced by bastions, angle towers, battlements, portcullises and drawbridges. Its cellars were large enough to hold huge quantities of meat and corn, oatmeal and wine, beans and fish, so that the castle's occupants could withstand a long siege. The screen wall is protected by further towers and an outer moat. The castle was more or less complete by 1277, and it taught King Edward

himself a useful thing or two about military architecture. After seeing this, he went home and rebuilt the Tower of London on a concentric plan with a moat.

The castle proper, with its living quarters, at the centre of this great complex, is surrounded by an inner moat, a middle ward or bailey, and curtain walls; the great hall is on the south side of the inner ward or courtyard. As well as the four angle towers there are heavily fortified gates at east and west. The castle's most distinctive feature in its ruined state is the south-east angle tower, in which the only vertical lines are the threads of resident spiders descending from the upper floors. The alarming angle of the leaning tower is attributed to Cromwell in some accounts and to Edward II's queen in others, but whoever attempted to demolish it failed because of the high quality of the masonry and cementing with which the castle was erected, and the whole 30-acre (12-hectare) fortress looks as if it would still take some mighty engines of war to reduce it to rubble, having stood solid for over seven hundred years.

Early in the present century the third Marquis of Bute took pains to preserve its fabric for posterity.

We might allow Gwyn Thomas the last word on Caerphilly Castle's remains. It is an apt enough comment on *all* romantic ruins:

On my last visit there a small boy was playing on one of the wall walks. His fancy was sunk deep in some Ivanhoe dream as he fired non-stop through the arrow slits, making with his mouth the zing of his invisible arrows. Then either he remembered some chore or his dream ran out of fuel. He called down to a man who was standing below, his eyes fixed on the West Gate to the Outer Ward.
'Hey, mister, what's the time?' The man looked startled and pulled himself slowly from his own well-furnished reverie. He asked, 'What sort of a question is that to ask in a place like this?'

Caerphilly lies just north of Cardiff, and the castle, which is in the care of the Welsh Office, is at the town's centre. There is a car park in Castle Street, and the main entrance to the castle is across the road from it. SO 155870.

PREVIOUS PAGES
*Caerphilly Castle
from the west.*

LEFT *The south gateway of Caerphilly Castle. This entrance leads on to a platform on top of the dam, fronted with huge buttresses between the inner and outer moats.*

Carisbrooke Castle

Isle of Wight

'I HAVE NOT seen many specimens of Ruins', John Keats wrote, 'I don't think, however, I shall ever see one to surpass Carisbrooke Castle.'

It is certainly the pre-eminent fortress on the Isle of Wight – indeed the only one of any considerable size, and it has a history second to none among the eventful castle chronicles of England. If it lacks anything in visual terms it is because some of its buildings are Elizabethan and still whole. Keats would have found more dramatic 'specimens of Ruins' with more time to seek them out. But in some of its fascinating details Carisbrooke has no rivals.

How many women fell and injured themselves while hurrying up that seemingly interminable flight of slippery stone steps (81 in number) in their long gowns, to the safety of the keep in times of danger? And did Charles I once sit on this stone window seat, stammering politely to his captors while looking out on the town of Carisbrooke – then the island's capital – and thinking of escape?

Carisbrooke's building history is as long as that of almost any castle in England and Wales. It is believed that a British camp was here long before the Romans came, and that when the imperial army took the Isle of Wight, they built a fort with a rectangular outer wall of stone. Nothing is known of Roman activity here, but a villa was discovered nearby, which perhaps belonged to one of the officers who retired here when the army moved on.

Then the Saxons occupied the site after a bloody slaughter, and it was probably the Saxon victors who raised the great artificial mound on which the Norman shell-keep was subsequently built. At the time of the Domesday survey, the mound or 'motte' stood between two baileys enclosed by earth banks. It had been the property since the Conquest of William Fitz Osbern and his son Roger.

The first stone building seems to have taken place around 1136, when Baldwin de Redvers held the island, and the shell-keep would have been built then, along with the curtain wall round the west bailey. In 1293 the castle became Crown property, and remained so for nearly a century except for a short spell in the ownership of Edward II's friend Piers Gaveston. Then it changed tenants at frequent intervals with the appointment of Lords of the Island and Captains of the Castle, until the Civil War. It had faced several attacks by the French, which it successfully withstood, and the Norman defences remained intact, though the domestic quarters of the castle were rebuilt and extended over a long period. The great hall and its adjacent buildings and the two chapels were in existence by 1299.

The gatehouse, which is perhaps the most imposing feature of the whole castle, was built about 1335, but did not then have its present machicolations and parapets, which were added about 1470. It was protected by three portcullises as well, to say nothing of the moat, crossed by a stone bridge.

In the Elizabethan period, when the threat was from Spain instead of France, the strategic value of the castle was sufficient to warrant extensive improvements by the governor of the island, Sir George Carey. These included bringing the domestic ranges up to date, and also the construction of outer defensive ramparts by the Italian engineer Federigo Gianibelli, who was the queen's favourite military architect. The outer archway built at this time bears Elizabeth's initials and the date 1598. She gave four thousand pounds towards the cost of these artillery defences, and the outer ditch was dug by island volunteers without pay. At this time also Carisbrooke's famous well was probably sunk, 200 feet deep, to be operated by a donkey on a tread wheel; but a well in the keep is much older and, of course, considerably deeper.

So Carisbrooke Castle was very much in its present form when King Charles arrived here in November 1647, seeking refuge through the Governor, Colonel Hammond, whom he ex-

pected to be sympathetic. Hammond, however, had not only obtained his post through Cromwell, but had the leading Parliamentarian John Hampden for a father-in-law! Nevertheless, he received the king kindly and treated him as a guest at first, even having a bowling green made in the grounds for the king's recreation. But it was not long before it was made clear to Charles that he was the Governor's prisoner, and his movements were restricted.

During an earlier dissension between the island government and Parliament, when the Earl of Portland had been removed as Governor, it had been asserted indignantly that there was not one papist in the whole island, but Cromwell's men were wise to ignore this sweeping claim. Certainly several men (who may or may not have been papists) got to see the captive king under one pretence or another, and twice made plans for his escape. Both attempts were bungled, the first through the incompetence of one Captain Burley (who might have been executed by the king if Parliament had not got him first); and the second through the stupidity of the king himself.

It was proposed on this second occasion that the king should climb through a window from which the iron bars were to be cut. He would let himself down into the courtyard by a rope when signalled that it was safe, then be conducted by his friends over the outer wall and across the ditch to a waiting horse and two more friends who would accompany him to the coast, where another ally would be waiting with a boat to take him wherever he wished. Charles approved of this plan except for one detail. He feared discovery if they should use a saw on the iron bars of the window and was confident he could escape without this being necessary.

At last the appointed time arrived. The castle was in darkness. A signal was given from below by the throwing of a pebble up against the king's window. All the accomplices were ready at their posts. The fresh horse champed at the bit and trod the ground impatiently. Everyone waited with bated breath. It would be one of the most famous escapes in history. The king's moment had come. Nervous and perspiring, no doubt, he climbed to the window, put his head through the bars, then his shoulders, and got stuck!

In due course, the bars were removed for another attempt, but this time the king was deterred from descending by a reception party larger than he had expected, including an officer who was prepared to shoot the king if he came down the rope.

After these anti-climaxes Charles resigned himself unhappily to his fate. Following his execution his two youngest children, Henry Duke of Gloucester and Princess Elizabeth, were also held at Carisbrooke in lenient confinement, but the princess, thirteen years old, died of a fever within a month, and two years afterwards the young duke was allowed to leave for the Continent. Parliament then used the castle as a state prison, and its most modern buildings continued to be kept in good order, as they still are. They served as the island Governor's residence until 1944, after which the main house was converted into the Isle of Wight Museum.

Carisbrooke is near the western outskirts of Newport, with the castle on the south side of the village. There is a large car park on the west bulwark of the castle, which is in the care of the Department of the Environment. SZ 486877.

Carisbrooke Castle. Charles I may have sat on this stone window-seat, looking out towards the island's chief town and dreaming of freedom.

Carreg-Cennen Castle

Dyfed

IT PERCHES aloft on a rocky hilltop in quiet Welsh countryside, and has been there since the thirteenth century, with precipitous crags on three sides of one of the most spectacular castle sites in Britain, rising 300 feet above the river.

No one knows who built the original castle here, but he had a choice spot, not only from the point of view of defence, but also as a source of pleasure, if he was a man of sensibility, for the castle affords fine views of the surrounding Welsh landscape. After Edward I's second campaign against the Welsh, the old castle was granted to John Gillard, who built the present castle round a rectangular inner ward, with the classic Edwardian

The beautifully situated castle of Carreg-Cennen.

projecting angle towers and twin-towered gatehouse. The domestic quarters had reasonable comforts, with fireplaces, garderobes and the customary private chapel, and the castle's defences included ditches, portcullises, drawbridges and machicolations. Later on an outer bailey was added with a curtain wall encompassing an area twice that of the original castle. There was no trusting those Welsh rebels!

Historical fact is in short supply at Carreg-Cennen, but picturesque legend associates the earlier castle with Lord Rhys, who held extensive lands in these parts in the twelfth century, and is romantically credited with the construction of the long dark tunnel cut through the solid rock from the south-east corner of the castle to a cave which was supposed to contain a spring. It is said this was done after the castle had been besieged and had run out of water. Lord Rhys's young ward Geraint heroically climbed down the face of the cliff to fetch water from a spring, but was shot in the attempt, and Rhys then resolved to make a secret passage by which the spring could be reached in safety when the need arose. The tunnel makes an exciting exploration for the visitor, and ends now with a cistern popularly treated as a wishing well.

The castle was badly damaged by Owain Glyndwr's men, and subsequently repaired, and was then the scene of action in the Wars of the Roses, when it was taken by the Lancastrians. After that Carreg-Cennen became a haunt of bandits, and in 1462 it was destroyed by William Herbert of Raglan Castle to preserve the local country from the criminal elements who had turned the place into a sort of thieves' den.

Carreg-Cennen Castle, which is in the care of the Welsh Office, is four miles south-east of Llandeilo and is reached by a signposted minor road from the village of Trapp. There is a car park and picnic area at the foot of the hill, which you must climb to reach the ruins. A torch and some care are needed in exploring the long dark tunnel. SN 664192.

Castle Rising

Norfolk

WHEN that shadowy king of England, Henry I, died in 1135, reputedly from eating too many lampreys – blood-sucking eel-like creatures that were then regarded as a great delicacy – his widow Adelaide of Louvain recovered from her grief well enough to be married again in two years, this time to William de Albini, Earl of Arundel, who built this castle as a mark of his new status as the husband of a former queen. Rising was then a place of greater significance than now, as a local verse tells us:

> Rising was a seaport when Lynn was but a marsh.
> Now Lynn it is a seaport town and Rising fares the worse.

The change of fortune was due to the sea receding so far as to leave the former port stranded. The castle rises from enormous earthworks, the most impressive feature of which is an extremely deep ditch, with a high rampart on the inner side, surrounding a more or less circular bailey on which the surviving though roofless great square keep squats like a broody hen. The earthworks may be Roman in origin. The castle is among the finest twelfth-century keeps remaining in England.

It was built with some taste for style and comfort as well as defence, with much ornamental stonework on the outside, and several rooms on each of the original two floors. Entrance was by a stone staircase to the upper storey, the ground floor being inaccessible from outside.

In the fourteenth century the castle passed into Crown hands, and Edward III installed his mother Isabella here after the execution at Tyburn of Roger Mortimer, her 'adviser' as some references quaintly put it, who had slaughtered the king's father Edward II in appalling fashion. The dowager queen, known to some as the 'She-wolf of France' lived in retirement here on a reduced income, and was visited regularly by her son the king and by the Black Prince, who subsequently owned the castle.

At that time the great keep was accompanied by other buildings on the site – granaries, stables, chapel and lodgings – which have now disappeared, only a fragment of the Norman gatehouse remaining besides the tower; even in the reign of Edward IV the castle was said to have no room in it but let in rain, wind and snow.

Castle Rising lies on the south side of the village of the same name, off A149 between King's Lynn and Sandringham. There is a car park at the site, which is in the care of the Department of the Environment. TF666246.

Castle Rising's great square keep may appear remarkably complete at first sight, but the interior is a cavernous ruin open to the sky. Entrance is by the small doorway on the left, leading to the first floor by a stone staircase; the ground floor is only accessible from inside.

The enormous circular towers of Cilgerran Castle were built of thin slatey Welsh stone, and must have given the masons long employment. Note the thin arrow slits. This is an aggressive-looking castle standing high above the River Teifi, but makes a picturesque scene from a distance and attracted the Romantic painters to the spot.

Cilgerran Castle

Dyfed

CILGERRAN was not mightiest among the castles of Wales, but it occupied a spectacular and apparently unassailable position on a promontory high above the River Teifi, and its ruins brought Richard Wilson and Turner here, among others, to paint the scene. Turner used it as an excuse for his growing obsession with light and the elemental forces of nature, as reflected in his characteristically long title, *Kilgarran castle on the Twyvey, hazy sunrise, previous to a sultry day*. And not only painters

came to see it. The castle was a major tourist attraction in the Romantic period, when boat excursions were made up the river from Cardigan to see it.

The castle was erected – or at any rate rebuilt – early in the thirteenth century by William Marshall, second Earl of Pembroke, who captured Cilgerran from the Welsh in 1223. Its chief remaining features are the gatehouse and two circular towers, with sections of the curtain wall which defined the inner ward or bailey. Little is now visible of the outer defences. Its 'ingeniator', as military architects were called in the Middle Ages, used thin slatey stone, dark and unappealing, and sustained the impression of harshness and aggression in his design of some of the doorways, especially the postern gate leading out to the ditch, where the voussoirs in the arches jut inwards with spiky ferocity.

Towards the end of the fourteenth century, the castle was repaired and reinforced against anticipated French invasion. It then passed into the possession of Griffith ap Nicholas, Lord of Dinevor, who was made captain of Cilgerran by Henry VI with a commission to keep the king's peace in South Wales, in recognition of Nicholas's powerful influence over his own people. It was a rare honour for a Welshman in those days, but it hardly softened the lord's hostility towards the English. In due course he was deprived of the office for harbouring thieves and bandits; the castle was taken by the then Earl of Pembroke, and eventually passed to the Vaughan family who remained in occupation until early in the seventeenth century, when it was abandoned as a ruin. Further collapse was caused by slate quarrying near the castle in the nineteenth century, but some repairs were carried out later, and in 1938 the castle came into the ownership of the National Trust.

Cilgerran is on minor roads between A478 and A484 two miles south of Cardigan. The castle's entrance is in the village, where there is limited parking space. The castle is a National Trust property in the guardianship of the Welsh Office. SN 195431.

Conisbrough Castle

South Yorkshire

THE REMAINS of this castle, dominated by the great Norman keep, stand on an area of ground which rolls and swells so much with natural mounds and artificial earthworks that the place resembles a galleon riding out a rough sea. But it has survived the storms of eight centuries, having been built around 1180 by Hamelin Plantagenet, the illegitimate half-brother of Henry II. He married Isabel, the heiress of the Warenne family who had been granted the manor by the Conqueror and built the first castle here of timber.

Hamelin's new stone keep was of unique design in England. It is circular, ninety feet high, with walls fifteen feet thick at the bottom, and supported by six enormous projecting buttresses which continue up the full height of the keep to double as defensive turrets at the top. The whole is faced in squarely dressed pale limestone which gives the keep a curiously modern look in its smoothness and clean lines. It has remarkably few windows, and must have been a gloomy place to live in, although its upper floors were certainly built with comforts in mind.

The castle has the two earliest hooded fireplaces known in England; a wide staircase with steps of a height that was easier on the legs than most of that period; water cisterns to avoid having to descend to ground level all the time to draw water from the well; a garderobe in each of the main living rooms; and a pigeon loft from which birds could be despatched with messages. Many of these conveniences were built into the thickness of the walls and into the buttresses, and the east end of the chapel on the third floor was also accommodated in a buttress.

The wall and other buildings of the inner bailey were added later, in rougher stonework, and were reached via a narrow zig-zag barbican from the outer bailey, which is now a public park.

In an area of heavy modern industry the castle has a struggle to exude a great deal of romance today, but it impressed Sir Walter Scott sufficiently, as he passed by in a coach, to find out more about it and use it to advantage in *Ivanhoe*.

Conisbrough lies on A630 between Rotherham and Doncaster. The castle is in the care of the Department of the Environment. There is limited parking space in the roads near the entrance gate. SK 517989.

Conisbrough Castle's round and heavily buttressed keep is unique. The neatly dressed pale limestone gives it a modern appearance compared with the coursed rubble stonework of the rest of the castle, but in fact the keep was probably built first.

151

Corfe Castle

Dorset

THE BUILDING of Corfe Castle took place over a very long period, from its timber origins before the Norman Conquest to its more or less complete state in the thirteenth century, after extensive rebuilding in stone by King John and Edward I. At that time, and for four hundred years afterwards, it must have been one of the most impressive fortresses in the kingdom. Even in its ruined condition, it remains among the most formidable examples of military architecture in England, standing starkly on its conical hilltop site and dominating the landscape for miles around.

It was built to guard a gap in the Purbeck Hills once known as Corvesgate, formed by one of the two streams that cut through the limestone to isolate the castle's hill, before joining to form the Corfe river flowing towards Poole Harbour. The Norman builders used the local Purbeck limestone which also went into the building of the attractive village at its foot, though not until much later, as stone was rarely used for domestic building in those days. Even then, however, it was a village of quarrymen and stone carvers, the menfolk being in the service of the castle's master masons. Teams of horses dragged tons of stone up the steep hillside to the men who were slowly shaping the material into a great royal citadel. Kings and their retinues must have been almost familiar figures to the generations of humble villagers whose streets they passed through regularly. The castle was virtually impregnable during the centuries before fire-power was capable of reaching it from neighbouring high ground, and wandering among its shattered walls today one wonders at the forces of destruction which brought it to its present condition.

Corfe's story is one of foul deeds, however, and we will come to that which brought about its ruin presently. It is most famously associated with the murder of the Saxon king who became known as Edward the Martyr. In 978, when the castle probably consisted of no more than an inner ward of stone surrounded by a timber palisade, Edward was stabbed to death at the instigation of his step-mother. His horse dragged his body along the ground when he tried to ride away and collapsed with his foot caught in the stirrup. One version of the legend says that the corpse was brought to the cottage of a blind old woman, who recovered her sight, and seeing white cytisus in flower, vowed to place some on the king's grave regularly, the plant thus becoming known as Martyr's Broom.

William the Conqueror, needless to say, built a stronger castle on the site, referred to in the Domesday Book as Wareham Castle, but it was with the building of a keep, around 1100, with an outer bailey of stone, that the castle began to assume an appearance that we might recognize today. The keep, commonly known as the King's Tower, was an austere fortified dwelling some 70 feet high, with a few windows cut through its great thick walls. It was reached by a winding route up the slopes, passing through successive outer defences. Nevertheless, King John, that insecure builder of so many fortresses, further strengthened and extended the castle's defences, using it both as a state prison and as a repository for the royal regalia. Miners dug out of the rock a huge ditch along the line of an inner wall to isolate the living quarters from the long outer bailey, which stretched down to the gatehouse at the foot of the hill. A drawbridge originally crossed this inner ditch where the right hand tower now stands. When the towers were built, a double portcullis was incorporated in the gateway, notwithstanding the fact that to get this far one would have had already to negotiate the drawbridge at the outer gate and pass through the long outer bailey guarded by towers and a curtain wall of seven feet or more in thickness, fully exposed to the castle's soldiers all the way.

The Butavant or Dungeon Tower was at the western extremity of the west bailey, where precipitous slopes provided a natural defence on that side. Among the king's prisoners here

OPPOSITE *The so-called 'King's Tower' at Corfe.*

153

were twenty-two French noblemen whom John denied food and water until they died of starvation, adding another grim item to the catalogue of Corfe's dark deeds. He also imprisoned here Eleanor, the sister of his nephew Arthur whom he had murdered. Eleanor spent many years at Corfe and was then moved to Bristol, where she died, having spent the greater part of her life in unhappy captivity.

Despite all the strengthening of existing buildings and extending of curtain walls, the Gloriette range was built in King John's time round an open courtyard without its own defences, though fairly unapproachable, and in an advanced if restrained architectural style which can still be detected in its ruins. It is clear that this range was considered an important addition to the existing castle, but its purpose has not so far been determined with any certainty.

It seems likely that what is thought to have been the chapel was built by Henry III. Henry also issued orders that the castle was to be whitewashed. It was a common custom to whitewash the interior walls of medieval buildings, whose tiny windows let in little light, and sometimes the outside stonework too, although Corfe's pale stone would scarcely have benefited from such treatment. It would be nice to think that Henry intended a symbolic erasing of the castle's lamentable past, but its cruelties were not over yet. In 1326 the homosexual Edward II was imprisoned here before being taken to Berkeley Castle, where his murder was perpetrated by those whose orders were to leave no marks on his body. The king's brother, the Earl of Kent, was convinced that Edward was still alive and in the dungeons at Corfe. The Constable of the Castle, encouraging him in this delusion, pretended to take messages from Kent to the king, but betrayed him to the queen and Mortimer, who made sure that Kent quickly followed his brother to the grave.

In 1572 Queen Elizabeth sold Corfe Castle to Sir Christopher Hatton, and in the following century it passed into the ownership of the Attorney General, Sir John Bankes. In 1643, Lady Bankes had to defend the castle in her husband's absence against siege by Parliamentary forces. She held it successfully for three years – an isolated Royalist stronghold in the middle of a vast area of southern England held by Cromwell's troops. Then the castle fell, through the treachery of one of its defending officers, Colonel Pitman, who was persuaded to bring in Parliamentary soldiers on the pretence of fetching reinforcements.

In 1646 Parliament ordered the slighting of Corfe Castle, and it was effectively destroyed by undermining the foundations and blowing up the buildings with gunpowder. The effect of Joshua's trumpets on the walls of Jericho can hardly have been more electrifying to the spectator than this demolition job. Some of its great walls crashed to the ground and rolled down the slopes in scattered fragments; others collapsed into their undercrofts like falling towers of dominoes. Some of the towers were blasted out of perpendicular to remain partly standing at an alarming tilt, and the southern tower of the south-west gatehouse, called Edward the Martyr's gate, was rent from its foundations, but the massive block of masonry remained intact and upright some feet from its original position.

The job was done so thoroughly that continued habitation was impossible, although the Bankes family recovered their property at the Restoration, and owned it for a further three centuries until it passed to the National Trust in 1982. The castle's ruins have remained little altered since the villagers of Corfe turned at the noise of explosions to gasp and stare in disbelief as the great citadel, which had been their familiar daily sight through so many generations, suddenly crumbled to the ground in clouds of smoke and dust.

Corfe Castle is the quintessence of romantic ruined fortresses in England. Its tumbled fabric attracts more visitors than many a fine castle which remains in its pristine state. Unlike those castle ruins where you have to seek out their particular atmosphere in exploring their venerable stones, Corfe's impression is immediate as you approach the village from any direction. In all weathers, at any time of year, it has an air of fantasy rather than grim foreboding about it. When the morning sun lights it from the east, you see it shining white, its keep soaring skyward like a castle in a fairy tale. In a November fog, it looms up suddenly, gigantic and compelling. Even from a distance – as from the Wareham road or across the barren heathland to the south – it makes an irresistible scene which has few rivals among our man-made landscapes. I wonder what Cromwell would have thought if some soothsayer he trusted, such as William

Lilly – Merlinus Anglicus as his detractors called him – had had the temerity to suggest that posterity would treasure the remnants of this symbol of royal power even more than its owners had treasured it in its prime.

The village of Corfe stands on A351 halfway between Wareham and Swanage. There are parking places at the foot of the castle hill within easy walking distance of the village centre, from which the castle gatehouse is approached across a bridge over the outer ditch. The ruins are the property of the National Trust. SY 958823.

This aerial view of Corfe Castle shows the long outer bailey (centre foreground) leading up the hill to the castle proper. King John's ditch is seen crossing the bailey, eastward from Edward the Martyr's Gate.

Donnington Castle

Berkshire

NOT A GREAT DEAL of Donnington is left to feed the hungry imagination, but the remains of its tall gatehouse make a striking picture on rising ground above the River Lambourne. Sir Richard Abberbury was granted licence to crenellate in the 1380s, at the same time as Sir Edward Dalyngrigge of Bodiam, and he built a castle on similar lines except that his had no moat. There was a tower at each corner of the outer walls, which enclosed domestic buildings round a courtyard, and square turrets in two walls with the gatehouse occupying a

The ruined gatehouse of Donnington Castle.

third. But the castle was small in comparison with Bodiam, and the domestic quarters may have been built only of timber.

Legend associates the poet Chaucer with Donnington, but there is no evidence that he ever visited the castle, let alone owned and lived in it, as is sometimes said. What happened was that Abberbury sold it to Thomas Chaucer, the poet's son, but he re-sold it to his son-in-law Sir John Phelipp, the first husband of his daughter Alice. Elizabeth Tudor owned the castle at one time and retired here once or twice in the dangerous period when her half-sister Mary occupied the throne.

Its subsequent history was uneventful until the Civil War, when it was garrisoned for the king and commanded by Colonel Boys, who ably defended it during two lengthy sieges by Parliamentary troops, led first by Major General Middleton and then by Colonel Horton.

The second siege involved heavy and continual bombardment which reduced most of the castle to its present sorry condition, but Colonel Boys refused to surrender and managed to hold out. The king knighted him for his services, especially as he had successfully secured the king's guns and ammunition here after the second Battle of Newbury, and King Charles himself was able to come and take them away ten days afterwards without the Puritan army realizing that he was there. Eventually, however, Colonel Boys was forced to surrender, and marched out with his two hundred men, colours flying proudly and drums beating.

The four-storey round towers of the gatehouse, flanking the entrance passage, are the only convincing evidence of a once-substantial military structure, and even they show red brick repairs to a tower in which a large hole was blown by a huge mortar in the final attack.

Donnington Castle is one mile north of Newbury, off west side of B4494 Wantage road. It is in the care of the Department of the Environment, and there is a car park at the site. SU 461692.

Dunstanburgh Castle

Northumberland

DUNSTANBURGH is not imposing as you approach it from the golf course which has to be crossed to reach it from the north, though its situation is impressive enough, on a remote hill at the eastern extremity of the Great Whin Sill, which crosses Northumberland and bears Hadrian's Wall along much of its ridge. The hill ends dramatically here in a hundred-foot cliff dropping into the North Sea, which throws up thundering waves at the castle's battlements in stormy weather through a funnel in the basalt rock. But from the north you see only a smattering of jutting broken turrets against the skyline, and wonder if the walk is worth it. It is. It is as gaunt a castle ruin as any to be found, sprayed by the lashing sea and the missiles of warring Scots.

The castle was built by Edward I's nephew Thomas, second Earl of Lancaster, and begun in about 1313. Edward II granted him a licence to fortify the castle in 1316, but by that time it was already finished. It was chiefly the king against whom Lancaster wished to defend himself! His great hall was in the huge gatehouse which, though formidable, was both the first and the last line of defence from that side. He who took the gatehouse had the castle at his mercy. The sea protected it on two sides, the open and easily watched country lay to the west, as well as a great ditch, and the castle's own defences to the south; but it could hardly have been built with any grand military strategy in mind, and was conceived as a place of refuge. Its outer defences, such as they were, enclosed eleven acres (4.5 hectares) of land.

Lancaster refused to take refuge in it himself, against all advice, when his long opposition to Edward and his favourites became too dangerous, and in 1322 he was captured at Boroughbridge and messily executed at Pontefract. The castle then assumed minor military value in the wars against Scotland, under successive constables. It had its own little

port, and ships were despatched from it to aid the king against his queen and her lover Mortimer.

Towards the end of the fourteenth century the castle came into the ownership of John of Gaunt, who had succeeded to the barony of Embleton and was guardian of the northern Marches. Gaunt was never a man to take the defensive architecture of others for granted, and he set about reinforcing Dunstanburgh at once, turning the gatehouse into a strong keep and erecting new defensive walls and towers, and a barbican on the south-west side where he made a new gateway. These changes were well advised. Scottish raiders were unable to take the castle when they overran Embleton in 1385. Henry Bolingbroke, Gaunt's son, took the castle into royal hands with the Duchy of Lancaster when he became Henry IV, and it was kept in good repair until 1462, when it surrendered under siege by ten thousand of Edward IV's men, and from then on gradually fell into ruin.

Some interest was shown in the state of the castle and its possible repair by Henry VIII and Elizabeth, but nothing was actually done, for its value as a border stronghold was negligible. In 1514, however, men-of-war from Henry's fleet, which had been lost for three weeks during a voyage to Scotland, were found sheltering in Dunstanburgh's little harbour.

The castle was sold by James I and was owned by a series of landlords for the next three centuries, in which it was battered by sea and storm. If a brave visitor ventures toward it from the north in bad weather, he may be reminded of nothing so much as a pair of skeletons, stranded in this bleak wilderness and waving their arms in a signal for help.

Dunstanburgh is a National Trust property in the guardianship of the Department of the Environment. It stands on the coast seven miles north-east of Alnwick. No motor road reaches it, and the visitor must walk one mile from the southern, or a mile and a half from the northern approach, signposted from the villages of Craster and Embleton respectively. NU 258220.

RIGHT *Dunstanburgh Castle from the air, showing the spectacular position of the castle on the Northumberland coast.*

Goodrich Castle

Hereford & Worcester

The solar and adjoining north-west tower of Goodrich, looking out over the Wye valley far below. The slender column seen here rose through two floors to form a double-arched screen in the solar.

THE RED sandstone mass of Goodrich Castle rises from foundations of solid rock as if it had grown there naturally instead of being man-made. It sits majestically aloof across a wide and deep moat (now dry) cut out of the rock which forms a high ridge dominating an important crossing of the River Wye. Doubtless the rock excavated from the ditch was used for the building – an economical piece of military construction.

Godric's Castle was here before the great stone fortification was built. Records show that it existed in 1102, but that must have been a timber structure erected by one of the Conqueror's barons, and the first stone building was a small keep dating from around 1150, which was followed at the end of the century by a curtain wall with angle towers. The castle we see today, however, is largely late thirteenth century, built by Edward I's uncle, William de Valence, Earl of Pembroke, as one of the great Welsh border strongholds. It looks compact but very powerful, and even in ruin it has a strange air of impregnability about it.

The Norman keep still stands beside the courtyard of the inner ward. It is a square three-storey tower of greyer stone than the rest, and was originally entered by an outer staircase to the first floor. It still has its fine Norman windows of two narrow lights with shafted piers between, within ornamental round arches, though many of the other doors and windows in the castle have triangular-headed arches. And there are stone window seats where medieval ladies in their long gowns and wimples must have sat looking at the Wye valley scene more than a hundred feet below.

This tower was flanked by a dungeon and a kitchen in the later rebuilding, when a more or less square plan was adopted, with buttressed circular angle towers at three corners and a vaulted gatehouse tower at the fourth, and portcullises at each end of the passageway. The chapel was beside the gatehouse, and the great hall and solar were on the opposite side of the courtyard. Subsequently a barbican was added to afford protection to the main gate, which was approached by an arched bridge or causeway across the moat. Before the barbican was built, the gate would have been protected by a drawbridge. At the same time as the building of the barbican, an outer ward was constructed, with two further towers on the west side where the wall enclosed stables.

The largest of the castle's towers is the south-west one, adjoining the great hall, and it

housed the buttery and pantry in traditional medieval arrangement, with the baron's private quarters at the other end of the hall. The essential well is beside the south wall of the solar. The solar, however, was separated from the dais end of the hall by a vestibule, above which was a private chapel with a trefoil-headed piscina where the priest cleansed the sacramental vessels. An unusual feature of the solar is a slender column rising through two floors. It supported a dividing screen with two pointed arches, while in the hall itself, where we might have expected a central hearth, is an early example of a walled fireplace with a corbelled hood.

The range between the gatehouse tower and the south-east tower must have housed the castle's garrison, overlooking the moat and alert to anyone approaching the entrance. A garderobe block with three cubicles projects from its wall and drains into the moat; it would have been known to medieval soldiers as the jakes.

In the fourteenth century Goodrich became the property of the Talbots, later Earls of Shrewsbury, and it remained in their family for over two hundred years. During the Civil War it was held for the Royalists by Sir Henry Lingen, but its south walls were eventually breached, reputedly by a cannon or mortar called Roaring Meg, which fired balls of 200 pounds. Amid much noise and confusion, with startled horses neighing and their agitated hooves clattering on the cobbled stable yard, the citadel might have been expected to surrender, but it did not; it was only after the king's capitulation in 1646, when the castle's water supply was cut off, that the garrison delivered itself up to the Parliamentary forces led by Colonel Birch. The castle was then rendered uninhabitable, and has never been occupied since, except by the house martins which nest in its ample niches and swoop around its broken towers.

The village of Goodrich lies just east of A40 halfway between Monmouth and Ross-on-Wye. The castle is in the care of the Department of the Environment. There is a pleasant parking and picnic area adjacent to the site. SO 577200.

Goodrich Castle. This sandstone fortress was one of the most powerful of non-royal castles.

Harlech Castle

Gwynedd

CROWS FLY OUT of the high empty towers round Harlech's deserted courtyard as you peer into its dingy recesses, like reincarnations of medieval men-at-arms rushing to their battle stations at the least sign of disturbance. Inside, the castle is like a gutted carcass, but its exterior is that of a strong and well kept fortress ready for action. It rises from the solid rock like Goodrich, but its builder was the same Master James of St George who built Beaumaris, for Harlech was one of the great arc of forts erected round North Wales by Edward I. None of them has a finer or more unassailable site than this.

The castle was begun in 1283 on a huge precipice overlooking the sea, to which it had access below, but the sea has since receded, leaving the castle land-locked. Twenty quarrymen and masons formed the vanguard of the work force, which by 1286 consisted of nearly a thousand men, a quarter of whom were masons. The castle was built on a square plan with circular angle towers and a giant of a twin-towered gatehouse, which was protected by a wide and deep ditch cut out of the rock. This latter work was an immense feat for the labourers who accomplished it. The rock they removed was used in the coursed grey stone building, and the townspeople must have stood in awe of the prodigious engineering that went on for about six years in order to maintain the king's stranglehold on Wales. When the castle was completed James of St George stayed on as its constable.

A mere thirty-seven men defended Harlech successfully against Welsh attack in 1294, but in 1404 Owain Glyndwr took it after some treachery, the French fleet cutting off the castle's supplies by sea, and it became his headquarters for four years. It then fell again to the English under the notorious John Talbot, Earl of Shrewsbury and 'scourge of France', who needed cannon and an army of a thousand to achieve his victory. Some say that Glyndwr was formally crowned Prince of Wales in the castle during his tenure of it.

Margaret of Anjou held it for a short time during the Wars of the Roses, after which a Welsh chieftain, Dafydd ap Jevon ap Einion, held it for the Lancastrians against a siege by Sir Richard Herbert, brother of the Earl of Pembroke. To the messengers who came for his surrender, Dafydd said defiantly: 'I held a castle in France for so long that all the old women in Wales talked of it; and now I intend to hold this castle in Wales until all the old women in France shall talk of it.' He held out for seven years until forced by famine to yield. Dafydd had won the respect of his adversary by his courageous resistance, and when at first King Edward refused to countenance sparing his life in return for his surrender, which Sir Richard had promised him, Herbert is said to have retorted: 'Then by God, I will put Dafydd and his garrison into Harlech again, and your highness may fetch him out again, by any one who can, and if you demand my life for his, take it!' Harlech was the last fortress in England and Wales to fall. 'Kyng Edward', wrote a contemporary chronicler, 'was possessed of alle Englonde, excepte a castelle in Northe Wales called Harlake.' The hardships and endurance of its defenders inspired the famous and stirring song 'Men of Harlech'.

The castle was well equipped to withstand lengthy periods of isolation. It had good plumbing and drainage. The gatehouse, which had been built so that it could be defended even if the enemy had gained access to the castle's inner ward, had four fireplaces in each of its towers, with quadruple chimney stacks. There was a granary, a bakehouse and a chapel as well as the kitchen and normal domestic accommodation of the time. There were also dungeons in the inner towers, and access to the water-gate beneath the cliff by a steep and twisting path. Fine views could be enjoyed from the ramparts, with the mountains of Snowdonia to the east and the sweep of the coast to the west.

During the Civil War, although by then it had been allowed to fall into 'great decaye',

Harlech Castle. This engraving shows the castle's dramatic cliff-top site.

Harlech once again held out for the king against a lengthy siege, before submitting to the Parliamentary forces of General Mytton, being again the last castle to fall. It is fine testimony to the military engineering abilities of Edward I's French architect, or 'inge-niator', that a castle he built in the thirteenth century should still be capable of such stubborn resistance in the seventeenth, after more than three hundred years of development in the weapons of war. And despite all the crumbled neglect of its interior living quarters, its outer walls are a credit to the craftsmanship of the masons who worked under the supervision of Master James.

Harlech is above A496 road between Porthmadog and Barmouth. The castle is in the care of the Welsh Office, and is entered from the town's market place, where cars can be parked when space is available. There is an alternative car park some distance away, Harlech's streets being narrow, steep and twisting. SH 581312.

Hedingham Castle

Essex

ONE WOULD hardly call this ruin romantic in its outward appearance. Its great four-storey keep of flint and rubble faced with neatly coursed Barnack limestone rises like an immense prehistoric monolith from the middle of an earthwork now devoid of all outer defences, and sheltered by trees. It looks square, solid and very plain. But it is among the best remaining examples of Norman military towers, and its story is chiefly that of the de Vere family, Earls of Oxford, through four and a half centuries, for it was to them that William the Conqueror granted the manor.

The keep was built around 1130 by Aubrey de Vere within a bailey surrounded by a moat. It was over a hundred feet high, and its walls were twelve feet thick at the base. An annexe on the west side, of which only broken lower

The four-storey keep of Hedingham Castle, built around 1130 with walls up to twelve feet thick.

walls remain, may have been a prison. Entrance to the keep was also on this side, by an outer stair to a doorway at first floor level, with columns and a round arch with zig-zag ornament. Inside, a spiral staircase wound its way up from basement to battlements, where four angle turrets and a parapet rose above the roof. The stone staircase was made characteristically to be mounted in clockwise direction, the theory being that the defending owner had space for his sword-arm (always assuming he was right-handed) while retreating up the stairs, and his pursuer would be hindered by being too close to the newel post.

The keep was also provided with wall fireplaces, and was among the first castles in England to be built with chimney flues, which are set into one of its buttresses. Clearly the de Vere builders planned early on for some domestic comfort as well as military efficiency. The hall on the second floor was a lofty room with a gallery all the way round it and a great round arch – the widest Norman arch in England – supporting the floor above.

King Stephen's consort, Matilda of Boulogne, is said to have died at Hedingham Castle in 1152. The castle was captured by King John when the de Vere earls sided with the barons against him, and later members of the family paid with their lives for their support of the Lancastrian cause. This might have been expected to stand them in good stead when Henry VII came to the throne, but Sir Francis Bacon tells us that sentiment played no part in the Tudor monarch's policy. When John de Vere, the fifteenth earl, entertained the king here in sumptuous fashion, he made the mistake of assembling a large number of retainers in the Oxford livery to impress His Majesty, who coldly pointed out on his departure that the earl had broken a recent statute forbidding this medieval practice, and fined him fifteen thousand marks.

The castle's present condition is due, by way of a change, not to the Civil War, but to the character of the seventeenth earl, whose chief talent was delighting Queen Elizabeth with his dancing. He married Lord Burleigh's daughter Anne, but turned out to be a thoroughly unsatisfactory husband – not only a spendthrift and a drunkard, but an atheist and a homosexual to boot! He dismantled and disposed of the property at the end of the sixteenth century, and thus it has remained since.

The name of the village is Castle Hedingham, and it is off B1058 four miles north of Halstead. The ruin, which is still in private ownership, stands on the north side of the village, and is open to the public on summer afternoons. TL 787360.

Kenilworth Castle

Warwickshire

THERE COULD hardly be a mightier fall than that which brought down this great and sometime royal castle, a place associated in history with Simon de Montfort, John of Gaunt and Robert Dudley, Earl of Leicester, and in fiction with Sir Walter Scott's famous novel, *Kenilworth*, about the fate of Amy Robsart. The facts about the building and destruction of this fortress of red sandstone are told easily enough, but between these events were five hundred years of history-making in one of the principal castles of the kingdom.

The first stone castle here was probably the huge rectangular keep, built by Henry II on a bluff of high ground previously occupied by a Norman motte-and-bailey castle of earth and timber. It may have been begun in 1174, when the king gave some land in Buckinghamshire to the Clinton family in exchange for their property here. During the reigns of King John and Henry III, further buildings were erected at considerable expense, and it was Henry who constructed the elaborate water defences which became such an important and influential part of Kenilworth's security, and which have now, alas, entirely disappeared. They were far more extensive than those at Caerphilly, and involved the damming of several streams to create a huge artificial lake called 'the mere', which extended nearly a mile to the west of the castle and defended it from south and west, while further moats and pools were made to north and east.

In 1253 Henry III – rather unwisely – gave the castle in trust for life to Simon de Montfort, Earl of Leicester, whose wife Eleanor was the king's sister. Within three years, de Montfort had assumed leadership of the barons in their opposition to royal weakness and extravagance, and soon a purely political rivalry escalated into a military one, de Montfort winning an important victory at Lewes and capturing the king and his son Edward. De

Montfort was now king in all but name, until Prince Edward escaped and, gathering an army to march against de Montfort, defeated and killed him at Evesham in 1265.

De Montfort's son, also Simon, continued to hold Kenilworth, however, and in the following year the castle was besieged by troops directed personally by King Henry and the future Edward I. The castle was able to hold out for many months, mainly owing to the water defences, which made undermining and close assault impossible. Prince Edward mounted an attack across the narrowest moat, using two wooden siege-towers from which catapults hurled boulders at the defenders, and he also had barges brought all the way from Chester in order to attack by water at night. At last lack of provisions and an outbreak of fever forced the garrison to surrender, and the king granted the castle to his son Edmund, Earl of Lancaster, whose descendants witnessed the abdication of Edward II here under duress from the queen, Isabella, and her lover Mortimer, Earl of March. In 1361 the castle passed by marriage to John of Gaunt, afterwards Duke of Lancaster.

It was he who built the palatial great hall over a vaulted undercroft, to the west of the keep, and in a few years added comfortable and civilized living quarters to the needs of defence. In 1399 the castle became the property of Gaunt's son, Henry IV, and then it remained in royal hands for more than a century and a half, until Queen Elizabeth bestowed it on her favourite Robert Dudley, shortly to enjoy the earldom of Leicester. Dudley made further extensive alterations to the castle, spending sixty thousand pounds on increasing its comforts and laying out fine Tudor gardens with arbours and parterres, and here he entertained the queen and her court in stupendous style in 1575, for three weeks, at an estimated cost of a thousand pounds a day. It was the queen's third visit to Kenilworth. She was accompanied by thirty-one barons and attended by her ladies-in-waiting, with four hundred servants besides,

and all were accommodated in the castle for the duration of Her Majesty's visit. Among the entertainments Dudley provided for her were music and dancing, hunting in the park, prize-fighting, bear-baiting, tournaments, pageants, acrobatics, fireworks, masques and other performances by Leicester's renowned company of players, and of course banquets galore, for which ten oxen a day were slaughtered.

The Italian expert who had been engaged to arrange the firework displays wanted to send live dogs and cats up to the heavens in a blazing dragon and have them, as it were, spat out, but he abandoned this plan, no doubt in deference to English sensibilities. The queen would probably not have minded. She enjoyed the bear-baiting well enough, with the bear biting, clawing and tossing himself free of the dogs and then shaking himself 'with the blood and the slaver about his visnomy' all making a very pleasant sport, according to the principal witness.

When the queen arrived, to the sound of trumpets, the clock on the keep (then called Caesar's Tower) was stopped, as if time were suspended for the duration of the royal visit. The queen signalled her pleasure at the lavish reception by knighting Thomas Cecil, Lord Burghley's eldest son, and four other gentlemen, and on 27 July continued her progress, going on to Chartley in Staffordshire, with regal impartiality, to undermine the finances of Lord Essex.

The great spectacle of the queen's visit in that hot July was the high point of Kenilworth's long history. After Leicester's death the castle passed through various royal and noble hands until the Civil War, when commoner hands took over and reduced it to indefensible condition. Cromwell's men wrecked the walls and towers, uprooted the gardens and – perhaps the greatest crime of all, from the point of view of posterity – they drained the lake. The local Parliamentary commander, Major Hawkesworth, converted a gatehouse built by Leicester into a house for his own use, but after the Restoration the

OPPOSITE *Kenilworth Castle. Looking across the ruins of John of Gaunt's Tower and the inner bailey to the twelfth-century keep built by Henry II.*

castle became unoccupied, open to the elements, and only a shadow of its former self.

Nevertheless, it is not difficult to visualize the magnificence of the place in its prime. John of Gaunt's great hall, built 90 feet long by the master mason Robert Skyllington to be worthy of the Duke of Lancaster and nominal King of Castile, is still impressive, even though it has lost both its roof and its floor. Its huge Gothic windows survive, flanking fireplaces in the latest fourteenth-century fashion, in front of which the duke and his third wife, his former mistress Catherine Swynford, would have sat through many a winter evening. Before the Civil War an eye-witness described it as—

a large and stately Hall, of twenty Paces in length, the Roofe whereof is all of Irish wood, neatly and handsomely fram'd. In it is five spacious Chimneys, answerable to soe great a Roome: we next view'd the Great Chamber for the Guard, the Chamber of Presence, the Privy Chamber, fretted above richly with Coats of Armes, and all adorn'd with fayre and rich Chimney Peeces of Alabaster, blacke Marble, and of Joyners worke in curious carved wood...

Nathaniel Hawthorne said of this ruined pile in the nineteenth century, 'Without the ivy and the shrubbery, this huge Kenilworth would not be a pleasant object'. The Office of Works took over the castle just prior to the Second World War and set about clearing it of vegetation and debris. What we see now is not so much 'pleasant' as awesome, justifying the would not be a pleasant object.' The Office of before its mighty fall, 'the glory of all these parts', and the third most stately castle in England.

The Department of the Environment maintains Kenilworth Castle and a large car park nearby, close to B4103 on the west side of the modern town between Coventry and Warwick. SP 278723.

Kenilworth's easily incised sandstone walls are covered with the graffiti of centuries of visitors eager to make their marks on history.

The lofty keep at Launceston sits on top of a man-made hill.

Launceston Castle

Cornwall

BEFORE the rise of Truro, Launceston was the chief town in Cornwall, and its castle had been important since the Conquest, guarding one of the crossings of the River Tamar. It stands on an artificial mound, conical in shape, which John Leland described with his usual graphic conciseness as 'large and of a terrible height'.

The circular keep which now surmounts the hill was built by Richard, Earl of Cornwall and titular head of the Holy Roman Empire, on whom the country had been settled by his brother, Henry III, under pressure from the barons. But the oval shell-keep round it is older, and enclosed the original castle built by Robert of Mortain, who received Cornwall from *his* brother, William I, as his share of the spoils. The site was already an ancient stronghold.

The Black Prince owned the castle during the fourteenth century, but it gradually fell into neglect until the Civil War, when it was hurriedly repaired as a Royalist garrison and subsequently changed hands several times before again becoming derelict.

By that time it had won some notoriety as a prison, since a fourteenth-century building by the north gate had long been used as the town dungeon and was known as Doomsdale. George Fox the Quaker spent some months in it, after much ill-treatment, while waiting to be brought before the Assize court, where most local people seem to have expected him to be sentenced to death for his unorthodox behaviour. 'The place was so noisome', he wrote, 'that it was said few that went in ever came out again alive. There was no house of office in it; and the excrements of the prisoners that from time to time had been put there, had not been carried out (as we were told) for many years. So that it was all like mire ...'

Over a century afterwards, the prison reformer John Howard came here and still found prisoners chained together on the damp floors of a gaol without sewers, chimneys or water. Among other prisoners, one called Charity was kept here until sentenced to be stripped naked and her back whipped as she was led round the town. Her crime was stealing tenpence worth of beef from the market. The outer bailey of the castle was long used as a place of execution, and men were hanged where children now play in the shadows of the dark stone tower.

Launceston is on A30 between Okehampton and Bodmin. The castle is approached by a gateway near the town centre, and there is a car park opposite the entrance. The outer bailey is now a public park, and the ruins are in the care of the Department of the Environment. SX 331847.

Ludlow Castle

Shropshire

THIS GREAT sandstone pile was once the palace from which the princes of Wales ruled their turbulent domain. Its walls rise from the top of a high cliff above the River Teme, and the market town which grew up in the shadow of the citadel spreads out eastwards from its gateway. Roger de Lacy, one of William of Normandy's powerful feudal lords of the Welsh Marches, built the original castle around 1085, and it was – like Corfe – among the first English castles built of stone.

Five generations of Mortimers conducted

their baronial politics from this border stronghold, and the Wars of the Roses, which arose largely from the conflicts between the too-powerful Marcher lords and the king, led to the fateful journey to the Tower of London of the twelve-year-old Edward v, who had lived here since he was three.

One enters the castle from the town's market place to find oneself in the great courtyard or outer bailey, which immediately impresses the visitor by its size, as no conception of the scale of this mighty fortress is obtainable from outside. The inner bailey is in the north-west corner, where a stone bridge crosses a ditch to give access to the gateway beside the Norman keep. The towers, dun-geon and battlemented walls enclose the inner courtyard in which stands Ludlow's unique feature, the ruins of the chapel of St Mary Magdalene. The chancel has long gone, but what remains is a circular nave, built around 1140, with castellated walls and decorated Norman doorway and windows. The young Prince Edward worshipped in this chapel, for the boy's father, the king, had laid down strict rules for his upbringing at Ludlow, including regular morning attendance at Mass.

A medieval romance concerning Ludlow related how a beautiful maiden, Marion de la Bruyère, a ward of the baron, fell in love with one of her guardian's prisoners, Arnold de Lisle, and helped him to escape. After some

time, pining for her absent lover, the damsel sent the young knight a message saying that the baron and his men would be away one night and he could safely come to visit her, but the treacherous de Lisle brought an army to take advantage of the castle's unguarded situation. Marion stabbed him to death and threw herself on to the rocks far below. Fables of this sort would have been in the repertoire of the itinerant minstrels and troubadours who sang to noble families in medieval castles throughout the land.

A real tragedy occurred here in 1502 when Arthur, Prince of Wales, eldest son of Henry VII, came with his Spanish bride, Catherine of Aragon, to spend his honeymoon, receive the homage of the local lords and preside over the Council of the Welsh Marches. Consumption carried off the fifteen-year-old heir to the throne within four months, leaving the crown – and the bride – to his brother Henry.

Sir Philip Sidney was another familiar figure here in his youth, when his father was Lord President of the Marches. Philip and his sister Mary, who became Countess of Pembroke, spent much of their childhood here. Sir Henry Sidney carried out much alteration and improvement to the castle at his own expense, and his coat of arms is above an inner gateway. Fifty years after his time, Milton's masque *Comus* was staged for the first time in Ludlow Castle's great hall, on Michaelmas Night 1634, to celebrate the Earl of Bridgewater's appointment as Lord President of Wales.

The Council of the Marches was abolished in 1689, and the royal castle which had for centuries made Ludlow virtually the capital of Wales became neglected and gradually fell into decay. It is not easy to feel friendly towards the castle now. It is a brooding, restless and eerie place, and even the ghosts who walk its gloomy passages must still keep one eye on the road from Wales.

Ludlow lies near the southern extremity of Shropshire beside A49 Shrewsbury–Hereford road. The castle is in the ownership of the Earl of Powys, but is open to the public daily. SO 508746.

Ludlow's unique circular Norman nave of the chapel of St Mary Magdalene, in which the young Prince Edward, later murdered in the Tower of London, worshipped regularly.

Middleham Castle

North Yorkshire

MIDDLEHAM is a heavy grey northern giant, brooding darkly over the village, though not from any great height, and we might think its situation was chosen with that apparent self-confidence which so often distinguishes Yorkshiremen, until we discover that it was put up by a Norman lord to guard the road between Richmond and Skipton. The earliest stone building was the thuggish rectangular keep, built around 1170 on the site of an earlier motte-and-bailey castle. This was closely surrounded by a ditch and a curtain wall, the keep itself being one of the biggest in the country.

Building operations continued at Middleham through three centuries, at the end of which it was a well appointed and rock solid castle, though not among the largest. It contained stables, a smithy and a slaughterhouse as well as the usual trappings of noble households, but it had precious little military value and it was already in ruins long before the Civil War.

Its principal role was as a baronial stronghold and it served the Nevilles in this guise in the fifteenth century. Warwick the Kingmaker held court here among his extensive local domains and kept Edward IV captive under the guardianship of the Bishop of York – providing Shakespeare with a good scene in Henry VI, Part III, set in the castle grounds:

Thus stands the case: you know our king, my
  brother,
Is prisoner to the bishop here, at whose hands
He hath good usage and great liberty;
And, often but attended with weak guard,
Comes hunting this way to disport himself.
I have advertised him by secret means,
That if about this hour he make his way
Under the colour of his usual game,
He shall find his friends, with horse and men,
To set him free from his captivity.

The speaker is Richard, Duke of Gloucester, who is credited by Shakespeare with many

other devious acts 'by secret means' both before and after he became Richard III.

It was common custom among the nobility of the time to place their sons in other great households to be schooled in the arts of chivalry and given their education, and the young Richard came to one of the greatest of them all. He made a lifelong friend here of Francis Lovell of Minster Lovell Hall in Oxfordshire. He also befriended Anne Neville, Warwick's daughter, and when he later married her, he acquired Middleham Castle as well. The young couple came straight to Middleham for their honeymoon.

Richard held court here as a strong, worthy and responsible northern landlord and local ruler on behalf of the king. He supervised the management of his estates, encouraged trade, obtaining licence for the village to hold two fairs a year, and dispensed justice. Above all, he won the respect of the no-nonsense northerners.

He must have dined with the abbot of Jervaulx, whose monks he had known since childhood, for the abbey was only a short ride down the road. Perhaps he purchased horses from them, and sent his kitchen staff to bring supplies of their cheese to the castle.

Here the duke led an uneventful family life with his wife in surroundings long familiar to them both, with their memories of early morning Mass in the second-floor chapel, meals in the great hall with Warwick's retainers, lessons in French and Latin, hunting in the afternoons, and listening to minstrels in the evening. But Richard's life was changed dramatically when a messenger came from Lord Hastings of Ashby to tell him of Edward IV's death. If Richard's tortured spirit sought sanctuary after his own death on Bosworth Field, it must have come back here to Middleham, where he was surely happy.

Middleham Castle, where Richard III was brought up in the household of Warwick the Kingmaker, and met his future queen, Lady Anne Neville.

The village of Middleham is in lower Wensleydale on A6108 two miles south of Leyburn and three miles north-west of Jervaulx Abbey. The castle is in the care of the Department of the Environment. SE 128877.

Montgomery Castle

Powys

SOME GUIDE BOOKS do not even mention Montgomery Castle. Its remains are only fragmentary and the town itself is, after all, no more than a glorified village. But the castle was one of that great string of fortifications along the Welsh border, and its subsequent history gives it much interest, not so much as a military stronghold but as the property of a distinguished family.

It had been built by the teenager king Henry III on the promontory site pointed out to him as 'a suitable spot for the erection of an impregnable castle', and was held by Mortimers among others during its later military life, but even in their time it was in a state of disrepair, having become strategically redundant after Edward I's conquest of Wales. But early in the sixteenth century the castle came into the possession of the Herbert family, who continued to own it for more than four hundred years.

In the time of Sir Edward Herbert the castle was in a very sorry condition, with no furnishings and only 'one lytle peece of waynscotte remayninge in the grett hall or dyning Chamber'. There were glassless windows and missing doors, and it was damp everywhere. The tiles on the gatehouse roof 'wanteth mending by reason whereof the wett putrifieth the Tymber'. I am reminded of the more or less contemporary concern by the Paston family in Norfolk over the condition of Caister Castle, which they had inherited from Sir John Fastolf (Shakespeare's Falstaff). Advising his brother to carry out urgent repairs there, John Paston warned him: 'And if it be not done this year, many of the walls will lie in the moat ere long...'

But a later Sir Edward Herbert, who became Lord Herbert of Cherbury under Charles I, built a new house in the castle grounds, which was called 'an elegant and noble pile'. It lasted less than thirty years. In the Civil War Lord Herbert surrendered the

*Only fragments
remain of
Montgomery Castle,
the one-time chief seat
of the Herbert family.*

temporary with Lord Herbert's work and serves to bring Edward a little closer, for he must have spent many hours poring over his books in this castle, in the attitude of the 'philosopher', and if the illumination of his study was not quite so dim, nor his surroundings quite so dusty and austere, his deep meditation was certainly as intense. Edward was considered eccentric in a time when private libraries were not yet fashionable, for he had two – one in the castle and one in London.

Lord Herbert was one of the brightest spirits of the age. An Oxford scholar, accomplished in languages, he was a diplomatist, historian, biographer of Henry VIII, musician, horseman and fencer, as well as a poet (though in that department his brother took precedence) and a soldier, having joined the army of the Prince of Orange in 1614.

He took a nice line in defence of infidelity:

> Inconstancy no sin will prove,
> If we consider that we love
> But the same beauty in another face,
> Like the same body in another place.

He was English Ambassador in Paris under James I, and numbered among his friends John Donne and Ben Jonson. But above all, he is remembered as a philosopher, who wrote the first purely metaphysical treatise in English, distinguishing truth from revelation and probability, etc., and 'De Religione Gentilium', which set out to show that all religions have the same five basic tenets; it has been called 'The Charter of the Deists'.

The Lord Primate of Ireland refused to administer the sacraments to Lord Herbert because his religious convictions on his deathbed were no more dogmatic than his Royalist ones had been in the Civil War, but his lordship died serenely all the same. His last words, spoken an hour before he died, were 'Then an hour hence he shall depart.'

Donne came here as a guest of Magdalene Herbert, whom he flattered fulsomely, and after her death he told his congregation at her memorial service that her corpse 'is mouldring, and crumbling into lesse, and lesse dust,

castle to Parliament on condition that the house should not be destroyed. But after his death both the old and the new castle were demolished, with the consent of his son, though perhaps some vain hope of saving the new house is implied in the owner's statement that it was already weak and indefensible, 'being after the modern fashion of brick, and not able ... to resist the weather'. Further collapse has occurred since.

The remaining broken walls do not give us much help in conjuring up the spirits of those civilized products of the Elizabethan age, Lord Herbert and his younger brother George, the poet and divine. They were both born during Queen Elizabeth's reign, and George was born in the castle. Their father was Sheriff of Montgomery, and their mother, Magdalene, was a woman of wit, who after her husband's death married a man twice her age. Lord Herbert himself was a dandified figure, with curly locks, long moustaches and a goatee beard, unlike George, who was of more ascetic appearance. Rembrandt's oil painting known as *The Philosopher* was con-

and so has some motion, though no life.' I dare say her relatives were not especially comforted by this macabre sentiment.

The castle stands on a rocky spur above the north-west side of the town of Montgomery, seven miles south of Welshpool, and is in the care of the Department of the Environment. There is a small car park at the entrance to a farmyard, through which you must walk to reach the ruins, and the official guide is obtainable at the house. SO 221968.

Nunney Castle

Somerset

HARDLY to be reckoned among the great military structures of England, the castle sits almost sedately in the middle of Nunney village with the parish church, farms and houses as close neighbours, and, so far is it from being a mighty and forbidding lord's

The cylindrical angle-towers of Nunney Castle give the moated keep an appearance of formidable strength, but the castle was a status symbol rather than an effective fortress.

castle, you can almost imagine the cook next door calling round for a gossip in the kitchen.

That is not to say that Nunney Castle is not an impressive building of its kind. It is a four-storey tower-house, built by Sir John de la Mare in 1373 with his profits from the Hundred Years War. The rectangular tower or keep had projecting cylindrical towers at its corners and was surrounded by a moat, which is still there. This compact symmetrical arrangement originally stood within a bailey enclosed by curtain walls on three sides and the local brook on the fourth, but these mock fortifications would hardly have kept out an enterprising burglar, let alone a hostile army. Clearly Sir John, whose effigy is in the church among his kinsmen, did not feel threatened. He had served his country well and he was appointed Sheriff of Somerset in due course. The castle was a status symbol of a proud old soldier of wealth and position rather than a defensive fortress.

Consequently the place has not found its way into the history books. It was owned by Paulets and Praters after the de la Mares had gone, and it put up a little resistance to Cromwell's men in the Civil War before surrendering. It was then slighted, the north side of the castle having been so much damaged and weakened by gunfire that as recently as 1910 the north wall came crashing down, so that it now looks like one of those exploded diagrams in which are revealed all the interior details – the floor levels, fine windows and fireplaces, an oven, garderobes, the tower in which a spiral staircase rose to the upper floors, and the altar slab of the chapel on the top floor.

It takes little imagination to people this hulk with medieval personages come to dine amid rich furniture and tapestries, as guests of Sir John and his lady on his home-made island with its ring of bright water.

Nunney lies just off A361 three miles south-west of Frome. There are various pleasant approaches in the village to the castle ruins, which are in the care of the Department of the Environment. ST 736457.

Pevensey Castle

East Sussex

IF ONE WERE to go straight from Nunney to Pevensey, as I am able to do on the printed page, there could hardly be a greater contrast in two ruins both with the title of 'castle'. Where Nunney is small, lacking in military might, and insignificant in history, Pevensey is enormous, magnificently fortified, and packed with incident of national significance.

To begin with, if its site had not had instant appeal for the Norman invaders, it would

have qualified unarguably for a place in the first section of this book as one of the most impressive Roman remains in Britain. It was *Anderida*, a fort built by the imperial forces in the third century AD to guard the Saxon Shore. It was virtually an island in the marshy Pevensey Levels which, at that time, the sea lapped at high tide. 'Into Pevenscie haven', the Holinshed Chronicles tell us, 'divers waters doo resort.' So the Romans took no chances with the foundations of their walls, though the ground they built on was well drained.

They sank a deep bed of clay and flints fifteen feet wide, on top of which they placed oak beams set in concrete. Then they built their wall twelve feet wide and nearly thirty feet high, of flint and rubble embedded in mortar, faced with dressed stone, and with courses of tile running through it. The giant work, punctuated with bastions, enclosed more than eight acres (3.2 hectares), and most of it, incredibly, still stands intact after sixteen hundred years, despite repeated attack and bombardment.

The first major attack on it that we know of is described in the *Anglo-Saxon Chronicle*: 'In this year Aelle and Cissa besieged Andredesceaster and slew all the inhabitants; there was not even one Briton left there.' The year was 491, and the assailants were the Saxon hordes who came across the Channel in waves to raid and plunder the south-east coast when the Romans had departed and left it defenceless. What an unspeakable massacre that short sentence describes. But the fortress walls were intact six hundred years later when Duke William of Normandy landed in Pevensey Bay with sixty thousand men. That shrewd Norman general occupied the Roman fort at once and hurriedly erected his first castle of timber within it, realizing that he could hardly improve on the Roman bulwarks as the curtain wall of his outer bailey.

Gradually the inner, Norman castle of stone replaced the timber structure, as William's half-brother Robert of Mortain strengthened the fortress the king had granted him. He took hints from the Roman defensive system and incorporated Roman building in his own works when convenient. The inner defences which gradually took shape up to the thirteenth century were protected from the outer bailey by a moat and a twin-towered gatehouse. Three D-shaped towers in the curtain wall imitated the Roman bastions, and a deep well was sunk in the inner bailey close to the keep to supply the garrison with water in times of siege, which were not infrequent. (The skulls of wolves were among rubbish brought up from the bottom during excavation.)

Narrow staircases lead down to dark basements below the Norman towers, which are often assumed to be dungeons, but seem in fact to have been cellar chambers, with carved vaulting and corbels. Pigeons and starlings inhabit them now, covering the floors with feathers and droppings which suggest the state of the average lord's great hall in England, according to Erasmus of Rotterdam, '... strewed with rushes, beneath which lies an ancient collection of beer, grease, fragments, bones, spittle, excrement of dogs and cats, and everything that is nasty.' In our preoccupation with the military aspects of our ruined castles, it is easy to overlook the domestic circum-

stances in which people of the time spent their lives. Here at Pevensey, however, domestic niceties were always overridden by the needs of defence. Although there were a few fireplaces for the winter months, the accommodation was generally sub-medieval, with few garderobes compared with, say, Middleham. Even the chapel was primitive.

William Rufus starved the castle into surrender, but King Stephen and Simon de Montfort both conducted abortive sieges of it during the twelfth century, and at the end of the fourteenth it was defended successfully by Lady Jane Pelham against the deposed Richard II's allies, when her husband was away in the north of England. The valiant lady wrote to her beloved husband, much concerned about his welfare, and almost casually added: 'And my dear Lord, if it like you to know my fare, I am here laid by in manner of a siege ... so that I may not out nor no victuals get me, but with much hard.'

The port of Pevensey was probably silting up by this time, and the castle lost some of its strategic importance as a coastal defence, though clearly not as an internal baronial fortress. But it was fortified against Philip of Spain's Armada in 1588, and a gun called a 'demi-culverin', made locally of Wealden iron, still stands in the inner bailey; while during the Second World War gun emplacements were built to defend the long-vulnerable south-east coast against anticipated invasion by Hitler's forces. But the castle had already fallen into neglect and ruin by the Civil War period, when Parliamentary commissioners surveyed it, and has lain like a grounded hulk for over three hundred years, with the Roman walls still arguably in better condition than the Norman ones.

Pevensey is situated near the coast four miles northeast of Eastbourne. The castle ruins are in the care of the Department of the Environment. There is a car park close to the main entrance, and public footpaths through the former outer bailey lead to the entrance to the inner castle via the Norman gatehouse. TQ 644048.

Raglan Castle

Gwent

WHEN IT COMES to picturesque and romantic architecture, Raglan has no peer except Bodiam among the castles of England and Wales. It is arguably more of a fortified mansion than a military structure, but as Cromwell's lieutenants judged it enough of a fortification to order the partial destruction of its keep or tower house, it is entitled to its place in this section rather than the next. It makes a 'rare and noble sight' as the Elizabethan poet Thomas Churchyard put it, and it requires little imagination to see that this was once one of the most sumptuous of Welsh palaces.

Its relatively uneventful history is told in a trice. The castle was begun by Sir William ap Thomas around 1435, probably replacing an earlier building on the site. Sir William died in 1445 and his son William Herbert, subsequently first Earl of Pembroke, continued the building. His successors to the property made various additions and improvements up to the time of the Civil War, when the castle became the local Royalist headquarters and was besieged by a Parliamentary force of three and a half thousand men under the command of Colonel Morgan. After a long resistance, the castle was surrendered in August 1646 to Sir Thomas Fairfax, the commanding officer of the New Model Army, who had come in person to supervise the siege of Raglan. It was among the last of the Royalist strongholds to fall to Cromwell. The household watched from the hall as the victorious troops entered the castle.

The undermining of the keep was followed by years of plundering Raglan's stone and fittings until the mid-eighteenth century, when the fifth Duke of Beaufort, who had succeeded to the estate through the marriage of his ancestor Charles Somerset with Elizabeth Herbert, prevented further damage to the ruins. Thereafter the castle was preserved as a tourist attraction, the Beauforts having by then built Badminton as their chief seat. That is Raglan's history, but a tour of the superb remains brings to life a building full of intriguing incident.

The oldest building at Raglan is the hexagonal keep, long known as the Yellow Tower of Gwent. It is entirely surrounded by a moat and was originally accessible only by a drawbridge from the main body of the castle. A new fixed bridge has now taken the place of an earlier arched bridge of stone. There is a theory that the tower was erected so that the lord of the castle could isolate himself from his own household in the event of a change in their loyalties. The castle was built, after all, as the Wars of the Roses were looming on the horizon. Lord Herbert, the son and heir of the first Marquis of Worcester, installed an

The oriel window of Raglan's great hall faces across the Pitched Stone Court, made in the sixteenth century. The doorway on the left led into the parlour.

OPPOSITE *A photograph c.1890 showing the ivied towers of Raglan's gatehouse as they appeared to the Victorian romantics. Stripping the vegetation from many ruins such as this has revealed architectural detail and possibly prolonged the life of the buildings, but has diminished their aesthetic quality.*

ingenious device in the tower which caused panic among a group of commissioners who had come to search the castle for arms. It was a hydraulic engine which roared into action to raise a large quantity of water to the tower's machicolations and pour it on the heads of those below. Such was the noise of the engine in the hollow echoing tower that even before they had got wet the men were tumbling over one another in their attempts to escape from what they thought were lions let loose. The tower was strong enough to withstand Colonel Morgan's artillery, and after the castle's surrender, the Parliamentary troops had great difficulty in destroying it, resorting to medieval undermining after an abortive attempt at demolition with pickaxes from the top floor downwards.

The more palatial parts of the castle are reached through a romantic-looking gatehouse, flanked by machicolated towers, which were cloaked with ivy in the nineteenth century, and protected by portcullises. Beyond the gatehouse, in the so-called Pitched Stone Court, a splendid cobbled courtyard with drainage channels carried away rainwater from the roofs of surrounding buildings. How the hooves of horses must have clattered on this surface once, as they brought guests to stay with the owners!

Dominating the courtyard along its western length is the great hall, and even its ruined shell provides a glimpse of the magnificence in which the occupants lived. A great oriel window, once fitted with heraldic glass, lit the high table end, and the hall was heated in winter from a huge fireplace. The room had a hammerbeam roof of Irish oak. Coats of arms and rich panelling covered the walls, which would have supported tapestries in an earlier age, and a minstrels' gallery stood over the screens passage at the lower end.

In 1502 Sir Walter Herbert entertained Henry VII's queen, Elizabeth of York, at Raglan. Her retinue included the 'Quenes mynstrelles', and when she left, servants were paid to make an eight days' journey to carry her baggage to London. The king, though not present on this trip, was familiar with Raglan, having been deposited here as a boy to be brought up for a time by Anne Devereux, Countess of Pembroke.

Beyond the great hall is the Fountain Court, so named because it once contained a fountain surmounted by a statue of a white horse, and on the far side of this grassed courtyard were palatial domestic apartments; a grand staircase leads to the upper storey. Between the Fountain Court and the hall was a range of buildings which included the chapel, and on the upper floor of the range was a long gallery – a recently invented domestic luxury – which was hung with family portraits in King Charles's time, and had windows at its northern end looking out over the Welsh hills to the west.

The climax of Raglan's story came around the period of the Civil War. It is not surprising to learn that the Marquis of Worcester, who contributed vast sums of money to the Royalist cause and was duly rewarded for what we might call his services to the conservative party, was reputedly the richest man in England (and presumably in Wales, too). He is supposed to have used the Great Tower to keep his treasure in. He entertained the king here in such lavish style that Charles feared his visit would do more injury to the resources of the Royalists than a siege of the castle by the enemy.

The old millionaire marquis was a man of taste, with a large and unique library (it had the best collection of Welsh bardic manuscripts in existence), a fine art collection, magnificent furniture and a well-stocked wine cellar. It is said that he would not tolerate drunkenness or coarse language. When the castle was taken the library was deliberately destroyed by fire, along with many other treasures and fittings. The earl himself was imprisoned, though an octogenarian, with the promise that he would be buried at Windsor, to which he is said to have replied: 'God bless my soul, they will give me a grander castle when dead than they took from me when living.'

When he died soon afterwards they did

bury him in St George's Chapel at Windsor, but one feels his spirit must reside among the broken walls of Raglan, the castle which his forefathers had built and lived in for two hundred years in considerable luxury for the time. It drew lavish praise from those who saw it whole, and does so still from visitors to its ruins. It is necessary only to walk through its courtyards and see its battlemented towers, with stone heads looking down from the parapets, its bridges and windows, and the huge extent of its residential apartments, to transport oneself into a lost world of chivalry and courtly splendour.

The village of Raglan is just off A40 between Monmouth and Abergavenny, west of the junction with A449. The castle, which is in the care of the Welsh Office, is half a mile north, on the opposite side of A40. Cars can be parked round a circular green in front of the entrance gate. SO 415083.

Rochester Castle

Kent

ALL THAT REMAINS of this castle, apart from stretches of its curtain wall, is the enormous brute of a keep standing square, unornamented and glaringly unromantic in the former bailey which is now a public park. You could almost mistake it for some sort of abandoned industrial building and pass it by. But venture into its cavernous, echoing interior and you pass from this world into another, chilling in its damp emptiness. Its floors and roof have gone, but it is a honeycomb of galleries and arcades that remind me of the architectural fantasies of Piranesi or, seen from the top, an eerie and outsize sewer shaft. It could be the set of a horror film.

It was built around 1130 (how often that significant date has appeared in this section!) by Henry I's Archbishop of Canterbury, Wil-

liam of Corbeuil, and guarded the approach to the town and the London-Dover road from the River Medway – a highly important strategic site. It had five floors, and still stands to its original height of 125 feet – the tallest keep in England. It was built with twelve-foot-thick walls of Kentish ragstone, with Caen stone for its dressings, on a site where previous forts and castles had stood since the Roman occupation of Britain. The river crossing was the Roman road known to us as Watling Street. Attached to it was a fore-building giving access to the keep at first floor level. A partition wall, five feet thick, divided the keep into two equal halves, with access to rooms on either side of it by round archways decorated

Rochester Castle. The Norman keep built by Archbishop Corbeuil is the tallest in England.

with chevron ornament and supported on massive round piers. A well-shaft built into this wall ascended to the top level of the building and was accessible from every floor. A stone newel staircase also rose to the top of the keep, while another shaft in the walls from top to bottom is supposed to have been made so that supplies could be brought in secretly from the river. Only small windows and openings in the walls allowed light and air to enter these gloomy chambers, and smoke to escape from the fireplaces, which were among the earliest wall fireplaces in Britain. The keep, not surprisingly, took thirteen years to build. It dominates the modern city's cathedral, and can be seen from twenty miles away.

The archbishops did not hold on to this solid fortress for long: Thomas Becket included in his quarrels with Henry II the accusation that the king had improperly deprived him of Rochester Castle, which, indeed, he had. Half a century afterwards, the baron in occupation, William de Albini, defended the castle for three months against the forces of King John. The garrison's supplies were cut off so successfully that for lack of other food they were forced to eat their own horses. At length they surrendered and a great many soldiers were hanged. In the following year Louis the French Dauphin took Rochester from the king in his support of the barons, but Simon de Montfort tried and failed to take

The labyrinthine interior of Rochester's keep, built of Kentish ragstone with decorated arches and dressings of Caen stone shipped from Normandy.

it when it had once again become Crown property.

The castle had fallen into decay long before the Civil War, and its interior was demolished in order to use the valuable timber elsewhere. It stood here for a long time empty and untouched, and consequently no later style of architecture intrudes on its Norman purity. It is not difficult to work out the layout of the place in its heyday, with the lord's great hall on the third storey, arcaded through the cross-wall to form one large, high room, but enormous imagination is required to picture furnishings and tapestries and a roaring fire making this a cheerful place on a peaceful winter's night, with masques and revels, everyone feasting noisily, and minstrels trying to make themselves heard above the din.

It is much easier to evoke its spirit of menace and brutality in time of battle. Its sinister purpose is all too evident in the mouldering walls and arches of this awful hollow tower. An odour of damp dungeons or catacombs clings to it and a shudder of revulsion attends our inspection of its awesome, echoing void.

Rochester is on A2 about halfway between London and Canterbury. The castle is owned by Rochester Corporation. It stands near the cathedral at the city centre, and close to the bridge over the Medway. There are car parks nearby. TQ 742686.

Skenfrith Castle

Gwent

SKENFRITH is the simplest and most austere of three castles built to guard the routes in and out of Wales between the Black Mountains and the River Wye. They are known as the Trilateral Castles, the others being Grosmont and White Castle, a few miles north-west and south-west respectively.

The first castle at Skenfrith was a timber affair built soon after the Conquest, but the more substantial castle of sandstone we see today was almost certainly the work of Hubert de Burgh, Earl of Kent and Justiciar of England in the time of Henry III. It stands on the west bank of the River Monmow, in the centre of the village, with higher ground rising on all sides, and it is difficult to imagine that it ever had any great military value. Beside most of the great fortresses of the Welsh Marches, it looks almost pathetic, consisting as it does merely of a quadrilateral curtain wall enclosing a round tower or keep, which appears to be built on the original Norman motte. Excavation has shown, however, that the 'mound' actually consists of earthworks built up round the foundations as the tower was built. The castle was moated on the three sides not protected by the river, and it was improved throughout the course of the thirteenth century. Round towers buttressed the four corners of the curtain wall, which still stands almost to its original height, though crumbling at its face, with parts of the wall walk intact along the top, and on the west side a bastion was added later in the century to strengthen the most vulnerable flank.

The castle was owned, with its neighbours, by the Duchy of Lancaster until the end of the fourteenth century, but it cannot have been long after that when it fell into neglect and became derelict. The earls of Lancaster had resided at Grosmont, and no one can have wanted to dwell in this primitive place any longer than was dictated by military expediency. The western range of living quarters was below ground level when originally built, and must have flooded every winter. Now roofless, these chambers collect rainwater which has no escape route, and steps lead down into deep pools, though you can see the doorways and fireplaces of rooms where the medieval occupants spent their miserable days always on the alert against Welsh attack.

Skenfrith stands on B4521, ten miles east of Abergavenny. The castle is owned by the National Trust, and is in the guardianship of the Welsh Office. The official guide can be bought from the village post office. SO 457202.

OPPOSITE *Skenfrith Castle. The round tower of one of the so-called Trilateral Castles built to guard one of the major routes in and out of Wales.*

Tintagel Castle

Cornwall

THE AUTHOR of the twelfth-century *History of the Kings of Britain*, Geoffrey of Monmouth, describing the birthplace of King Arthur, has a lot to answer for. 'For it is situated on the sea', he wrote, 'and is on every side encompassed thereby. Nor none other entrance is there save a narrow rock doth furnish, the which

The fyrſt boke.

¶Here begynneth the fyrſt boke of the mooſt noble and worthy prince kyng Arthur ſomtyme kyng of grete Brytayne/now called Englande Whiche treateth of his noble actes and feates of armes & chyualrye/and of his noble knyghtes of the table roũde and this volume is deuyded in to.xxi.bokes.

¶How Utherpendragon ſente for the duke of Cornewayle and Igrayne his wyfe/and of theyr ſodayn departynge agayne.   Capitm.j.

¶It befell in the dayes of y noble Utherpen dragon whã he was kynge of Englande and ſo regned/there was a myghty and a noble duke in Cornewayle that helde longe tyme warre agaynſt hym. And y duke was named the duke of Tyntagyll/& ſo by meanes kynge Uther ſente for this duke/char gynge hym to brynge his wyfe wt hym for ſhe was called a ryght fayre lady/& a paſſynge wyſe/& Igrayne was her name. So whan the duke & his wyfe were comen to y kynge/by the meanes of grete lordes they were bothe accor ded/& the kyng lyked & loued this lady well/and made her grete chere out of

three armed knights could hold against thee, though thou wast standing there with the whole might of Britain beside thee.' These two sentences by an exceedingly unreliable chronicler have made Tintagel a place where romance has gone berserk. 'There's a fascination frantic in a ruin that's romantic', as W.S.Gilbert put it, and the village thrives on coach-loads of tourists who pour down the headland slopes to see the spot where the immortal once-and-future king was supposedly fathered on Igraine, the Duke of Cornwall's wife, by King Uther Pendragon, and delivered into the waiting hands of the magician Merlin, while the Atlantic waves lapped the shores of Lyonesse.

What actually stood here at the time when Arthur is supposed to have led the British against the Anglo-Saxons was a Celtic monastery, and the castle whose remains we see now was not built until six hundred years after the legendary hero's death. That, however, does not make it any the less spectacular. The ruins stand on a rugged promontory, part of which is called 'the island', being almost cut off from the mainland by erosion. When the stone castle was built, about 1240, the isthmus was higher and wider. The relentless seas broke it down during the next hundred years, taking some of the buildings with them, and leaving only a narrow ridge which one crosses by a precipitous path, with steps cut into the rock in the nineteenth century, when Sir Walter Scott and Tennyson had created a new surge of interest in the Arthurian legends.

Reginald, Earl of Cornwall, was the castle's chief builder, and we see the upper and lower wards of his magnificently sited citadel on the mainland, leading to the inner ward on the 'island', with its great hall, once probably over a hundred feet in length. Part of the cliff on which it stood has been devoured by the waves. Beyond are the excavated remains of the monastery where the medieval castle's owners planted a walled garden.

Truth is quite as fascinating as fiction on this highly atmospheric site. The castle is totally unlike the usual Norman concept of military architecture, and it was already in disrepair by the fourteenth century, presumably being considered useless by that time, although the Duchy of Cornwall refortified it at the end of the century as a precaution against French attack. By 1540 it was in ruins, but the romantic situation must have appealed to its medieval lords as much as it does to modern visitors. Richard, Earl of Cornwall, was among its owners as was the Black Prince later. They were both Christian crusaders against what they saw as the powers of darkness, and the medieval taste for tales of chivalry and romance being what it was, they both doubtless knew that this was sacred soil to the British – a symbol in imagination, if not in fact, of the Celtic twilight.

Geoffrey of Monmouth's choice of site was an inspired one, and as the spectral whispers of holy hermits and medieval knights are drowned by the screaming gulls and crashing waves, it is easy to substitute a dream of the valiant Arthur consulting his bearded practitioner of the occult here, marrying his chosen bride Guinevere, planning his strategy against the heathen invaders from the east, and setting off in quest of the Holy Grail, with always at his side the sword Excalibur. But a dream is all it is – a myth of an idealized champion which arose to satisfy the psychological needs of an oppressed people, who comforted themselves with the illusion that he would return, like Christ to the Christians or Frederick Barbarossa to the German peasants.

The village of Tintagel is on Cornwall's north Atlantic coast on B3263, between Boscastle and Camelford. The castle ruins are in the care of the Department of the Environment. There is a car park near the entrance to the long path by which one must walk to the ruins. SX 050890.

FAR LEFT *Tintagel Castle as illustrated in Wynkin de Worde's 1498 edition of Malory's* Le Morte d'Arthur. *It shows the 'Duke of Tyntagyll' bringing his wife to Uther Pendragon at the king's command, 'for she was called a ryght fayre lady and a passynge wyse, and Igrayne was her name.'*

LEFT *Part of Tintagel Castle on its dramatic island site.*

189

Tintagel Castle – a highly romanticized view of the ruins, engraved by George Cooke after a painting by Turner.

191

Tretower Castle

Powys

The twelfth-century shell-keep at Tretower Castle with the later tower-keep inside it.

THIS IS ANOTHER of the small ruined border castles of Wales of which this volume can only touch on a tiny proportion, and if it should be asked 'Why this one?', the answer is that it shows an interesting development of the medieval lord of the manor's social and political situation through the feudal period of Britain's history.

The castle is of the motte-and-bailey type, and was first built very soon after the Conquest by a lord named Picard, to guard the Usk valley against Welsh rebels. It was constructed of timber on its artificial mound which was no doubt surrounded by wooden

palisades – the common type of stronghold from which early Norman lords ruled their little empires. The Picard family remained in control here for two centuries, however, and by the mid-twelfth century they had built a shell-keep of stone in place of the palisades, and a circular tower-keep of three storeys was later added inside it, with walls eight feet thick; to make way for this the earlier great hall and other domestic buildings were demolished.

The Picards were involved at that time in the Welsh uprising led by Llywelyn ap Gruffydd, and in 1403 Tretower was defended for the king against the revolt of Owain Glyndwr, but was partly destroyed. Soon after that the male line of the Picard family died out, but by then they had built the fortified manor house known as Tretower Court which stands in front of the castle, and has a gatehouse complete with machicolations and arrow-slits. The castle was clearly considered too uncomfortable a residence for the lord of the manor in times when his security was not threatened, but for a while the castle was kept more or less intact and probably accommodated the lord's retainers when it was not in use for military purposes. Then when private castles went out of fashion in more peaceful times it was allowed to fall into decay.

In the shattered interior of the cylindrical keep can still be seen the carved stonework of fireplaces, and windows with stone window seats. The hall occupied the second floor and on the third was the lord's solar. This inner keep towered high above the level of the shell-keep so that in time of war the garrison had a clear field of fire over the outer wall, and in peace the occupants had a fine view of the surrounding country from their lofty living rooms.

Tretower is on A479 just north of A40 between Abergavenny and Brecon, and three miles north-west of Crickhowell. You can park in the lane in front of Tretower Court, through which you must pass to reach the castle. Tretower Court and Castle are in the care of the Welsh Office. SO 184212.

Tutbury Castle

Staffordshire

OF ALL the castles and fortified mansions in which the wretched Mary Queen of Scots suffered her prolonged death throes (for as Oscar Wilde said, 'all sentences are sentences of death'), Tutbury was the one she most abhorred.

The castle already had a long history when she was brought here under house arrest to be guarded by George Talbot, Earl of Shrewsbury, who leased the place. It had been founded soon after the Norman Conquest, when the Ferrers family held it for a long period, and was rebuilt and extended over the centuries, eventually becoming a property of the Duchy of Lancaster. John of Gaunt and Henry IV were among those who spent much time in state here, sponsoring, as well as more civilized pursuits, the Tutbury bull-running, in which a bull despoiled of his horns, ears and tail was smeared with soap and let loose to be captured before being cruelly baited in the market place.

But it is always to Mary Stuart that we return inevitably in considering Tutbury. The castle stood on high ground near the Derbyshire border overlooking the River Dove, with fine views on all sides, but Mary, naturally enough, had no eye for its attractions, and said it was 'exposed to all the malice of the heavens'. It was in rather neglected condition then, and very damp and draughty, and the Scottish queen became chronically ill there.

At first her captivity was lenient, and she spent much time sitting with Shrewsbury's wife, Bess of Hardwick, doing her needlework, but as time went on, the conditions of her confinement grew steadily worse. The formidable and malevolent Countess grew jealous of her and spread ugly rumours of her husband's improper relationship with the State's prisoner, and baited the delicate royal prisoner as if she were the Tutbury bull. The castle's drainage system was atrocious, and what with the foul smells from this and the

One of the remaining towers of Tutbury Castle. Built over a long period, it was started within five years of the Conquest, and was for a time the prison of Mary Queen of Scots.

refuse heap beneath her windows, to say nothing of the marsh below the castle, from which noxious fumes arose, the unfortunate lady's illnesses – which she ascribed to rheumatism but which may have been porphyria – grew steadily worse, and her hair turned white beneath her coloured wigs.

It was less than sixty years after Mary's execution at Fotheringay when Tutbury Castle itself was sentenced to death. Parliamentary commissioners ordered its demolition, and brought it to the state it is in today: a rather odd jumble of buildings of both red

and white sandstone, surrounded by a ditch. Children now play on the grass of a former courtyard where once, no doubt, the warhorses of John of Gaunt champed the grass, and messengers arrived through the entrance gate with letters of national moment from London concerning the future of the Scottish queen.

Tutbury Castle is still in the ownership of the Duchy of Lancaster. It stands on the north-western side of the town, and there is limited parking space near the entrance gate. SK 209210.

Domestic Ruins:
SILENT HALLS

Lowther Castle

Spofforth
Castle

Thorpe Salvin Manor

Hardwick Old Hall
South Wingfield Manor
Sutton Scarsdale Hall Newstead Abbey

Moreton Corbet Castle

Bradgate House Grace Dieu

Stokesay Castle

Kirby Hall Lyveden New Bield

Bishop's Palace

Houghton House

Minster Lovell
Hall

Greys Court

Old Wardour Castle

Scotney Castle

Cowdray House Nymans

Appuldurcombe House

Hallsands

THE RUINS of great houses and mansions, built after castles had been made redundant by peace and democracy, have received very much less attention in literature than the castles, abbeys and Roman remains which are among the nation's chief tourist attractions. This can only be because they are much closer to us in time, and seem somehow commonplace by comparison with the giant building works of prehistoric and medieval England and Wales. In my view it is high time domestic ruins were given their due, for they are not less romantic, nor less beautiful in their echoing emptiness, than most of the more famous specimens of fallen splendour. Besides, how poor will posterity think the architectural remains of the last two or three centuries if we now treat houses and mansions as less worthy of preservation than castles and abbeys.

Because of the relative neglect of domestic ruins as potential tourist attractions, we have lost many fine mansions which ought to have been cared for as zealously as any castle. There was Old Ragdale Hall in Leicestershire, for instance – the fine timber-framed Tudor mansion of the Shirley family, upon which a demolition gang descended in 1958. And there was Bayons Manor in Lincolnshire, the spectacular Victorian baronial extravaganza of the Tennysons, in which the National Trust had already expressed interest when it was ruthlessly blown up by the landowner. Then there was Witley Park in Surrey, with its 'manor house' built in neo-Gothic style by the financier Whitaker Wright around 1900 (with a glass-roofed billiard room beneath a lake) and completely demolished after only half a century. Cassiobury, at Watford in Hertfordshire, was built by the Earl of Essex in 1661, and was a superb mansion with fine woodcarving by Grinling Gibbons, described by the fifth earl's wife, the actress Kitty Stephens, as '. . . a very pretty house and more full of comforts,

curiosities and pretty things than any house I ever saw'. But in 1927 it was demolished.

Other houses have disappeared for other reasons. Shelley's house at Cwm Elan, where the poet lived for a short time and was influenced by the magic of the valley on his lonely walks, is now submerged beneath the waters of the Elan Reservoirs. Agecroft Hall, a half-timbered Tudor house in Lancashire, was dismantled and shipped to America for re-erection in Virginia in 1926 – a black year for English houses, several having been demolished at that time. The cottage in which George Fox was born at Fenny Drayton in Leicestershire was also taken to the United States. But there is no point in dwelling on what we have lost. Fortunately an enormous number of magnificent houses have survived, though some are in ruins. Most of these have been brought to their knees not by royal whim or military action, but by fire or the prohibitive cost of upkeep, the sort of eventualities that we are familiar with today.

It is possible in ruined houses to feel a little closer to the daily life of their one-time occupants than we are able to do in abbeys and castles; the very scale and layout of domestic ruins is something with which we can more easily identify. At Gorhambury in Hertfordshire, we might catch the ghostly echo of Queen Elizabeth, being welcomed at the threshold as she visits Sir Nicholas Bacon for the first time, scornfully remarking to her Lord Keeper of the Great Seal: 'My Lord, what a little house you have gotten.' Almost any one of the old halls included in this section of the book could be the scene of Walter de la Mare's haunting poem 'The Listeners', and the visitor may or may not be aware that the house is full of silent phantoms in the shadows, listening to the sounds he makes, as his presence disturbs the still air and causes a faint tremor among the cobwebs.

Appuldurcombe House

Isle of Wight

THE WORSLEY family inhabited Appuldurcombe from 1713 until 1805, and in spite of being ruinous their house is still patently the most impressive on the island, next to Osborne. The architect is not known with certainty, but it was very probably John James, a young man who had worked for Sir Christopher Wren on St Paul's Cathedral, and who was certainly in attendance at the site on one occasion to 'fix the best manner in conveying the water from the roofs'.

The Worsleys had long been lords of many manors in the south of England when the fourth baronet, Sir Robert, dismantled the old family mansion here in order to build a fashionably symmetrical baroque mansion in its place. Although building work had started in 1701, the house took a long time to complete, owing to lack of finances, and Lady Worsley – formerly Frances Thynne, Viscount Weymouth's daughter – made scathing remarks about the rate of progress. In fact, it was not completely finished when Sir Robert died, and as his two sons pre-deceased him, interest in the house waned for a time, until Sir Richard Worsley carried out further work towards the end of the century and had the park landscaped by Capability Brown.

The house had been built of local stone with dressings and ornamental sculpture in Portland stone. Two hundred and eighty tons of it were brought across to Cowes and then carted overland, and it cost £178 13s 5d, of which £103 was the freight charge. Although many local men supplied materials and minor services during the building, provincial artisans were not equal to the quality of work required for such a grand design, and master masons were brought from London, their wages accounting for well over half the cost of the house.

Sir Richard Worsley married Seymour Dorothy Fleming (as Gibbon put it, 'for love and £80,000'), but the love did not last as long as the money. Lady Worsley was evidently given to receiving her visitors in bed: she confessed to twenty-seven lovers when her husband divorced her. He directed most of his passion to collecting thereafter, though reserving a little for his 'housekeeper', Mrs Smith. Appuldurcombe was so full of paintings that in some rooms they were stacked on the floor. Sir Richard also had a fine collection of Greek marbles, brought home during his Mediterranean travels before Lord Elgin rifled the Parthenon.

Appuldurcombe must have been a splendid place to see, but in due course the works of art were dispersed throughout the country and overseas, and the house was bought by an absentee landlord who leased it for use as a

hotel, in which role it was short-lived. Then it was occupied by the Benedictine monks who were rebuilding Quarr Abbey – a nice reversal of fortunes for it was more usual for the homes of monks to be taken over as private dwellings. Finally, in both world wars the house was commandeered to billet troops, and its fate was then sealed and decay inevitable, even if a land-mine had not exploded nearby and done considerable damage.

The east front is the most spectacular and best-preserved side of the house, and appears to want only glass in its windows to make it perfectly habitable; but it is nothing more than an empty shell which, since 1945, has been threatened with both total demolition and removal stone by stone for re-erection in

some city which, through severe bomb damage, could do with an injection of bygone stylishness. Fortunately, neither of these proposals has come to pass.

Man proposes, as the Latin proverb has it, but God disposes, and at Appuldurcombe House the still night air is stirred only by phantom sighs of love among the ruins.

Appuldurcombe House. Glassless windows still look out over the Worsleys' landscaped grounds, but only their ghosts enjoy the view.

Appuldurcombe House stands half a mile west of the village of Wroxall, which is on B3327 between Ventnor and Godshill. The ruins are in the care of the Department of the Environment. There is a car park at the end of the drive, from which you must walk the short distance to the house. SZ 543799.

Bishop's Palace

St David's, Dyfed

THE PALACE of the bishops of St David's lies close to the cathedral where the principality's patron saint, known to the Welsh as Dewi, may be buried, and where there is a shrine to his memory in this most holy corner of Wales. The cathedral and the palace are separated only by a trickling stream, which rejoices in the grand name of River Alun, just as the village through which it flows blushes under the title of cathedral city. But there is nothing modest or diminutive about the Bishop's Palace. It is unquestionably one of the finest medieval ruins in the whole of Wales.

Its chief builder was Henry de Gower, who was elected bishop in 1328. He came of a noble family and was an accomplished linguist as well as a dedicated ecclesiastic and clearly a man of taste. Between his election and his death nineteen years later he supervised the building and completion of almost the whole of the magnificent palace whose ruins still show the splendour in which he and his successors entertained their distinguished visitors. The bishops had been wealthy men almost since the days of the Norman Conquest. William I had himself worshipped at the shrine of St David during a visit here on more temporal matters, and in 1115 the bishopric passed from Welsh to English hands.

The palace built by Bishop Gower was not the first on the site, of course, and some parts of the building pre-date his period, but his master mason ingeniously brought all the work to a unified whole, mainly by the introduction of sumptuous arcaded parapets which are a principal feature of the palace architecture, and by the use of local sandstone of buff and purplish hues which now looks so mellow and picturesque with its covering of yellow lichen. The buildings occupy three sides of a more-or-less square courtyard, and across this, facing the main entrance, is the elaborate porch leading to the great hall. External steps lead up from the courtyard through an ogee archway, above which are two canopied niches once occupied by statues. The hall itself was built above a vaulted undercroft, and the roof was covered with lead, the parapets rising above it. At the east end of the hall, where the entrance from the porch led into the screens passage, was a door to the kitchen and service rooms, and above it in the gable a beautiful rose window.

The usual private rooms found in medieval halls at the opposite end to the screens passage do not occur here, and it seems clear that the bishop's hall and solar on the east side of the courtyard, which had been built before Gower's time (probably by Bishop Bek around 1290) were considered adequate, apart from some refinement of their architectural style. A chapel for the bishop's private use was built between the solar and the main gate, despite the presence of an earlier chapel flanked by the great hall and the older western range, which was probably used after the rebuilding as a lodging for palace guests. The bishops would have lived comfortably in the eastern range, with its fireplaces and its windows looking towards the cathedral, while the great hall was used only for state occasions. A passage added to the eastern corner of the courtyard, linking the bishop's hall with the great hall, allowed the kitchen between them to serve both.

Although the principal floors of the palace were above ground level, there was no serious attempt to build defensive features into it. The bishops must have felt secure both in the hands of God and in the remoteness of their situation near the Pembrokeshire coast, looking out towards Ramsey Island and the uninhabited rocks known as Bishops and Clerks, and the coastline to the north. Beyond, beneath the sea, was said to be the lost land of Rhys Ddwfn, although the bishops would have regarded this as mere pagan supersition. The bishops owned Ramsey in medieval times, and kept cattle, sheep and horses there, where St David is popularly supposed to have met St Patrick – though it can only have been the Irish saint's ghost that Dewi saw.

OPPOSITE *The ruins of the Bishop's Palace at St David's, from the cathedral precincts.*

Despite the apparent safety of this far western outpost of the English Church, both the Reformation and the witch craze (neither of which was as early or as dramatic in its effects in Wales as in England) seem to have visited St David's with alacrity, showing that there was no hiding place from private fanaticism or public inconstancy. Around 1500 a case was brought against a man accused of hiring a witch to kill the bishop, and it was not long after that when the decay of the palace began. Bishop Barlow proposed the removal of the see to Carmarthen, and it was he who began the destruction of the palace by stripping all the lead from the roof of the great hall. Legend has it that he took the lead to provide dowries for his five daughters, who were all married to bishops. His successor, Dr Robert Ferrar, was one of the Protestant bishops burned at the stake by order of Bloody Mary in 1555. Early in the seventeenth century some of the buildings were demolished by Bishop Milborne; and his successor, William Laud, soon to become Archbishop of Canterbury, conducted half-hearted enquiries into local

witchcraft here in 1625. Before the end of the century the place was derelict. It was taken over by the Commissioners of Works in 1932.

Jackdaws are the only residents of this richly decorated shell now. Perhaps they are the spirits of the thieving bishops who profited from the destruction of this place. They sit chattering on the parapets, looking down on the empty hall where matters of seemingly great moment were once discussed by bishops, noblemen and clergy, on the site of the Celtic monastery founded by St David of whom it was popularly believed, as Defoe reported, that he was 'uncle to King Arthur, that he lived to 146 years of age, that he was bishop of this church 65 years, being born in the year 496, and died ann. 642; that he built 12 monasteries, and did abundance of miracles.'

St David's lies on A487 at its most westerly point between Fishguard and Haverfordwest. There is a car park at the approach to the cathedral, and visitors must walk through the cathedral close to reach the ruins of the palace, which are in the care of the Welsh Office. SM 754257.

Bradgate House

Leicestershire

BRADGATE PARK, in the Charnwood Forest area of north-west Leicestershire, is one of the most romantic spots in England. It is an estate of nearly a thousand acres (404 hectares) which was given by the industrialist Charles Bennion in 1928 to the people of Leicestershire 'to be preserved in its natural state for their quiet enjoyment'.

The place has been preserved in its natural state since the fifteenth century, and this fact contributes a great deal to Bradgate's romantic atmosphere. One dreads to think what capabilities Lancelot Brown might have perceived here. The ruins of the old house stand among rock outcrops, ancient oak trees and herds of deer, and a meandering stream – the River Lyn – trickles along by your side as you walk from the gates to the remaining brick walls of a house which has witnessed some of the more shady events in England's history.

It was Thomas Grey, first Marquis of Dorset, who built the mansion of red brick here at the end of the fifteenth century. It was the first country house in Leicestershire, and one of the first in England. Bricks were made on the site by itinerant craftsmen, and stone was probably brought from Ulverscroft, a former Augustinian establishment nearby.

The marquis was the eldest son of Sir John Grey, Lord Ferrers of Groby, and his wife Elizabeth Woodville. After her husband's death at St Albans, while fighting for the Lancastrians, she married the Yorkist king, Edward IV, and became the mother of the princes murdered in the Tower.

Henry Grey, the third marquis, married Lady Frances Brandon after divorcing his first wife. Frances was the daughter of the Duke of Suffolk and granddaughter of Henry VII, and here at Bradgate House in October 1537 she gave birth to the first of her three daughters. The child was called Jane. Her father eventually became Duke of Suffolk when all his father-in-law's heirs died.

Lady Jane Grey grew up to be a comely and accomplished girl. Her parents secured for her the most learned tutors of the day, and she soon mastered Latin, Greek, French and Italian. When the rest of her family were out hunting in the park, she was usually to be found in the house reading Plato. But this rare being soon became a helpless pawn in the political ambitions of her scheming relatives. When she was sixteen she was married to Lord Guildford Dudley, son of the Duke of Northumberland, who had virtually made himself Protector during the minority of the consumptive Edward VI, and who induced the young king to bequeath the throne to Jane to preserve the Protestant succession. When Edward died the unsuspecting Leicestershire girl was proclaimed Queen of England. She had no aspirations to power, and fainted when she was told.

However, Northumberland and Suffolk had reckoned without the possibility of the people rallying to Mary Tudor's side, and when they did so, Jane was thrown into the Tower, her reign having lasted nine days. At length she was executed for treason – a human sacrifice by her parents at the altar of ambition. She was not yet seventeen when they chopped off her head within the Tower precincts. Legend has it that the oak trees in Bradgate Park were pollarded as a mark of mourning for her.

Jane's husband and her father-in-law had preceded her to the block; her father followed her within the month and her uncle Lord Thomas Grey not long afterwards. The Greys had been brought down wholesale to a humbler level, and their fortunes declined until the Stuart period, when James I made Henry Grey Baron of Groby again. There is a fine monument of alabaster to him in the chapel which survives at Bradgate, and beneath its floor, earlier members of the Grey family still lie in a sealed vault.

Bradgate was brought to ruin, according to legend, in 1694, when the lady of the house set fire to it one night and ran away by the light of the blaze. The Countess (the head of the house

had by now been elevated to Earl of Stamford) was said to be quite unable to tolerate the place. This story is a romantic fiction. A fire did occur at Bradgate but the damage was not extensive. The Greys deserted the house soon after, however, and the building gradually fell into decay. They owned Bradgate until the early years of the present century, and continued to use the unspoiled park for hunting, but the ancient house was never restored; peacocks now strut and scream round the old brick walls while deer roam freely among the trees and bracken.

If only these ruins could be made to give up their secrets, what glimpses of life in a great Tudor family would be revealed to us! The beautiful Katherine Grey, sister of Lady Jane, was doomed to die at twenty-seven after enforced separation from successive husbands, and has become known to us as 'the lady of lamentations', of whom it was said that 'though the roses in her cheeks looked very wan and pale, it was not for want of watering'. The third sister, Mary, who was deformed, lived a little longer, into her thirties – but in disgrace, having married beneath her. Sad though their stories are, they had known happiness, and it does not stretch imagination far to visualize the scene here on May Day, for Lady Mary left us her impressions of it: 'Then

Bradgate House – the ruins of the brick-built country house of the Grey family.

when the merrie May Pole and all the painted Morris dancers with Tabor and Pipe beganne their spritelie anticks on oure butiful grene laune, afore that we idel leetel Bodyes had left ower warme Bedds, would goode Mistress Bridget the Tire-woman whom our Lady Mother alwaies commanded to do ower Biddinge, come and telle us of the merrie men a-dancing on the Grene.'

Yet even such celebrations seem to have been marred by tragedy. On a hill above the ruins stands a stone folly called Old John, where a windmill had once stood. Tradition has it that a huge bonfire was erected in the park round a large pole, and lit to celebrate the coming of age of the fifth Earl of Stamford's son, but when the pole burnt through it fell on the head of an old miller and killed him, the tower being built afterwards as a memorial to him. No wonder the Greys grew weary of this house of sorrows.

The ruins of Bradgate House stand in the park whose entrance is from the village street of Newtown Linford, on B5327 six miles north-west of Leicester. Cars are admitted to the park on Thursdays in summer, pedestrians only on other days; but there is a large car park at the entrance. The park and ruins are administered by Leicestershire County Council. SK 534102.

Cowdray House

West Sussex

ON 24 SEPTEMBER 1793 a workman at the magnificent Tudor mansion of the Montague family near Midhurst left a charcoal fire unattended. By the end of the day, Cowdray House – one of the finest houses in Sussex – had been destroyed by a blaze which swept through every corner, leaving it gutted and roofless. A few days later Lord Montague was drowned in Germany while attempting to navigate the Rhine Falls at Schaffhausen. The double disaster seemed like the fulfilment of a curse put on the family by a monk, thrown out of Battle Abbey at the Dissolution and displaced by the Brown family whose heads became Viscounts Montague.

The house had stood for over three hundred years. It had been started in 1492 by Sir David Owen, the son of Owain Glyndwr, and continued by Sir William Fitzwilliam who purchased the estate in 1529. On his death in 1542

the house, still incomplete, passed to his half-brother Sir Anthony Brown, who owned Bayham Abbey and several other suppressed religious houses as well as Battle. He was Henry VIII's Master of the Horse, and was so highly regarded by the king that he was entrusted, as one of a three-man embassy, with the delicate diplomatic mission of obtaining the hand of Anne of Cleves for Henry after the death of Jane Seymour. Sir Anthony acted as wedding proxy for the king in a quaint custom of the day, dressed in blue and white, one leg being entirely clad in white satin to be thrust into the princess's bed as a token of the king's marital rights over her. But when the king first set eyes on her at Rochester he disliked her immediately and, as Horace Walpole said, only put his own leg into bed to kick her out. Sir Anthony's fortunes did not suffer by this brief misadventure with the 'Flanders Mare', however, and by the time of his death in 1548, Cowdray was complete and resplendent. Set in its great park (landscaped by Capability Brown later on), it had provided lavish hospitality for the young King Edward VI, who wrote that he was 'rather excessively banqueted' there. Sir Anthony's son, the first Viscount Montague, entertained Queen Elizabeth – not one to complain of excessive hospitality – and she was pleased to shoot deer with a crossbow in the park. Royalty still frequents Cowdray Park, though now the sport is polo.

The ruins of the house present a fine study in unspoiled Tudor architecture, with the turreted gatehouse, great hall with huge bay window and many mullions and transoms, and other remnants of buildings ranged round a more or less square courtyard. The consistency of style is impressive, and helps us to imagine what the rooms must have been like when they were alive with the noise and colour of a Tudor house-party.

There was a long gallery where occupants could take exercise in bad weather and look at the family portraits on the walls; there was a parlour decorated by pupils of Holbein; the grand staircase was painted by Pellegrini. The hall, which had a fine hammerbeam roof of oak with tracery in the spandrels, was known as the Buck Hall because it had life-size bucks on the walls bearing shields with the arms of England and of the Brown family. The chapel had a three-sided apse with a window in each facet and a battlemented roof, added when Sir William Fitzwilliam was granted a licence to crenellate by Henry VIII. The kitchen, which was the only corner of the house to escape the conflagration, was a hexagonal room with large fireplaces and turreted chimneys.

And so this once-noble house stands, rising out of the long grass on an outcrop of sandstone along the foot of the South Downs, with its brick exposed here and there by the removal of the stone facing. Though its interior was consumed by the fire, its walls and towers are sufficiently recognizable and unchanged for the ruined house to have been called 'an absolutely consistent epitome of Tudor architecture at its plainest and most sober'. Cowdray remains a national treasure not quite lost.

The ruins of Cowdray House, which happily have not been subjected to the usual cosmetic treatment, lie half a mile east of Midhurst, from where they can be approached by a road off A286. There is parking space by some cottages forming an estate courtyard near the entrance. SU 893220.

The remains of Cowdray's Tudor gatehouse.

Grace Dieu

Leicestershire

IN THE north-west corner of Leicestershire, on the high ground of Charnwood Forest, a small Augustinian nunnery was founded in the thirteenth century by Roesia de Verdun. It housed fifteen nuns and a few poor people and dependants 'of virtuous conversation and all desirous to continue their religion there'. This testimony was given by those who defended the nunnery against the charges of Henry VIII's commissioners – those same Doctors Leigh and Layton who reported to Cromwell on Fountains Abbey. In this instance, the case for suppression was that two nuns had given birth to children, and that the nuns venerated the girdle and tunic of St Francis, super-stitiously held to assist women in childbirth. Enough said, as far as the rapacious king and his henchman the Lord Keeper – a man of 'prying eyes and gripple hands' – were concer-ned. The nunnery was duly suppressed, the nuns turned out and their scant property sold.

The buildings passed in due course to Sir John Beaumont, descendant of a long line of powerful Leicestershire landowners stretch-ing back to the Conquest, and it is to him that we owe the conversion of the nunnery into a dwelling house, which entitles Grace Dieu to its place in this section. For however interest-ing the original nunnery might have been, it can hardly compete with the subsequent story of the Beaumont home that grew out of it.

John Beaumont himself was not a specially admirable character. As Master of the Rolls he indulged in forgery and misappropriation of funds and had to resign his position and forfeit the property, which went for a time to the Hastings family of Ashby. But after John Beaumont's death, the Earl of Huntingdon restored Grace Dieu to Beaumont's widow, who was a Hastings herself, and it was here that one of Leicestershire's greatest sons was born in or about 1584: Sir John Beaumont's grandson Francis, whose name became as inseparably linked with that of his friend and collaborator John Fletcher as Gilbert's with Sullivan or Marks's with Spencer. It is safe to assume that something, at least, of the Beaumont and Fletcher partnership was con-ceived and written in this converted nunnery.

Even at this time the Beaumonts were busy exploiting the coal deposits in the area, and their increasing fortune led them to abandon

Little is left of the mansion built out of the former nunnery at Grace Dieu, but the poet and dramatist Francis Beaumont was born in this house, and Wordsworth was familiar with its ruins.

Grace Dieu in the seventeenth century for nearby Coleorton Hall. The former nunnery passed to Sir Ambrose Phillipps, who demolished most of the buildings, including the church, which the Beaumonts had left untouched. Eventually the Phillipps, too, abandoned Grace Dieu to nature.

The Beaumonts, meanwhile, had produced another important figure in the world of the arts, Sir George Howland Beaumont. When he was not attending to his coal mining interests, Sir George was delighting in the company of writers and artists. He was one of the founders of the National Gallery and a friend and patron of Wordsworth and Constable, among others. Wordsworth stayed with him at Coleorton and wrote some lines on Grace Dieu, by this time in ruins:

Beneath yon eastern ridge, the craggy bound,
Rugged and high, of Charnwood's forest ground,
Stand yet, but, stranger, hidden from thy view,
The ivied ruins of forlorn Grace Dieu.

If Wordsworth ever wrote a worse verse than this, I do not know it, and for a more worthy celebration of the place and the Beaumont connection with it we have to go back to Thomas Bancroft, who must have known Francis Beaumont:

Grace Dieu, that under Charnwood standst alone,
As a grande relicke of Religion,
I reverence thine old but fruitful worth,
That lately brought such noble Beaumonts forth,
Whose brave heroic muses must aspire
To match the anthems of the heavenly quire . . .

There is not much left of either the relic of religion or the house now, and what there is hides under a cloak of vegetation, as this is one ruin which has not (so far) been rescued, tidied up, and opened to public inspection. But it occupies an important niche in English cultural history.

The ruins stand in a field on the south side of A512 Loughborough–Ashby de la Zouch road, just north-east of Thringstone. The land is private property, and visitors are strongly advised by the owners not to enter the field. The presence of the farmer's bull may be a more powerful deterrent than the danger of falling masonry. However, the ruins can be seen from the roadside. SK 436184.

Greys Court

Oxfordshire

IN THE grounds of the Tudor mansion known as Greys Court, where the Earl and Countess of Somerset were kept in the custody of Sir William Knollys after their conviction for the murder of Sir Thomas Overbury, stand the scanty brick and flint remains of a fortified manor house built here by the de Grey family in the fourteenth century.

They had owned the manor since the time of the Domesday survey, and Sir John de Grey was licensed to crenellate in 1347. The property consisted of a rectangular courtyard surrounded by a curtain wall with an octagonal tower at each corner, and against the west wall a square four-storey tower-house or keep, built partly of brickwork which may well have been the earliest in Oxfordshire. The 'keep' had small square-headed windows, and all the towers except one were topped with battlements. Between the de Greys who built this house and the Knollyses who built the later one, the place was owned by the Lovell family.

The Saxon village of Rotherfield was already here when the de Greys came. The name comes from 'Hryther' and means land where cattle graze. After the Conquest it soon became known as Rotherfield Greys. Walter de Grey was Archbishop of York in the time of Henry III, and Sir Robert de Grey helped Edward I subdue the Welsh. In due course the family was granted a barony, but nearly lost it when the second Lord Grey offended Edward III by drawing a knife in anger in the king's presence. In any case, the barony was short-lived, as the fifth Lord Grey died without issue in 1387.

The house itself survived until the early sixteenth century, when the new house was built using material from the old one and incorporating some parts of it in the new building, in particular the kitchen. A drawing of about 1600 shows the outer walls and two gatehouses intact, and the foundations of these can be detected in the parched grass in very dry summers.

Rotherfield Greys is two miles west of Henley-on-Thames, and Greys Court lies north of the village, well signposted, between A423 and B481. The house and ruins are owned by the National Trust, and there is a car park at the site. A well-known feature of the house is a donkey wheel used to draw water from the well, like that at Carisbrooke Castle. SU 725834.

Clothed in vegetation, the remains of Greys Court incorporate some of the region's earliest brickwork.

Hallsands

Devon

AT THE END of the nineteenth century there was a thriving village at this spot on the Devon coast, occupied chiefly in crab fishing. It had been known as Hall Cellar once, but was latterly called Hallsands. Its houses, post office, grocer's shop and public house were built along either side of a tiny village street, on a narrow shelf of rock protected by tall cliffs behind and with a natural bank or beach of shingle in front, looking out over Start Bay. More than 120 people made up the coastal community, which had been here for centuries, and generation after generation of children grew up in close communion with the sea, learning from their forefathers how to live in harmony with the ocean, making a living from it when it was compliant and treating it with proper respect when it was in violent mood.

In 1897, plans to extend the naval dockyard at Devonport involved dredging the sea-bed for large quantities of gravel, and the Board of Trade granted a licence for this to be done off the coast in Start Bay. During the next four years contractors dredged more than half a million tons of gravel, shingle and sand from the area. The old men of the village shook their heads and said this interference with nature would come to no good, while the younger men complained that it was damaging their livelihoods.

Local fears were brought to the notice of the House of Commons, and the government appointed an inspector to look into the matter. As a result, some compensation was paid to the fishermen, and the villagers were assured that any sinking of the shingle beach because of dredging operations would be of little consequence, as the sea would of course quickly re-form the bank it had put there naturally in the first place. But the old men still stubbornly wagged their heads as if they knew more about the sea than did the pin-striped bureaucrats in Westminster. It was

over four years before anyone took any notice of them, and dredging operations were then stopped. But it was too late.

In the winter of 1903, waves that would previously have been held at bay by the pebble ridge, which had subsided by as much as six or seven feet, lashed the very threshold of the village, bringing down parts of the sea-walls and making three houses uninhabitable. In the following autumn and winter more damage was done when high tides, whipped up by strong east winds, wrecked part of the village pub, carried away sections of the road, exposed the foundations of sea-walls and caused widespread damage to houses as forty-foot storm waves crashed over them, smashing windows, breaking down walls and roofs, and leaving them awash. One family moved out lock, stock and barrel when its house was left standing three feet from a deep fissure in the rock where the road had been. All the houses on the seaward side of the village street were badly damaged – some beyond repair – and they were totally exposed to the next severe storms to come along, all semblance of sea defences having by now been swept away.

It was eleven years before another tempestuous combination of high tides and easterly gales hit Hallsands. By that time the village had to some extent recovered its equilibrium. Houses and the road had been repaired, a new sea-wall built and foundations reinforced, and life had returned to something like normality, though the old men still shook their heads and muttered dark warnings.

The end of January 1917 brought the prophesied tragedy to Hallsands. Heavy seas threw tons of water at the village in frightful storms. A great barrage of wind and waves lashed the houses for two days, and at the end of this relentless onslaught only one house was left standing. The villagers had gathered what furniture and belongings they could and retreated to the top of the cliffs. When the storms abated, twenty-nine houses had been destroyed, the village street had vanished into crevasses between the rocks, and an entire village population had been made homeless.

PREVIOUS PAGES
Hallsands. The shattered ruins of the village destroyed by the sea in 1917 stand as a permanent and startling warning against ill-advised interference with nature.

The Board of Trade said the disaster was due to natural causes.

In due course, which is a euphemism in this case for lengthy enquiries and the slow process of law, some compensation was paid to the villagers of Hallsands, and a new community grew up in the safety of the cliff-top, but after nearly seventy years the terrible havoc wreaked on the place can still be seen here. Houses, burst apart as if by explosions, cling to the edges of rocks shattered by the raging ocean. Empty fireplaces remain in walls almost unaccountably left standing, only hard granite and strong mortar having saved them from collapsing into the sea along with the rest of the village. The pebble beach where the fishermen moored their boats is about twelve feet lower than it used to be, and in stormy winters waves still wash over what remains of the once-protected shelf of rock that formed the foundation of a hard-working and resilient village community.

Hallsands lies north of Start Point near the southernmost tip of Devon. It is reached via winding and narrow lanes from A379 between Kingsbridge and Torcross, and there is a car park at the entrance to the new village above the cliffs, from which the visitor must walk the rest of the way. SX 820375.

Hardwick Old Hall

Derbyshire

ONE OF Bess of Hardwick's more admirable achievements was the building of great houses. She and her second husband, Sir William Cavendish, built Chatsworth and founded the Devonshire dynasty, and during the last years of her fourth husband's life, when she was separated from him, she set about rebuilding the manor house which her father had owned, and in which she grew up until her first marriage – and her first widowhood – at the age of thirteen. She had married

Sir William St Loe after Cavendish, and after outliving her third husband, this redoubtable woman ensnared the rich George Talbot, who was eight years her junior, but did not permit his accession to her boudoir until she had steered his wealth to her own account.

Her father's manor house became a mansion which now stands in ruins beside the vast Hardwick Hall built by Bess (never one to let the grass grow under her feet) after the Earl of Shrewsbury's death. The ruin is known today as Hardwick Old Hall, and even in its dereliction it is a monument to its builder's energy and ambition in old age. Her taste was grandiose and her purse apparently bottomless. She was in her seventies when she began this house, with the new Hall yet to come.

The façade which the visitor first approaches is a 200-foot-long stone wall pierced by many mullioned and transomed windows on its six floors. It might seem to be merely characteristic of the time and somewhat cheerless, but behind it was a lavish remodelling of John Hardwick's modest manor, in which Bess employed some of the finest craftsmen of the day in her interior decoration. The most sumptuous work of all was the plaster friezes of forest scenes round the walls, such superb examples of Elizabethan art that the same craftsmen were employed to work again in the new mansion. Principal among them was Abraham Smith.

Stone staircases now ascend to roofless chambers in this old mansion, which was well equipped with windows, fireplaces, privies and all the comforts that the period was able to provide, with gardens and summerhouses outside and a stone cistern into which water was pumped. But the place was not, finally, a fit enough palace in which to entertain a queen, and Bess left it as a servants' lodging when she moved to her newest building close by to await the royal visit that never came.

The Countess of Shrewsbury was expert with an embroidery needle, though it is difficult to imagine this woman sitting demurely in her chamber embroidering a petticoat for one of her daughters. She had numerous business interests, including mining (one writer even went so far as to call her a coal merchant); she was a farmer and a landlord; she involved herself in ceaseless building projects; she was highly ambitious and an inveterate political schemer.

According to legend, some soothsayer (or possibly an architect with an eye to the main chance) told Bess that as long as she kept building, her life would be preserved. She *did* keep building, and died at eighty-seven, when her masons had to stop work during a hard frost.

Hardwick Hall and Hardwick Old Hall are National Trust properties, reached from A617 Mansfield–Chesterfield road at Glapwell. The ruins of the Old Hall, which is in the guardianship of the Department of the Environment, are undergoing repair, but can be seen from outside. There is a car park at the site. SK 468632.

The ruins of Bess of Hardwick's Old Hall.

Houghton House

Bedfordshire

YOU MUST be prepared to walk a quarter of a mile from the nearest parking place to see this ruined Jacobean mansion, but the effort is well rewarded. Bedfordshire is not a major tourist county, so the ruin is also relatively little known, yet distinguished men and women have walked its passages and been familiar with its every corner.

The house was built around 1615, of brick with dressings of white stone, on an open site

looking over the Bedfordshire landscape, and was the property of Sir Philip Sidney's sister Mary, by this time Dowager Countess of Pembroke. It was built on the H-plan in favour at the time, and was on two storeys with a basement on the east side where the land sloped away from the house. The building had all the typically Jacobean features – shaped gables, mullioned and transomed windows and tall chimneys – as well as rather more unusual turrets at the corners. The south porch, with huge keystones over the doorway, gave direct access to the great hall without a screens passage, and this fact, together with

Houghton House. An engraving by Lodge showing the mansion as it appeared in its prime.

House Beautiful? Bunyan may have based his allegorical mansion on Houghton House, the home of Lady Mary Sidney, sister of the famous Sir Philip. The house was dismantled by the Duke of Bedford in 1794.

the central features of the north and west façades of the house, lead experts to the conclusion that alterations were made to the house some years after the Countess's death, perhaps by the first Earl of Elgin. In particular, the spectacular west front, often attributed to Inigo Jones, was given a classical three-tier centrepiece with Tuscan columns, of which only the ground floor remains standing.

The Duke of Bedford purchased Houghton House in 1738, and it was occupied by the Marquis of Tavistock, the duke's son, and then by the Earl of Upper Ossory, no less, until in 1794 the then Duke of Bedford dismantled the house, leaving it roofless and floorless as it has remained ever since. We know from an old engraving what a splendid place this was once, and even in its present state we can sense its stylishness and the former excellence of its situation. But now it stands not only shattered and derelict, but has as its distant prospect the multitudinous chimney stacks of Bedfordshire brick factories belching their acrid smoke across the landscape.

How different this place must have been when the house was new-built and shining bright, and Mary Sidney sat looking out of the windows in her old age, perhaps remembering her childhood at Ludlow Castle. At sixteen she married Henry Herbert of Wilton House. (Despite her marriage, however, she distri-

buted her favours freely.) A beautiful young woman of wit and learning, she built up a fine library at Wilton. She was patron to many men of letters, including Ben Jonson, John Donne and Edmund Spenser. After the earl's death, she either married or co-habited with Sir Matthew Lister, a member of the College of Physicians.

She spent ten thousand pounds building this house, bringing architects from Italy, according to the diarist John Aubrey, and having it modelled on the description of a house in her brother Philip's poem 'Arcadia', which she had inspired, for he loved her dearly. But she did not long enjoy her retirement here: the house was hardly finished when she died in 1621 at the age of sixty.

According to tradition, John Bunyan, whose home was not far away, based his 'House Beautiful' in *The Pilgrim's Progress* on Houghton House. From the top of it Christian was shown the 'Delectable Mountains' to the south – undoubtedly the Chiltern Hills for, like Hardy, Bunyan used familiar local scenes as the models for his locations.

The ruins of Houghton House are in the care of the Department of the Environment. They stand a mile to the north-east of Ampthill, and are reached by a track leaving A418. There is parking space about a third of a mile along the track, and you must walk the rest of the way. TL 039395.

Part of the beautiful
two-storey west range
of Kirby Hall.

Kirby Hall

Northamptonshire

KIRBY HALL is such a patently magnificent mansion, though it is but an empty shell, that one is almost reluctant to call it a ruin. It seems nearly possible to live in it still. But its empty halls are mostly roofless, its windows mostly unglazed, and starlings nest in its niches. If any footsteps are heard at night when all the visitors have gone, they can only be the ghostly tread of Sir Christopher Hatton, lamenting the sorry state to which his splendid home has come in four centuries.

It was Sir Humphrey Stafford who began the building here in Rockingham Forest in 1570, bringing Oolitic limestone from the quarries at Weldon, only two miles away. The design of the two-storey mansion made use of the giant pilaster and other motifs popular in France then but not in England, giving Kirby Hall an architectural distinction among English houses of the period.

219

Hardly had Sir Humphrey's house been completed when he died, in 1575, and the estate was purchased by Sir Christopher Hatton, then thirty-five years old. He had already impressed Queen Elizabeth to such an extent that she gave him Corfe Castle – and he had been so impressed by her that he was in the course of building Holdenby Hall, near Northampton, as a 'shrine' for her. Hatton was a gay and handsome cavalier who had apparently danced himself into the queen's affections, and been made captain of her bodyguard. 'To serve you', he wrote to her, with the extravagant flattery expected of him, 'is heaven, but to lack you is more than hell's torment.' The queen showered him with gifts and called him her 'sheep' and her 'bell-wether', and Mary Stuart accused him of being the queen's paramour.

Meanwhile, Hatton continued building at Kirby Hall, in the process of which the village of Kirby-in-Gretton was demolished to make way for his park and the beautiful gardens which John Evelyn subsequently praised. The house was built round a square inner courtyard, the main entrance being from a forecourt on the north side. Passing through the north range where the service rooms were accommodated, one faced the south range across the courtyard, and here was the great hall, with guest rooms and lodgings to east and west.

In 1587 the queen made Christopher Hatton her Lord Chancellor (though he had never practised as a professional lawyer), but for her 'sheep' to be given the woolsack was scarcely compensation for his displacement in her intimate affections by Raleigh. In four years he fell fatally ill of kidney trouble, though some say he died of a broken heart because the queen demanded payment of a debt he could not meet. The queen attended his bedside in London, however, and fed cordial broths to the only favourite who had kept his vow to remain celibate for her sake.

Hatton's descendants lived at Kirby Hall, entertaining James I here. Some alteration was carried out in the 1630s, possibly by Inigo Jones, adding sumptuous Renaissance details such as the Italian loggia on the north side, and the unique gable over the porch in the south range, above a neat little balcony flanked by Corinthian columns.

Kirby Hall was lived in until 1820, after which it was allowed to fall victim to nature; it passed into the care of the Office of Works in 1930. Meanwhile, the quarries which had long before supplied its mellow stone, were becoming the scene of the spreading iron industry upon which Corby's growth was based, and the ruins of the house now stand in surroundings rather less romantic than those the mansion grew up in. Nevertheless, Kirby Hall is a spectacle not to be missed – a gleaming skeleton picked clean by the elements but refusing to collapse into a mere heap of bones.

The first stone of Kirby Hall was laid, way back in 1570, by a four- or five-year-old boy. He was John Thorpe, son of the master mason Thomas Thorpe, and we can easily picture the touching little family ceremony on the levelled and marked-out site, with the other workmen looking on.

He would remember the occasion all his life, probably, but whoever it is that finally removes the last stone at Kirby will think nothing of it. It is impossible to believe that ruined buildings will be preserved indefinitely. Their appreciation is but a passing fancy, and the day will come when this beautiful house vanishes entirely, to be replaced by ... what? A nuclear power station? A computer factory? A multi-storey car park? It might be said of such a worthy ruin that, like the monarchy, it no longer exercises power itself, but it effectively denies power to others, and therefore should not be abolished as a redundant institution. Sir Christopher Hatton's ghost would agree with that.

Kirby Hall is in the care of the Department of the Environment, and stands to the north-east of Corby, from where it can be reached by a minor road off A6116, or from the village of Deene just off A43. Cars are parked in the north forecourt of the house. SP 926927.

OPPOSITE *Kirby Hall – part of the north range from the courtyard, showing the Italian loggia.*

Lowther Castle

Cumbria

YOU WOULD hardly think it a ruin at all at first site. It looks like one of the Gothic fantasies of mad King Ludwig of Bavaria, or a film set for a Hollywood costume epic, left behind by Metro-Goldwyn-Mayer. But it is a roofless and hollow shell not two hundred years old, having been started in 1806, when lords of manors were wont to express their wealth and local power in lavish houses. It was abandoned in 1936, when they could no longer afford the upkeep.

The Lowther family had been here since the

It may not look like a *ruin, but Lowther Castle is a hollow shell, abandoned only 130 years after it was built.*

thirteenth century, and were empire-building capitalists from early on, their influence extending over territories as widespread as those of such other great northern families as the Percys and the Howards. They had mining, shipping and farming interests, as well as political ones, and their power rocketed in the seventeenth century when Sir John Lowther, MP for Westmorland, was made Viscount Lonsdale in recognition of his active support for William of Orange. He was First Lord of the Treasury, and was badly wounded in a duel with a Customs officer, who challenged him after being dismissed from his post. Fighting remained in the blood: it was the sixth earl who gave the Lonsdale Belt to boxing.

222

William Wordsworth's grandfather was Lord Lowther's estate superintendent, and his father, John Wordsworth, was his 'law-agent', which was a euphemism for Tory political agent. Wordsworth himself recovered a long-standing debt from the second earl, and suddenly found admirable qualities in the aristocracy after having been a left-wing revolutionary.

It was Wordsworth's patron Sir George Beaumont, of Grace Dieu – another coal-mining magnate – who recommended Robert Smirke as architect to Hugh Lowther, the fifth Earl Lonsdale, after the earlier Lowther Castle had been extensively damaged by fire in 1720. He built this sham-medieval pile in five years, with towers, pinnacles, mock-machicolations and battlements. The entrance hall with its grand staircase was 60 feet square and rich with pointed arches above clustered columns.

The earl who occupied it longest, known to his tenants as 'Lordie', was as flamboyant as his house. He rode about in a black and yellow coach drawn by a team of horses, and smoked large cigars. As a young man he had beaten the World Heavyweight Champion in an exhibition boxing contest, and the World Walking Champion in a hundred-mile walk up the Great North Road. When he entertained Kaiser Wilhelm II here, he had the lavatory seats electrically heated, but at the outbreak of the First World War he assembled a private army of his tenants and had them in uniform almost before the Army had opened a recruiting office.

By the 1930s, however, the baronial aspirations of pseudo-feudal landlords had been sunk once and for all by democratic institutions and declining wealth, and the Lowthers made the decision to move into a more modest home. Lowther Castle had been occupied by the Army, which had left it in a poor condition. A sale of its contents lasted for many days. It is a nice irony that the buyers included Sir Alexander Korda, who acquired, among other things, Lord Lonsdale's black and yellow coach for use in his film studios. Then the castle was demolished, leaving the outer walls intact as a symbol of the power that had once ruled half Cumberland. And here this spectacular ruin stands yet – a roofless and redundant Xanadu – with Emperor's Drive still stretching across the vast park where whole villages had been destroyed to enhance the views from the castle.

Lowther Castle is still owned by the family, and the public is allowed near the ruins only during a short period each summer, but it can be viewed from the road through the park between Askham and Newtown, four miles south of Penrith and a mile west of A6 at Hackthorpe. NY 522238.

Lyveden New Bield

Northamptonshire

THIS STRANGE – not to say eccentric – house is not, in the strictest sense of the word, a ruin at all, since it was never actually finished, and remains much as it was when work was abandoned in 1605 – a roofless shell.

The house was begun by Sir Thomas Tresham, a member of an old Catholic family of Northamptonshire, and was designed by Robert Stickells to please Sir Thomas's taste for religious symbolism – he had already built

Lyveden New Bield is the only building in this book which has never been occupied. It was abandoned before completion in 1605.

the famous Triangular Lodge at Rushton as an allegory of the Trinity. The design of Lyveden was similarly intended as an exhibition of Sir Thomas's faith, for which he suffered some years in prison as a 'Popish recusant'. The house was to be in honour of Christ's Passion. The ground plan is in the form of a cross, and much play is made on mystical numbers throughout the building, which was to have been a summer retreat from Sir Thomas's main house not far away.

The house is built of stone, and is of three storeys including the basement, with mullioned and transomed bay windows rising the full height of the house. Seven emblems of the Passion occur on the entablature above the ground floor, and on the frieze above the upper floor is carved an inscription from the Catholic Mass.

Muriel Throckmorton, Sir Thomas Tresham's wife, would no doubt have had much to do with the furnishing if her husband had lived. But, after years of harassment and incarceration in the notorious Fleet prison, he died in 1605, unaware, no doubt, that his son was implicated in the Gunpowder Plot and was about to forfeit all the family estates for his treason.

Perhaps the oddest thing of all about this house is that no one in nearly four hundred years has acquired the property and completed the building. What was already there in 1605 was a well-built stone frame of a house in quiet countryside with fine gardens. The gardens have now gone, but the house still stands on a more-or-less square terrace, amid fields and woodlands, awaiting the arrival of the roofing contractor and the glazier. They have never turned up, however, and alone among the buildings in this book, Lyveden has never served any useful purpose.

Lyveden New Bield was purchased by the National Trust in 1922. It stands a mile and a half south of Harley Way, between A6116 at Brigstock and A427 near Oundle. Visitors must park their cars in a lay-by at the roadside and walk the half-mile along a rough track crossing two fields. SP 984853.

Minster Lovell Hall

Oxfordshire

THIS ALWAYS seems to me one of the most haunting of domestic ruins, though there is little enough left above ground level of what was once a vast and magnificent manor house. Its layout and building history have been worked out in the finest detail by archaeologists, but they have not cast the smallest glimmer of light on its ancient mysteries.

The Lovell family owned this manor on the fringe of the Cotswolds from the twelfth century, and it was William, the seventh Baron Lovell, who built the great manor house of limestone here, on the site of a Norman priory, in the fifteenth century. It stood in a picturesque wooded landscape beside the River Windrush, and was on the scale of a palace, built round three sides of a courtyard with the river enclosing the fourth side. The great hall was on the north side, with solar and chapel adjacent. The east range contained a pantry, buttery, kitchen and stables. Along the west side were private family and guest rooms. A large circular dovecote, which remains intact nearby, housed birds which supplied meat and eggs for the lord's table and guano for fertilizing his fields.

William Lovell died in 1455, and his son John followed him to the grave ten years later. The property then came to John's son Francis, the ninth baron, who had been since childhood a close friend of the Protector, Richard of Gloucester. The boys had learned the rules of courtly conduct together in the household of the Earl of Warwick at Middleham Castle. Edward IV made Lovell a viscount, and he became Richard's Chief Butler of England. At his friend's coronation as Richard III he played a prominent role and subsequently became Lord Chancellor and a Knight of the Garter.

Lovell was no more popular than the king in some quarters, and was named in the notorious lampoon by a Wiltshire squire,

Tantalizing fragments remain of the palatial manor house of the Lovells. This traceried window was in an upper chamber in the west wing.

William Colyngbourne, a supporter of the Lancastrian cause, whose provocative verse was affixed to the door of St Paul's Cathedral:

> The Cat, the Rat, and Lovel our Dog,
> Rule all England under an Hog.

The other members of the king's unpopular trio, which exemplified his partiality for northerners, were Sir William Catesby and Sir Richard Ratcliffe. The author of the seditious libel was disembowelled and hanged for treason, for he was also alleged to have been in communication with Henry Tudor. It was an uneasy time, and Lovell added a strong tower to the south-west corner of Minster Lovell Hall. At the Battle of Bosworth Lovell fought at the king's side, but did not share his fate. He went into hiding, and later emerged as a supporter of Lambert Simnel's rebellion against Henry VII, but in the ensuing battle at Stoke in Nottinghamshire, Lovell once again managed to escape.

This much is fact, but it is what happened afterwards that brings us to the dark legends that drift round these old walls like a fog, and invest their stones with a touch of the macabre. One story of Lovell's fate says that he tried to swim across the Trent with his horse and drowned when he could not surmount the steep bank on the other side. This seems unlikely, but the viscount certainly vanished, and more popular accounts say that he made his way, undetected by his enemies, back to Minster Lovell, where he made his presence known in the dead of night only to one loyal retainer, who hid him in a secret vault or cellar, and fed him there daily, unknown to anyone else, for several months. But the king siezed the Lovell estates and the household was dispersed. The servant who possessed the only key to the inhabited chamber either died suddenly or was sent away before he could rescue his master, and Francis Lovell was buried alive, to die of suffocation or starvation.

Well, one may say, this is just a typical piece of local gossip – the sort of thing people dream up to account for a disappearance they cannot otherwise explain. In due course, the manor came into the possession of Thomas Coke, Earl of Leicester, who dismantled most of the house early in the eighteenth century and used the ruins as farm buildings. But a report to the Clerk of the House of Commons said that workmen at the hall – presumably the demolition gang – had come by accident upon a secret vault, in which they had just had time to glimpse the body of a man before it crumbled to dust in the sudden exposure to fresh air. He had been seated at a table with papers and books on it, and he had a dog at his feet. The story was told to Sir William Cowper by the third Duke of Rutland in 1728. Shades of Thornton Abbey! But there the subject was a victim of the death penalty; here, I suppose, of death by misadventure. Needless to say, perhaps, tales soon grew that the ghost of Lord Lovell haunted the place, and that the rustling

of papers was to be heard below the ground.

Who can say with confidence where fiction takes over from fact in this bizarre catalogue of events? We know enough about ingeniously constructed priest-holes in Tudor houses not to dismiss too lightly the possibility of a hidden chamber, and we have sufficient testimony from other sources about long-preserved corpses collapsing into dust when exposed to the air. But was it Francis Lovell? And if not, who was it?

We shall never have a certain answer to

This original diapered path of limestone and cobbles at Minster Lovell leads into a vaulted entrance passage or lobby, beyond which was the great hall.

these tantalizing questions, but the remaining stones of this great manor house know all the secrets, and the high Perpendicular windows which are now no more than holes in broken walls once lit rooms where dark deeds were plotted as well as magnificent banquets held. No doubt the much-maligned king came here to be entertained by his oldest and closest friend, and enjoyed himself. We know that he gave Lovell's sister several gifts over the years. But Lovell himself always remains a shadowy figure (Shakespeare gave him only two or three insignificant lines to speak). He was still a young man when he died – perhaps thirty-three, for he was two years younger than Richard. The Tudor propaganda which attributed a villainous character to the last Plantagenet king clearly extended also to his cronies, but it seems strange that one so close, and so favoured by his monarch, does not figure more prominently in Richard's alleged political acts. His evident instinct for self-preservation, thwarted only by a cruel turn of fate if the legend is true, might indicate that he had no personal ambition for power, were it not that he had raised an army in the north to march on Henry Tudor.

At any rate, his grandfather's house was built on an ambitious scale, and it must have given Francis a taste for the good life. Its picturesque ruins were taken over by the Ministry of Works in the 1930s, and have been given the usual cosmetic treatment which does nothing for their romantic atmosphere. But we can lay our hands on the ancient fabric and imagine that we feel the palm-print of a man – leaning on a wall to look out of a window at the pleasant scene, perhaps – who knew Richard III throughout his life and had the answers to all our questions about him.

The ruins of Minster Lovell Hall are in the village on north side of A40 between Witney and Burford. They are in the care of the Department of the Environment. There is a small parking area in the lane from which a path leads to the entrance. SP 324114.

Moreton Corbet Castle

Shropshire

THE CORBETS were powerful landowners in the Welsh Marches from the Conqueror's time onwards, and this fine ruin is called 'castle' because it replaced the castle held here by the family before the present house was built, towards the end of the sixteenth century. Part of the medieval stone keep remains behind the melancholy shell of the Elizabethan mansion.

It was Sir Richard Corbet who was mainly responsible for the house. The Corbets were not a particularly admirable lot. They demolished the village and re-routed the road to make space for their private park. Earthworks of the former village and outer defences of the castle can still be traced. Only the church was left standing, and in it are many monuments to the family, with their elephant-and-castle crest.

The house itself, however, was architecturally in advance of its time – a classical *tour-de-force*. It was built of red sandstone faced with pale ashlar, on two storeys with tall bell-shaped gables. The walls of the south façade still stand to their full height, with attached Tuscan and Ionic columns, large five-light windows, and fragments of decorative carving, and it is easy to see what a large and sumptuous mansion this was in its prime. If it had remained undamaged and occupied, it would undoubtedly have ranked as one of the great houses of England. But in 1644 the Royalist Corbets fortified it against siege by Parliamentary forces, who eventually took it and burnt it down.

The noble ruin has dominated the flat countryside around it for over three hundred years, little disturbed by either local residents or sightseers, but unfortunately it now has for its close neighbour the RAF base at Shawbury, and the job that Cromwell's men left half done may yet be completed as the tottering stonework trembles to the roar of low-flying jets.

The gabled Elizabethan mansion of the Corbet family was brought to ruin by Cromwell's troops.

228

The modern village of Moreton Corbet lies beside B5063 about eight miles north-east of Shrewsbury. The ruin is in the care of the Department of the Environment. There is limited parking space outside the gate. SJ 561231.

Newstead Abbey

Nottinghamshire

NEWSTEAD never was an abbey, and even if it had been its importance as an ecclesiastical ruin would be far outweighed by its subsequent fame as the home of the poet Lord Byron.

The place was founded by Henry II (still suffering attacks of conscience after the murder of Becket) as an Augustinian priory, and in the thirteenth century much rebuilding took place, including the west front of the priory church, which still stands to its full height. It is very impressive, with a huge central window, and a statue of Christ in the tympanum and of the Virgin Mary in the gable.

After the Dissolution the priory lands and buildings were purchased by Sir John Byron, who dismantled the church and priory buildings and built himself a mansion on the site with the cheaply acquired stone. The house itself, though much altered and repaired, is far from being ruinous, but the remains of the priory around are so closely linked with it that they qualify as part of Byron's house, and

Newstead Abbey. A nineteenth-century view of the priory ruins beside the Byron mansion. The remaining façade was the imposing west front of the priory church, which Lord Byron called 'A glorious remnant of the Gothic pile . . .'.

indeed it was the Romantic poet himself who encouraged posthumous promotion of the place to 'abbey' status.

Byron was ten years old when he succeeded unexpectedly to the family title on the death of his great-uncle. But what he inherited at Newstead was a liability rather than a great windfall. The fifth baron, an impoverished madman who had killed a neighbouring lord in a duel and lived here with one servant and a village tart, had cut down all the ancient oak trees and shot all the deer in the park, to say nothing of neglecting the house to the point of ruin. He finally expired in the scullery, the only room in the house with a watertight roof, where – so legend has it – he had trained the crickets to come out of their corners when he called them. The mansion was cheerless, damp and rotting. One room was said to be full of hay; another sheltered cattle. But Lord Byron came and lived here intermittently for eighteen years, doing what he could to look after the place; mourning the loss of his dog Boatswain and, to a lesser extent, his mother; getting some comfort from the pretty house-maids and infatuated shopgirls who made up his harem; and writing to his friends from what he called 'the melancholy mansion of my fathers'.

But the upkeep and restoration of this romantic place was beyond Byron's means, and he decided there was no option but to dispose of it. Attempts to sell Newstead by auction failed when bidding ended short of the reserve price. Then a prospective purchaser made a private offer, but the deal fell through after protracted negotiations. Again the property went to auction, with the same result. At length, in December 1817, Newstead went to a wealthy old friend of Byron's, Colonel Wildman, who expended a small fortune on restoration and what he conceived as improvement, until he, too, became impoverished when the Emancipation Act slashed his huge profits from slave labour in the West Indies. The ghosts of the black-cowled friars – one of whom Byron claimed to have seen – must have smiled in impious satisfaction at the fates of those who had usurped their ancient property.

Meanwhile, the poet limped off to voluntary exile in Italy amid dark hints of incest and national disgrace, leaving Newstead's ghosts behind him with the famous monument to Boatswain, which had been placed with premeditated blasphemy where the priory church's high altar had once stood.

Newstead Abbey, as it is still called, is now owned by Nottingham City Council. It lies west of A60 halfway between Nottingham and Mansfield. There is a car park in the grounds. SK 539533.

Nymans

West Sussex

THIS RUIN stands at the centre of a garden which is much more famous than the house itself. Nymans is, in fact, one of the great gardens of England, created by Ludwig Messel, and there in the middle of it are the ruins of a medieval manor house, with gables, Gothic windows and mullions of grey stone. At least, it *looks* like a medieval manor house. Actually, it was built little more than half a century ago.

The Edwardian house around which Ludwig Messel began his splendid gardens in 1890 did not satisfy his son, Colonel Leonard Messel, who commissioned the architect Sir William Tapper to convert the building into 'as faithful a reproduction as might be' of a West Country manor house. The result was remarkable. It was built around 1927 of brick faced and dressed with stone, and was designed in imitation of a fourteenth-century manor house that had been added to during the following two centuries. In 1932 it was described as 'so clever a reproduction' that 'some future antiquary may well be deceived by it'. Here the Messel family lived among rare trees, shrubs and plants laid out by such experts as William Robinson and Gertrude

ABOVE AND RIGHT
The south side of the beautiful 'medieval' manor house of Nymans, built by Leonard Messel in the late 1920s.

Jekyll. Oliver Messel himself, the renowned and highly original stage designer, could hardly have conjured up a finer set than the one his family lived in.

But in 1947 a disastrous fire destroyed the south side of the house, only twenty years after it was built, and left it, if anything, even more like a medieval manor house than it was before. Part of Nymans continues in occupation by the family, but the south side presents as romantic a domestic ruin as can be

found anywhere, with magnolias reaching up to the gable of the former great hall and climbing plants twining round the mullions of glassless windows. The house when complete could have been regarded by purists as a fake, but even they cannot deny that it is a genuine ruin, and a very handsome one at that.

Nymans is a National Trust property. It lies just off A23 on the south-east side of Handcross, between Crawley and Haywards Heath. There is a large car park and a tea-room at the site. TQ 268295.

Old Wardour Castle

Wiltshire

THE ORIGINAL 'castle' was built late in the fourteenth century by a branch of the Lovell family of Minster Lovell in Oxfordshire, but one glance at the ruin is enough to tell us that this building belongs in the domestic class, notwithstanding its position at the centre of a bailey which was surrounded by a curtain wall.

The original fortified house was built in 1393, in an odd shape round a small six-sided courtyard, when Sir John Lovell was licensed to crenellate, but it was much modernized in the second half of the sixteenth century when Sir Matthew Arundell purchased the property, and most of the detail of the ruined house is of that date. The Arundell family were staunch Catholics, and Matthew's son Thomas was made a Count of the Holy Roman Empire even before James I made him an English baron.

They were also Royalists, and in 1646 the house was besieged by well over a thousand men, against whom the house was defended by twenty-five men and a few female servants, all led by Lady Blanche Arundell. The household surrendered when the Parliamentarian troops undermined the walls, and after the women and children had been taken away in captivity, the soldiers plundered the house and did extensive and wanton damage to the property and its grounds. In the following winter it was again besieged, this time by Royalists intent on shifting the Roundheads who had garrisoned themselves there. The Parliamentarians managed to hold out longer than was expected, which was attributed by some to a well known Puritan preacher, Robert Balsom, who was inside the house with the troops and was believed to have used witchcraft on his side's behalf. By the time the Cavaliers in their turn had done great damage to the house in trying to restore it to Lord Arundell – who had directed that a mine should be detonated under it – it was hardly worth recovering, although the diarist John Aubrey, who saw the house the day after it was blown up, said that 'the mortar was so good that one of the little towers reclining on

ABOVE *A victim of the Civil War, Old Wardour Castle was defended against Parliamentary forces for a time by the sixty-year-old Lady Blanche Arundell and a handful of household retainers.*

RIGHT *This superb portal to the great hall at Old Wardour, from the central hexagonal courtyard, was part of Robert Smythson's classical remodelling of the mansion in the sixteenth century.*

one side did hang together and not fall in peeces.' It was called Wardour Castle, Aubrey says, 'from the conserving there the ammunition of the West'.

The Arundells built a new mansion nearby in the late eighteenth century, to which they removed their Catholic relics, but they did not demolish the old one, and its bleak ruin stands as a monument to the idiocy of the war, having been blown up by its rightful owner, who was killed himself not long afterwards. The grounds round the old castle were landscaped in romantic fashion and included a grotto of the kind then in favour – a fantastic construction of rock, brick and plaster on an elevation facing the main entrance. Bits of an expensive black marble fireplace, smashed up by Cromwell's troops, were built into it.

The ostentation of the Tudor alterations to Wardour is still evident in what remains. The compact medieval plan, inspired by French models, was retained by the Arundells, who employed Robert Smythson as their architect, but the romance of the ruin has since been destroyed to some extent by the removal of vegetation which sprang from every crevice in the Chilmark limestone. The shell-headed niches on either side of the front doorway; the Arundell coat of arms above, and above that a niche bearing a figure of Christ; the splendid entrance to the great hall from the courtyard, with its Tuscan columns and lions' heads – all these are now cold and bare and mildewed from exposure to the elements. It is no surprise to learn that the damp and draughty chambers are reckoned to be haunted: Lady Blanche Arundell drifts about the walls she defended with such spirit – loading the guns of her twenty-five men until the shot ran out, only to see the place she loved brought down by her own husband for the sake of his principles.

Old Wardour Castle is in the guardianship of the Department of the Environment. It lies a mile north of A30 between Shaftesbury and Wilton, near Donhead St Andrew, and is reached by narrow lanes and a long drive. There is car parking space at the site. ST 939263.

Scotney Castle

Kent

EVERYONE knows Scotney Castle: it has appeared on chocolate boxes, calendars, greetings cards and books about beautiful Britain for many years, and will no doubt continue to do so as long as there is a taste for the

picturesque scene. It is pre-eminent among the sort of English ruins-in-a-landscape favoured by landowners of the Romantic period.

Scotney is called a castle by virtue of its one remaining circular tower from a medieval castle built under licence by Roger Ashburnham at about the same time as Bodiam, and for the same reason. It was an elaborate defensive structure, with a moat creating two

islands, on one of which was Ashburnham's manor house surrounded by a curtain wall with four angle towers. It is one of these towers, built of stone and rising directly from the moat to its machicolated battlements, that survives.

In the Tudor period some reconstruction of the domestic quarters was carried out, and from this time dates a priest-hole where the

The idyllically romantic ruins of Scotney Castle reflected in their surrounding moat.

Jesuit Father Blunt was secreted during the Elizabethan persecution of Catholics. Then in the seventeenth century a more ambitious rebuilding began, an up-to-date manor house which was never actually finished. A carved boss from Bayham Abbey was built into it.

In 1837 a new Gothic Revival house was begun on a nearby elevated site for Edward Hussey, and the old Scotney Castle was incorporated in its garden as part of a romantic landscape almost obligatory for the landed gentry of the time. There was no need for follies here – the moated ruins of the medieval castle and the manor were a ready-made feature of the view from the new house. Only a little judicious touching-up was necessary to transform them into the artistic centrepiece of the beautifully laid-out gardens. The roof of the tower was given its conical shape and lantern to deprive it of what little military aggression it might have had left, and part of the seventeenth-century house was carefully demolished in order to leave the remainder, with its oriel windows and broken gables, looking even more picturesque. Stone for the new house was quarried from the sandstone rock between the castle and the new site, and then the quarry – where the footprints of an iguanodon were found – was transformed into a splendid rock garden.

The result was a *tour de force* of artificial landscaping, with the moat expanded into a lily-covered lake, fed by the River Bewl, in which a mirror-image of the ruins is reflected. A perfect balance is achieved between buildings and luxuriant vegetation, which has no rival in England. The colours of the ruin's grey stone and red brick are complemented by the blue water and greenery of summer or the dazzling display of autumn, and instead of a noble building crumbling into attractive decay, the place seems like an imaginative painting brought to life.

Scotney Castle is a National Trust property. It lies a mile and a half south-east of Lamberhurst on north side of A21, and three miles east of Bayham Abbey. There is a car park and a shop at the site. TQ 691355.

South Wingfield Manor

Derbyshire

THE MAGNIFICENT fortified manor house of South Wingfield was raised by one Cromwell and brought down by another two centuries later, and in between it became one of the great houses of England and one of the many prisons of Mary Queen of Scots through her nineteen years of captivity.

Its builder was Ralph, Lord Cromwell, Henry VI's Treasurer of the Exchequer, Master of the Royal Hounds and Falcons, Constable of Nottingham Castle, Steward of Sherwood Forest and, manifestly, the local big-shot. He began the work in 1441 after a twelve-year lawsuit in which he disputed his right to the manor with Sir Henry Pierrepoint. Having won it, he spent lavishly on this superbly sited mansion, built in squarely dressed Carboniferous sandstone on a steep hill above the village, and saw it taking shape over fourteen years, with its tall tower complete with dungeon cells, its huge banqueting hall with fine oriel window, tall chimneys, and state apartments rivalling almost any in the kingdom. His emblem as Lord Treasurer – a double purse – was carved over the entrance, and in other parts of the building too. But even as the place rose dramatically towards completion Cromwell died, and the reversion of his estate having been sold to John Talbot, the second Earl of Shrewsbury took possession and completed the house. He was the son of that John Talbot who was known as the 'scourge of France'.

The Talbot earls lived (and some died) here through the reigns of the Yorkist and Tudor monarchs, and in Elizabeth's reign the sixth earl, George Talbot, was charged with the custody of Mary, the unfortunate Scottish queen, who first came here from Tutbury Castle. Soon after her arrival in April 1569 she fell ill, allegedly because of the insanitary conditions of the house. Lord Shrewsbury indignantly retorted to her doctors, however, that the illness was due to the 'continual

The southern gable of the state apartments and the porch leading to the banqueting hall at South Wingfield Manor.

festering and uncleanly order of her own folk'. Nevertheless, Mary was removed to Chatsworth while Wingfield was cleaned up, but when she returned, she became ill once more. After that, she went back to Tutbury, which was even worse, and only returned to Wingfield fifteen years later, to be placed in the custody of Sir Ralph Sadleir, a stand-in for Shrewsbury who was frequently away at court. Sadleir had protested that he would rather keep the queen at Sheffield with sixty men than at Wingfield with three hundred, but here he stayed, with his royal prisoner grey with the strain of her long captivity.

Whether the Earl of Shrewsbury had gone grey too is not recorded, but it would hardly be surprising if he had. On the one hand he was responsible to Elizabeth I, who was full of suspicions and teased him with them, making him more severe in his treatment of the prisoner than he might otherwise have been. On the other, he had to endure the taunts of his wife, Bess of Hardwick, who fed the queen's suspicions with rumours that her husband had actually slept with his prisoner and given her a child. Shrewsbury must have been glad to be relieved of his unpleasant duty, and he called the female trio – two queens and an ambitious countess – 'three devils'.

South Wingfield Manor passed through various other hands from 1616, when the seventh Earl of Shrewsbury died, until 1774, when the then owner Immanuel Halton took much of the stone to build himself a new house not far away. It had suffered much in between times, having been attacked and partly demolished by Parliamentary forces in the Civil War, and then having its banqueting hall converted into a two-storey house.

Apart from the farmhouse which was eventually built beside the inner gateway and still remains there, the place has been in ruins for more than two centuries. And if the visitor can banish from his imagination the tractors in the south courtyard, and the runner beans growing up canes beside the ancient walls, he might picture the sad figure of Mary, grey at forty, attended by her servants in the range stretching northward from the high tower, while the lord of the manor dined in the great hall, hung with tapestries and lit at the dais end by a fine bay window. Below the hall is a vaulted undercroft almost as remarkable as that at Fountains Abbey, built to raise the hall above sloping ground.

At the time of writing, the ruins are undergoing extensive repair by the Department of the Environment, and only parts of the mansion are accessible, but these include the great hall and undercroft. The village is on B5035 two miles west of Alfreton, and the manor is reached by a drive off the street at the southern approach to the village. Cars are parked in the south courtyard – now a green. SK 358550.

Spofforth Castle

North Yorkshire

SPOFFORTH is a gaunt ruin, and unadorned except for a polygonal corner turret which contained a newel staircase and has a sort of conical cap or abbreviated spire. Its northern bluntness is slightly misleading, for though the castle looks dark and strong and ready to defy all-comers, it is actually a fortified manor house rather than a castle, and could hardly have stood up against an organized attack for more than ten minutes. Although it was built against a buttress of solid rock, it stood on low ground and both floors were accessible from the ground. Clearly its builders had no fears that their lives were in danger. Why should they? For they were those powerful northern barons the Percys, who had lorded it over these parts since the Conquest.

Licence to fortify his mansion was granted to Henry de Percy in 1308, and it was probably then that this house was built to replace an earlier one on the site. Because of the steep slope of the ground the great hall was built above a basement or undercroft, and this

Henry Percy – Shakespeare's 'Hotspur' – may have brandished his first wooden sword in this aisled undercroft at the former Percy manor house at Spofforth. Above was the great hall.

lower room probably survives from the earlier building. The solar wing also remains.

What is interesting about Spofforth, however, is not so much its architecture as the life that went on within. The Percy barons are known to history as a war-mongering tribe, but they were also hereditary benefactors of Fountains Abbey, and for that alone we owe them our gratitude. Nevertheless, their story is chiefly one of battle and bloodshed, and the great castle of Alnwick, in Northumberland,

which became their chief seat, seems a more fitting place for them than this unexceptional manor house.

Spofforth, however, is reputed to be the birthplace of that most celebrated medieval warrior, Sir Henry Percy, the famous 'Hotspur', son of the first Earl of Northumberland. Was it in these passages and chambers and winding stairs that he acquired his impetuous spirit and his taste for soldiering? He won his reputation (and his nickname) as a young man in France, supported Henry Bolingbroke's usurpation of Richard II's throne, but four years later joined his father in rebellion against the king, and died at the Battle of Shrewsbury, aged thirty-nine. He was buried at Whitchurch, but many of his supporters refused to believe that he was dead, so the king had him exhumed. His body was rubbed in salt and exposed between two millstones at Shrewsbury, then beheaded and quartered, and shown in the chief cities so that no one should doubt the king's victory.

After the death of the third earl of Northumberland at Towton in 1461, Spofforth Castle seems to have fallen into decay, probably as a result of extensive damage caused by the Yorkists. Leland said it was 'sore defacid' in his day. It was restored to a limited extent in Queen Elizabeth's time, only to be dismantled early in the seventeenth century.

At Spofforth it is not hard to see in the mind's eye Hotspur playing here as a boy six hundred years ago, preparing to become the valiant knight, the 'Mars in swathling clothes', who 'turns his head against the lion's jaws', as Shakespeare has it.

Spofforth is on A661 between Harrogate and Wetherby. The castle is in the care of the Department of the Environment, and is reached from a village street where cars can be parked. SE 365514.

Stokesay Castle

Shropshire

WHEN Henry James came to Stokesay, he 'lay on the grass beside the well in the little sunny court of this small castle and lazily appreciated the still definite details of medieval life.' The marvellous state of preservation does give us a very clear idea of the conditions in which a well-to-do medieval family lived.

Stokesay is really, like so many so-called castles, a fortified manor house, and as such, it is one of the earliest and best-preserved in Britain, although if local farmers had not used its buildings at one time, storing grain in the cellar and making barrels in the hall, it might have been in an even better state. Nevertheless, despite its remarkably intact appearance from across the millpond on the west side, it is a ruin, mostly roofless and uninhabitable.

Stokesay is a serenely peaceful place today, set among the south Shropshire hills, but it is a constant wonder to me that it could have been built in the thirteenth century with such open aspect, within a few miles of the Welsh border, at a time when the Marcher lords and their men-at-arms slept with their hands on their swords, only too conscious of the dangers from the Celts of Llewellyn the Great. The manor house had a moat round it, but that would hardly have had any deterrent effect on visitors with a hostile intent, and was only an early example of what was to become merely fashionable – the home-made island.

The north tower of the 'castle' dates from about 1240. The de Say family built it in the hamlet called South Stoke, which later took the family's name and became Stoke-de-Say. In choosing such a situation they must have been blessed with supreme optimism or profound faith: more probably the latter, for they also built or rebuilt the ancient church next door. It was Laurence de Ludlow, a wealthy wool merchant and clearly far more pessimistic, who bought the manor house and obtained a licence to crenellate from Edward I in 1291. His successors lived at Stokesay for three centuries.

From the south, with its solid tower and castellated wall, the manor, which is built of the local greenish-yellow sandstone, looks like a considerable fortification, but from the north it takes on the appearance of a castle from Grimm's fairy tales, with its half-timbered overhanging storey added to the north tower during Laurence de Ludlow's rebuilding. The two towers are joined by a long, gabled banqueting hall, notable for its surprisingly large pointed windows. It was originally aisled, like a church, with timber

The external staircase at Stokesay, characteristic of the time (c. 1285), leads to the lord's solar or sitting-room, and to the south tower via a wooden bridge. The original staircase was covered in, as can be seen by the line of the gabled roof in the stonework.

posts, and was accessible from the upper floor of the north tower. The timbered roof remains here, and is a fine piece of medieval craftsmanship. It is supported by three pairs of crucks, the upper parts of which are still in position, themselves supported on stone pilasters built to replace the lower parts of the timbers which had rotted.

At the southern end of the hall, a solar was accessible only by an outer staircase, originally covered in, and it had two 'squints' through which the room's occupants could see what was going on in the hall. The solar was furnished with fine timber panelling by the seventeenth-century occupants – the Baldwyn family who leased the place for six generations.

A so-called 'passage block' led from the solar to a small room between it and the south tower, but there was no access to this tower except from the courtyard. The south tower walls are more than five feet thick and have garderobes built into them which discharged into the moat. The kitchen block stood beside the north tower. It has disappeared now, but its foundations can still be traced. The well near the south tower is fifty feet deep.

Across the courtyard, an exuberant if somewhat incongruous gatehouse was added in the Tudor period, by which time one of Laurence de Ludlow's descendents had married into the Vernon family of Haddon Hall, Derbyshire. Legend has it that an outlaw lived in the gatehouse at one time.

Another legend about Stokesay is that two giants, who owned extensive lands here, kept their gold in a chest below the vaults of the castle, but one day the key of the vault was accidentally dropped in the moat and no one could ever find it. The treasure remains in the vault to this day, guarded by a raven, some say. I have never noticed this bird there, but the ground floor of the south tower, where the entrance to the secret chamber must be, is always locked – no doubt they are still searching for the key.

Stokesay was clearly never intended to stand up to any sort of organized attack, and in fact it came under threat more from the English than from the Welsh, when Cromwell's men laid siege to it in 1645. The occupants hastily surrendered without a fight, which meant that only minimal damage was done to the property. Only the curtain wall was demolished. It originally stood thirty-four feet above the moat, with battlemented parapets. A small section remains adjoining the north tower. It is a pleasing irony that for the unique survival of so much of this fine medieval house we are indebted to the owners' cowardice in the face of the enemy.

When Stokesay was eventually sub-let to local farmers, they brought the place to neglect and ruin faster than all the Welsh marauders and Puritan troops together. But the Allcroft family, who have owned it since 1869, have taken great care to restore and preserve what is left of this fine medieval building, one of Britain's most important domestic ruins.

Stokesay Castle stands just off A49 Ludlow-Shrewsbury road, half a mile south of Craven Arms. There is a car park up the signposted lane and past the church, only a few yards from the ruin. SO 436817.

RIGHT *Stokesay, the best-preserved medieval manor house in England.*

Sutton Scarsdale Hall

Derbyshire

THIS IS indeed a sorry sight. Where other ruins may harbour bats and owls and make us feel the uneasy presence of watching spirits, Sutton Hall seems only a place of cobwebs and mildew and flaking plaster looking out over a landscape of opencast mining. Some of its decorative features were long ago taken to the United States, where they can be seen in the Philadelphia Museum.

The house was built in the eighteenth century for the Earl of Scarsdale, and was a neo-classical mansion of the Corinthian order. It was built of brick with stone facing, on two storeys, with giant fluted pilasters all round, the front also having attached columns beneath a central pediment. The back had projecting wings enclosing a narrow courtyard, and the interior was lavishly decorated.

A branch of the Arkwright family lived in it later, when the inventive and ambitious barber from Lancashire who became Sir Richard Arkwright had made this territory his own, as the father of factory industry, and joined the ranks of the *nouveaux riches*.

There have been those who have applauded the gutting and partial demolition of this baroque mansion, on account of its incongruous proximity to the village church, but I am not among them. Neither, it seems, is the Department of the Environment, which – when I was there – had the ruins boarded up and fenced off with warnings of dangerous stonework. They are in the course of clearing the site of rubble and preparing the ruin for public inspection.

Only a few lanky trees growing close to the walls offer the hollow carcass any protection from the storms to which it stands exposed.

Sutton Scarsdale is four miles south-east of Chesterfield near Heath, north of A617, and about four miles north-west of Hardwick Hall. The ruin is reached by a drive from the village street, and there is limited parking space round a small green at the back of the house. SK 441686.

RIGHT *Sutton Scarsdale Hall, a once-superb baroque mansion.*

Thorpe Salvin Manor

South Yorkshire

JUST INSIDE South Yorkshire is the quiet and relatively isolated village of Thorpe Salvin, where for centuries the lords of the manor were the Sandford family, some of whose monuments are in the Norman parish church. Among them are Henry Sandford and his wife Margaret, who built the impressive manor house whose ruins stand close by.

It was in the reign of Elizabeth I when Henry Sandford, a loyal subject of Her Majesty, erected a fitting manor house of rugged stone. It was approached via a small gate-house with a stepped gable, which brings the visitor face to face with the southern façade of the great mansion. It is three storeys high and perfectly symmetrical, with a central porch flanked by straight walls punctuated with huge chimney breasts and ending in round towers. Square-headed windows in ranks of three are complete with mullions, transoms and drip-moulds. The angle towers were battlemented, and the chimney-stacks, now gone, must have accentuated the height of the house. Symmetry was an obsession with the Elizabethan gentry. They would have loved this place.

We can see at once that it was a house of style and importance, and our sense of expectation is aroused by the front elevation, stimulating our imaginations as we approach.

Alas, our expectation are not fulfilled, for the façade is all there is. It stands there like a piece of stage scenery, uncanny in its flatness, and ready to fall at one blow – like a cardboard cut-out – into the villagers' allotments which surround it. Many ruined buildings are reputed to have ghosts in them, but this house is itself a ghost.

The ruins of Thorpe Salvin Manor stand on private ground close to the church and facing the road beside a private estate, but can be seen quite clearly from the gateway. The village is four miles west of Worksop on minor roads south of A57. SK 523810.

RIGHT *The deceptive façade of Thorpe Salvin Manor.*

Bibliography

I must record my debt to the invaluable official guides to those ruins in the care of the National Trust, the Department of the Environment, and the Welsh Office. These are usually available on the spot, and give much more historical and architectural detail than I have had space for.

I have also consulted a large number of topographical and biographical works in writing this book, but must make particular mention of the following more specialised publications:

Alexander, Michael (Trans.), *Beowulf* (Penguin, 1973)
Anglo-Saxon Chronicle (Everyman's Library edition, 1972)
Ashe, Geoffrey (Ed.), *The Quest for Arthur's Britain* (Pall Mall Press, 1968)
Aubrey, John, *Brief Lives* (Penguin edition, 1972)

Barham, R. H., *The Ingoldsby Legends* (Richard Bentley, 1840)
Bede, 'The Venerable', *Ecclesiastical History of the English Nation* (Everyman's Library edition, 1910)
Beresford, Maurice & John G. Hurst (Eds.), *Deserted Medieval Villages* (Lutterworth Press, 1971)
Borrow, George, *Wild Wales* (Collins, 1955 edition)
Branston, Brian, *The Lost Gods of England* (Thames & Hudson, 1957)
Breeze, David J. & Brian Dobson, *Hadrian's Wall* (Allen Lane, 1976)

Caesar, Julius, *War Commentaries* (Everyman's Library edition, 1953)
Clifton-Taylor, Alec, *The Pattern of English Building* (Faber, 1972)
Chaucer, Geoffrey, *The Canterbury Tales* (Oxford Univ. Press, 1978)

Defoe, Daniel, *A Tour Through the Whole Island of Great Britain* (Penguin edition, 1971)

Forde-Johnston, James, *A guide to the Castles of England and Wales* (Constable, 1981)
Fox, George, *Journal* (Everyman's Library edition, 1949)
Frere, Sheppard, *Britannia: A History of Roman Britain* (Routledge & Kegan Paul, 1979)

Gibbon, Edward, *The Decline and Fall of the Roman Empire* (Everyman's Library edition, 6 vols., 1954)
Girouard, Mark, *Life in the English Country House* (Penguin edition, 1980)
Graves, Robert, *The White Goddess* (Faber, 1948)

Hair, Paul (Ed.), *Before the Bawdy Court* (Elek, 1972)
Hallam, H. E., *Rural England, 1066–1348* (Fontana, 1981)
Harper, Charles G., *Abbeys of Old Romance* (Cecil Palmer, 1930)

Harper, Charles G., *Mansions of Old Romance* (Cecil Palmer, 1930)

Harvey, John L., *The Tragedy of Hallsands Village* (P.D.S. Printers, Plymouth, n.d.)

Hawkes, Jacquetta, *A Guide to the Prehistoric and Roman Monuments in England and Wales* (Chatto & Windus, 1973)

James, M. R., *Abbeys* (Great Western Railway, 1925)

Johnson, Paul, *The National Trust Book of British Castles* (Weidenfeld & Nicolson, 1978)

Johnson, Stephen, *Later Roman Britain* (Routledge & Kegan Paul, 1980)

Little, Bryan, *Abbeys and Priories in England and Wales* (Batsford, 1979)

Macauley, Lord, *Critical and Historical Essays* (Everyman's Library edition, 1967)

Macauley, Rose, *Pleasure of Ruins* (Thames & Hudson, 1964 edition)

Maringer, J., *The Gods of Prehistoric Man* (Weidenfeld & Nicolson, 1960)

Muir, Richard, *The Lost Villages of Britain* (Michael Joseph, 1982)

Pevsner, Nikolaus, and others, *The Buildings of England* (Penguin Books, 46 vols., 1951–74)

Piggott, Stuart, *The Druids* (Thames & Hudson, 1968)

Richmond, I. A. *Roman Britain* (Penguin, 1963)

Southern, R. W., *Western Society and the Church in the Middle Ages* (Penguin, 1970)

Stanford, S. C., *The Archaeology of the Welsh Marches* (Collins, 1980)

Tacitus, *The Annals of Imperial Rome* (Penguin edition, 1971)

Thomas, Gwyn, *A Welsh Eye* (Hutchinson, 1964)

Thomas, Keith, *Religion and the Decline of Magic* (Weidenfeld & Nicolson, 1971)

Timbs, John, and Alexander Gunn, *Abbeys, Castles and Ancient Halls of England and Wales* (Frederick Warne, 3 vols., n.d.)

Wacher, John, *The Coming of Rome* (Routledge & Kegan Paul, 1979)

Warrington, John (Ed.), *The Paston Letters* (Everyman's Library edition, 1975)

Wood, Margaret, *The English Medieval House* (Ferndale edition, 1981)

Ziegler, Philip, *The Black Death* (Collins, 1969)

Index